WORLD TRADE ORGANIZATION

Tariff Negotiations and Renegotiations under the GATT and the WTO:

Procedures and Practices

Anwarul Hoda

CAMBRIDGE UNIVERSITY PRESS
Cambridge, New York, Melbourne, Madrid, Cape Town, Singapore, São Paulo

Cambridge University Press
The Edinburgh Building, Cambridge CB2 8RU, UK

Published in the United States of America by Cambridge University Press, New York

www.cambridge.org
Information on this title: www.cambridge.org/9780521804493

First published 2001
Third printing 2004

A catalogue record for this publication is available from the British Library

French edition and Spanish edition paperbacks of this title are both available directly
from WTO Publications, World Trade Organization, Centre William Rappard, 154 rue
de Lausanne, CH-1211 Geneva 21, Switzerland   http://www.wto.org

ISBN 978-0-521-80449-3 hardback

Transferred to digital printing 2007

TABLE OF CONTENTS

Page

PREFACE

1. The procedures and practices to implement the provisions relating to tariff negotiations and renegotiations have evolved considerably since the GATT was established in 1947. The provisions themselves have undergone some changes in the last 52 years. This study reviews the evolution of these provisions and of the procedures adopted and practices followed by the contracting parties to GATT 1947 and the Members of the WTO. The first chapter outlines the legal framework of tariff negotiations and renegotiations as it exists at present. The second deals with tariff negotiations held in the context of multilateral trade negotiations and includes accession negotiations. The third takes up bilateral and plurilateral negotiations held under GATT 1947 as well as under the WTO outside the context of tariff conferences and rounds of multilateral trade negotiations. The fourth is devoted to renegotiations under the various provisions of the General Agreement, and particularly Article XXVIII and Article XXIV:6. In the fifth chapter some issues on such technical aspects as rectification, consolidation and implementation of the Harmonized System are explored. The last chapter offers some conclusions and recommendations. The Appendices reproduce selected documents which might of use to the reader.

2. The source used for the research has been mainly the original records available in the archives of the WTO Secretariat and Secretariat notes.

3. I have benefited greatly from the comments made on the first draft by Mr. Ake Linden, Dr. Frieder Roessler, Mr. William Davey and Miss Yvette Davel, former staff members of the Secretariat. I have also had very useful suggestions from Mr. Heinz Opelz, Director, Market Access Division and Mr. Alberto Campeas, Director, Textiles Division, who was Director of the Tariff Division during the Uruguay Round. I am also very grateful for the help received from Mrs. Suja Rishikesh-Mavroidis and Ms. Nimala Liyanapatabendi, both from the Market Access Division, in finding and selecting the necessary resource material and in ensuring the correctness of the references quoted in the study. I must also acknowledge with thanks the secretariat assistance rendered by Miss Mary McCormack. However, I would like to take full responsibility for any errors of fact or analysis that might have remained and to emphasize that the opinions expressed are entirely mine and do not reflect the views of the WTO Secretariat.

Anwarul Hoda

CHAPTER I

LEGAL FRAMEWORK FOR TARIFF NEGOTIATIONS AND RENEGOTIATIONS UNDER GATT 1994[1]

1.   Several articles of the General Agreement have a bearing on the process of tariff negotiations and renegotiations. An analysis of all these articles and the ways in which the provisions impinge on the commitments made during tariff negotiations and renegotiations is outside the scope of this work. We take up only those articles which have a direct bearing on the subject of our study.

A.   Provisions Relating to Tariff Negotiations

2.   While GATT 1947 (like GATT 1994) prohibited quantitative restrictions as a general rule, it allowed the use of "duties, taxes or other charges" for the regulation of trade. Furthermore, the national treatment provision which required that, once goods had been imported, they should be treated on equal terms with domestically-produced goods, served to ensure that all discriminatory taxes (i.e. tariffs) aimed at protection were applied in a transparent manner only at the border. The plan envisaged in 1947 for the liberalization of world trade was to prohibit the application of quantitative restrictions, to allow regulation of import (and export) through transparently-administered non-discriminatory tariffs applied at the border, and then to work for the progressive reduction of these tariffs through successive rounds of negotiations.

Periodic tariff negotiations

Article 17 of the Havana Charter provided, *inter alia,* as follows:

> "Each Member shall, upon the request of any other Member, or Members, and subject to procedural arrangements established by Organization, enter into and carry out with such other Member or Members, negotiations directed to the substantial reduction of the general levels of tariffs and other charges on imports and exports, and to the elimination of the

---

[1]   The WTO Agreement provides that references to "contracting party" shall be deemed to read "Member". As for the term "CONTRACTING PARTIES" which refers to contracting parties acting jointly, it provides that, in the case of certain provisions (which are not of relevance in this study) the reference shall be deemed to be references to the WTO while, in the case of other provisions (which are of relevance in this study) the functions of the CONTRACTING PARTIES shall be allocated by the Ministerial Conference. No such allocation has, however, been decided upon so far.

In describing the provisions of GATT 1994, therefore, we have substituted "contracting party" by "Member" and the "CONTRACTING PARTIES" by the "Ministerial Conference". Since the functions of the Ministerial Conference are carried out by the General Council in the intervals between meetings of the Ministerial Conference, for all practical purposes references to the Ministerial Conference should be deemed to be references to the General Council. References to contracting party and CONTRACTING PARTIES occur only when an account is being given of what happened during the operation of GATT 1947.

preferences referred to in paragraph 2 of Article 16, on a reciprocal and mutually advantageous basis."

3.   The desiderata contained in this provision provided the basis for the initial rounds of tariff negotiations held under GATT 1947. It was not until the Review Session of 1954-55 that the present Article XXVIII *bis* was introduced, entering into force on 7 October, 1957. This Article envisages that from time to time the Ministerial Conference may sponsor negotiations directed to the substantial reduction of the general level of tariffs and other charges on imports and exports and in particular to the reduction of such high tariffs as discourage the importation even of minimum quantities. The report of the Working Party, on the recommendation of which this Article was added to GATT 1947, noted that "(t)he article would impose no new obligations on contracting parties. Each contracting party would retain the right to decide whether or not to engage in negotiations or participate in a tariff conference." Thus, under GATT 1947, participation in tariff negotiations was optional. The position remains unchanged in the WTO Agreement, even though the requirement for original membership of the WTO that contracting parties to GATT 1947 should have Schedules of Concessions and Commitments annexed to GATT 1994 besides Schedules of Specific Commitments annexed to GATS, made participation in the tariff negotiations (as well as the negotiations for specific commitments in GATS) obligatory during the Uruguay Round.

Principle of reciprocity

4.   A central requirement of Article 17 of the Havana Charter and Article XXVIII *bis* of the General Agreement is that the negotiations be held on a reciprocal and mutually advantageous basis. There is no provision on the manner in which reciprocity is to be measured and even the rules of various rounds of negotiations did not spell out any guidelines on the issue. The understanding has always been that governments participating in negotiations should retain complete freedom to adopt any method for evaluating the concessions.

Modalities of tariff negotiations

5.   On the modalities of tariff negotiations, Article XXVIII *bis* leaves it to participants to decide whether the negotiations should be carried out on a selective product-by-product basis or by the application "of such multilateral procedures as may be accepted by the contracting parties concerned". It envisages that the negotiations could result in the reduction of duties, the binding of duties at existing levels or commitments not to raise duties on particular products beyond specified levels. It stipulates further that "(t)he binding against increase of low duties or of duty-free treatment shall, in principle, be recognized as a concession equivalent in value to the reduction of high duties".

6.   Article XXVIII *bis* also provides for the negotiations to take into account the diversity of situations of individual participating countries "including the fiscal, developmental, strategic and other needs" and the needs of developing

countries for tariff protection to assist their economic development and to maintain tariffs for revenue purposes.

Concept of non-reciprocity

7.   In the 1960s and 1970s the concept of non-reciprocity was developed for trade negotiations between developed and developing countries and was embodied in paragraph 8 of Article XXXVI, which was introduced in Part IV of the General Agreement and became effective on 27 June 1966. This paragraph states that "(t)he developed contracting parties do not expect reciprocity for commitments made by them in trade negotiations to reduce or remove tariffs and other barriers to the trade of less-developed contracting parties". An interpretative note adds that the developing countries "should not be expected, in the course of trade negotiations, to make contributions which are inconsistent with their individual development, financial and trade needs, taking into consideration past trade developments". The interpretative note also extends the applicability of the concept of non-reciprocity to renegotiations under Article XVIII or XXVIII.

8.   The concept was further elaborated in the Tokyo Round Decision on "Differential and More Favourable Treatment, Reciprocity and Fuller Participation of Developing Countries", also known as the "Enabling Clause", which was adopted on 28 November 1979. This clause provided, *inter alia,* as follows:

> "The developed countries do not expect reciprocity for commitments made by them in trade negotiations to reduce or remove tariffs and other barriers to the trade of developing countries i.e. the developed countries do not expect the developing countries, in the course of trade negotiations, to make contributions which are inconsistent with their individual development, financial and trade needs. Developed contracting parties shall therefore not seek, neither shall less-developed contracting parties be required to make, concessions that are inconsistent with the latter's development, financial and trade needs....Having regard to the special economic difficulties and the particular development, financial and trade needs of the least-developed countries, the developed countries shall exercise the utmost restraint in seeking any concessions or contributions for commitments made by them to reduce or remove tariffs and other barriers to the trade of such countries, and the least-developed countries shall not be expected to make concessions or contributions that are inconsistent with the recognition of their particular situation and problems."[2]

---

[2]   GATT, BISD, Twenty-sixth Supplement, p. 204.

Supplementary negotiations

9.   In the years before Article XXVIII *bis* was introduced into GATT 1947, the practice had been established for negotiations to take place for tariff concessions even outside of general tariff conferences or rounds of negotiations. In fact, while adopting the procedures for the Torquay Tariff Conference, the CONTRACTING PARTIES had also established procedures[3] for negotiations between two or more contracting parties at times other than during general tariff conferences. These procedures require notification to other contracting parties about the date and place of negotiation and circulation of the request lists exchanged between contracting parties proposing negotiations. Other contracting parties are given the right to join in these negotiations. The procedures provide for a selective, product-by-product basis for the negotiations. These bilateral and plurilateral negotiations are known as supplementary negotiations and their results as supplementary concessions.

Tariff negotiations during accession

10.   Although tariff negotiations are a substantial component of the process of accession of governments, neither Article XXXIII of GATT 1947 (which is now no longer relevant) nor Article XII of the WTO Agreement gives any guidelines on how such negotiations are to be conducted. The latter article provides simply, as the former had done until it ceased to be in force, for the accession to take place on "terms to be agreed" between the applicant government and the full membership. One of the terms is in every case commitments for market access, including reduction and binding of tariffs. The negotiations for securing tariff commitments are made on a bilateral basis between the applicant-government and its main trading partners.

Tariff commitments on behalf of dependent territories

11.   The Protocol of Provisional Application of GATT 1947 provided for the acceptance of the Protocol by the contracting parties in respect of their metropolitan territories as well as on behalf of their dependent territories. Article XXVI 5(c) of GATT 1947 provided that when these dependent territories acquired full autonomy in the conduct of their external commercial relations they would become contracting parties when the responsible contracting parties certified that such autonomy had been acquired. The States which became contracting parties through the succession route of Article XXVI 5(c) were bound by the tariff commitments made earlier on their behalf. On their becoming new contracting parties, a new schedule was established for them on the basis of the corresponding entries in the schedules of the contracting parties which had made the commitments on their behalf. The provision has not been carried forward into the WTO Agreement.

---

[3]   GATT, BISD, Vol. I, p. 116.

Non-application

12.   Article XXXV of GATT 1947 provided for non-application of either the full Agreement or of Article II of the Agreement between two contracting parties if:

> (a)   the two contracting parties had not entered into tariff negotiations with each other, and

> (b)   either of the contracting parties, at the time either became a contracting party, did not consent to such application.

13.   The prerequisites for non-application of GATT 1947 were so formulated as to provide for such non-application only at the outset (in January 1948) or at the time of accession of a new contracting party. The contracting party invoking the article had the option of providing for the non-application of the entire agreement or only of tariff concessions.

14.   Article XIII of the WTO Agreement has a corresponding provision on non-application. However, it can be invoked between original Members of the WTO which were contracting parties to GATT 1947 only where Article XXXV of that Agreement had been invoked earlier and was effective as between those contracting parties at the time of entry into force of the WTO Agreement.

B.   Provisions Relating to Tariff Renegotiations

1.   Article XXVIII is the principal provision of GATT 1994 on renegotiations of tariff concessions. It provides for the possibility of modification or withdrawal of tariff concessions after negotiation (renegotiation) with:

> (i)   Members with which the concession was initially negotiated; and

> (ii)   Members which have a principal supplying interest. In addition consultations have to be held with Members which have a substantial interest in such concessions.

Such modification or withdrawal can be done:

> (i)   on the first day of each three-year period, the first of which began on 1 January 1958;

> (ii)   at any time in special circumstances on authorization; or

> (iii)   during the three-year period referred to above, if the Member concerned has, before the beginning of the period, elected to reserve the right to renegotiate.

In the negotiations the Member seeking modification or withdrawal is expected to give compensatory concession on other products. If agreement is not reached, the affected Members get the right to withdraw substantially equivalent concessions initially negotiated with the Member making the changes.

Initial negotiating rights (INRs)

2.   In the early days of GATT 1947, for every individual concession there were one or more contracting parties with INRs. When at a subsequent negotiation a concession was negotiated at a lower level of tariff on the same product, the contracting party or parties acquiring INRs could be the same or different depending on whether in the meantime there had been changes in the market shares of the product. Thus for each tariff line figuring in successive rounds of negotiations, there could be several layers of INRs held by the same or different contracting parties. The INRs other than those resulting from the latest negotiations are referred to as historical INRs.

3.   In the first five rounds of tariff negotiations the technique used was that of item-by-item negotiations on a bilateral request-offer basis. In these negotiations, before the tariff concessions were consolidated in a Schedule, there used to be bilaterally agreed lists of concessions exchanged by participants. In these negotiations, therefore, it was easy to identify the contracting party which had initial negotiating rights (INRs). However, there was no such clarity when, in the Kennedy Round, important trading nations decided to adopt a linear reduction approach. The CONTRACTING PARTIES, therefore, adopted a decision on 16 November 1967 which provided as follows:

> "In respect of the concessions specified in the Schedules annexed to the Geneva (1967) Protocol, a contracting party shall, when the question arises, be deemed for the purposes of the General Agreement to be the contracting party with which a concession was initially negotiated if it had, during a representative period prior to that time, a principal supplying interest in the product concerned."[4]

During the discussions of this decision in the Trade Negotiating Committee it was emphasized that the words "that time" referred to "when the question arises". Following the Tokyo Round in which a formula approach was also followed, a similar decision[5] was adopted on 28 November 1979 in respect of INRs. While another similar decision[6] was taken in 1988 in connection with the introduction of the Harmonized System, no such decision was adopted for the concessions agreed in the Uruguay Round.

4.   As we shall see in the account of the practices and procedures adopted during the tariff negotiations, INRs have also become a bargaining chip and sometimes they are granted in bilateral negotiations as a reward for important reciprocal concessions or used as an element for topping-up in the exercise for bilateral balancing of reciprocal concessions. There have been other instances during accession negotiations in which INRs were specifically excluded in respect of items figuring in bilaterally-agreed lists of concessions. INRs are

---

[4]   GATT, BISD, Fifteenth Supplement, p. 67.

[5]   GATT, BISD, Twenty-sixth Supplement, p. 202.

[6]   GATT, BISD, Thirty-fifth Supplement, p. 336.

presumed to exist if any concession is mentioned in a bilateral list drawn up in rounds of negotiations, bilateral or plurilateral negotiations, accession negotiations or renegotiations unless indicated otherwise. Where there are no bilateral lists it is presumed not to exist unless specifically indicated in the Schedule.

5. The Uruguay Round Understanding on the Interpretation of Article XXVIII of GATT 1994 made an addition to the concept of INRs. It is provided that, when a tariff concession is modified or withdrawn on a new product (i.e. a product for which three years' statistics are not available), a Member having initial negotiating rights on the tariff line where the product is or was formerly classified shall be deemed to have an initial negotiating right in the concession in question. The Understanding also adds the requirement that any Member having a principal supplying interest in a concession which is modified or withdrawn shall be accorded an initial negotiating right in the compensatory concessions, unless another form of concession is agreed by the Member concerned.

Principal supplying interest and substantial interest

6. Article XXVIII provides for the Ministerial Conference (CONTRACTING PARTIES) to determine the Members having a principal supplying interest or substantial interest. However, the procedures adopted for renegotiations with which we shall deal in detail in Chapter IV provide that, if a Member makes a claim of principal supplying interest or substantial interest and the Member invoking Article XXVIII recognizes the claim, "the recognition will constitute a determination by the CONTRACTING PARTIES of the interest in the sense of Article XXVIII:1".[7]

7. An interpretative note to paragraph 1 of Article XXVIII provides that a Member should be determined to have a principal supplying interest if it "has had, over a reasonable period of time prior to the negotiations, a larger share in the market of the applicant contracting party than a contracting party with which the concession was initially negotiated, or would...have had such a share in the absence of discriminatory quantitative restrictions maintained by the applicant contracting party". The interpretative note envisages that generally there would not be more than one or, in those exceptional cases where there is near equality in supplying status, two contracting parties with a principal supplying interest.

8. Another interpretative note mentions one other category of Member with a principal supplying interest: where the concession to be modified affects a major part of the total exports of a country. One more category of countries with a principal supplying interest has been created (and the possibility of consideration being given to yet another category on a future date has been envisaged) in the Uruguay Round Understanding on the Interpretation of Article XXVIII of GATT 1994, paragraph 1 of which provides as follows:

---

[7] GATT, BISD, Twenty-seventh Supplement, pp. 26-28.

"For the purposes of modification or withdrawal of a concession, the Member which has the highest ratio of exports affected by the concession (i.e. exports of the product to the market of the Member modifying or withdrawing the concession) to its total exports shall be deemed to have a principal supplying interest if it does not already have an initial negotiating right or a principal supplying interest as provided for in paragraph 1 of Article XXVIII. It is, however, agreed that this paragraph will be reviewed by the Council for Trade in Goods five years from the date of entry into force of the WTO Agreement with a view to deciding whether this criterion has worked satisfactorily in securing a redistribution of negotiating rights in favour of small and medium-sized exporting Members. If this is not the case, consideration will be given to possible improvements, including, in the light of the availability of adequate data, the adoption of a criterion based on the ratio of exports affected by the concession to exports to all markets of the product in question."

9.   The Uruguay Round Understanding has clarified two aspects relevant for the determination of principal supplying or substantial interest. First, in the determination of principal supplying interest or substantial interest, only trade which has taken place on an MFN basis is required to be taken into consideration. However, trade which has taken place under non-contractual preferences (such as the GSP) will also be taken into account if the preferential treatment has been withdrawn at the time of the renegotiations or will be withdrawn before the conclusion of the renegotiations. Second, if a tariff concession is modified or withdrawn on a new product (i.e. a product for which three years' trade statistics are not available), for the determination of principal supplying and substantial interests and the calculation of compensation, production capacity and investment in the affected product in the exporting Member and estimates of export growth, as well as forecasts of demand in the importing Member, have to be taken into account.

10.   There is no criterion laid down for determining substantial interest. The Interpretative Notes acknowledge that the concept is not capable of precise definition, but suggest that those Members could be construed as having a substantial interest when they have a significant share in the market. In practice, contracting parties (Members) having 10 per cent or more of the trade share have been recognized as having a substantial interest. Article XXVIII requires Members to negotiate modification or withdrawal with Members having initial negotiating rights or a principal supplying interest and to reach an agreement with them, and the Members with a substantial interest have only the right to consultation. But if there is no agreement with Members with INRs or a principal supplying interest, or if the Member with a substantial interest is not satisfied with the agreement reached among them, all have an equal right to withdraw substantially equivalent concessions initially negotiated with the applicant Member.

Types of renegotiations: open season, special circumstance and reserved renegotiations

11.   As already mentioned, there are three types of renegotiations envisaged in Article XXVIII: three-year (open season) renegotiations; special circumstance renegotiations; and reserved renegotiations. Article XXVIII:1 provides that on the first day of each three-year period (the first period having begun on 1 January 1958 and the next one at the time of writing beginning on 1 January 2000) any Member may modify or withdraw a concession after negotiation and agreement with Members having initial negotiating rights and a principal supplying interest and consultation with those with a substantial interest. Any other period may also be specified by a decision of the Ministerial Conference. The second type of renegotiations are those authorized in special circumstances by the Ministerial Conference under Article XXVIII:4. The third type of renegotiations envisaged in Article XXVIII:5 are those that may be held at any time before the end of the three-year period if any Member elects to reserve the right before the beginning of the period. In such cases other Members also get the right to hold renegotiations on concessions initially negotiated with the Member which has reserved the right.

12.   The substantive requirements in all three types of renegotiations are essentially the same. However, there is a major difference in regard to time limits. In the three-year renegotiations the notification about the intention to withdraw or modify has to be made no later than three months (but no earlier than six months) before the first day of the period and the whole process has to be completed before that date. The modification or withdrawal (whether or not after agreement) takes effect on that date. Thus in the three-year negotiations normally the request has to be made during the period from 1 July to 30 September, the renegotiations have to be completed before 31 December and the modification and withdrawal take effect on 1 January of the following year. Time limits are also prescribed for special circumstance negotiations. A decision on a request for such renegotiations has to be made within thirty days of its submission. The renegotiations have to be completed within 60 days of authorization, but a longer period may be prescribed if a large number of items is involved. If no agreement is reached within the prescribed period, the applicant Member has the right to refer the matter back to the Ministerial Conference for its examination and recommendations. Any determination in such renegotiations that a Member has unreasonably failed to offer adequate compensation must also be made within thirty days of the submission of the matter. As for reserved renegotiations, there are no time limits at all regarding when they are to be begun or concluded.

Compensation and retaliation

13.   The central requirement underlying the negotiation for compensatory concessions by the Member proposing a modification or withdrawal is the maintenance of "a general level of reciprocal and mutually advantageous concessions not less favourable to trade than that provided for in this Agreement

prior to such negotiations". When a developing country Member needs to modify or withdraw a concession, the provision in Article XXXVI:8 regarding the concept of non-reciprocity has to be taken into account. No other guidance is provided on the level of compensation. Some clarity is provided in the Uruguay Round Understanding on the Interpretation of Article XXVIII of GATT 1994 in respect of those renegotiations which involve the replacement of an unlimited tariff concession by a tariff rate quota. Paragraph 6 of the Understanding provides as follows:

> "When an unlimited tariff concession is replaced by a tariff rate quota, the amount of compensation provided should exceed the amount of the trade actually affected by the modification of the concession. The basis for the calculation of compensation should be the amount by which future trade prospects exceed the level of the quota. It is understood that the calculation of future trade prospects should be based on the greater of:

> "(a) the average annual trade in the most recent representative three-year period, increased by the average annual growth rate of imports in that same period, or by 10 per cent, whichever is the greater; or

> "(b) trade in the most recent year increased by 10 per cent.

> "In no case shall a Member's liability for compensation exceed that which would be entailed by complete withdrawal of the concession."

14.   The right of a Member to modify or withdraw a concession is absolute, provided the prescribed procedures are followed. It is not dependent on an agreement being reached with the Members with INRs and a principal supplying interest. However, as mentioned already, if the Member seeking a modification or withdrawal does go ahead without having reached an agreement with the Members with INRs or a principal supplying interest, these Members get the right to withdraw "substantially equivalent concessions" initially negotiated with the applicant Member. The Member with a substantial interest also gets the same right either when no agreement is reached, or even if an agreement is reached with the Members having INRs or a principal supplying interest but the Member with substantial interest is not satisfied with it. However, there are two time limits to be respected: first, the retaliatory withdrawal must take place within six months of the withdrawal or modification of the concession; and second, a 30-day period should be allowed after notification by the retaliating Member.

15.   An Interpretative Note to Article XXVIII makes an important point regarding the date of entry into force of the compensatory concession. When a modification or withdrawal of a concession is made, the legal obligation of the Member changes. The implication is not that the actual level of applied tariff is changed on that day: the Member may choose to delay the implementation of the applied level in light of the new commitment. If a tariff change following renegotiation is delayed, the Member concerned has the right to similarly delay the entry into force of the compensatory concession.

Renegotiation for promoting the establishment of a particular industry

16.   Article XVIII:7 of GATT 1994 is another provision for renegotiation of concessions, but it is open only to developing countries and can be used only for the purpose of promoting the establishment of a particular industry. This provision may be invoked by a developing country at any time and no authorization is needed. The Article requires the Member seeking to modify or withdraw the concession to enter into negotiations with Members with INRs and those having a substantial interest. It would be noted that, unlike in Article XXVIII, there is no reference to Members with a principal supplying interest and the requirement is to negotiate equally with Members with INRs and a substantial interest. In substance, however, these differences are of no consequence. In the event of disagreement the matter may be referred to the Ministerial Conference for prompt examination. The Member invoking Article XVIII:7 may proceed with the modification or withdrawal if it is found that the compensatory adjustment offered is adequate, or when it is not adequate if it is determined that the Member has made every reasonable effort to offer adequate compensation. The right of affected Members to withdrawal of substantially equivalent concessions is the same as in Article XXVIII.

Renegotiations in the context of formation of customs unions

17.   Article XXIV:6 stipulates that if, in the process of the formation of a customs union the duties have to be raised beyond the bound level in one or more of the constituent territories, the procedures for renegotiations in Article XXVIII are to be followed. In providing for compensatory adjustment in such renegotiations, due account has to be taken of the reduction brought about in the corresponding duty by other constituents of the union, sometimes referred to as internal compensation. The Uruguay Round Understanding on the Interpretation of Article XXIV of GATT 1994 adds little of substance to the provision in Article XXIV:6. On the question of a time-frame for the renegotiations, it reaffirms that the procedures must be commenced before tariff concessions are modified or withdrawn. If the renegotiations cannot be concluded within a reasonable period of time, the customs union can proceed with the modification or withdrawal of the concession, giving the affected Members the right to withdraw substantially equivalent concessions.

Withdrawal of concessions

18.   The last provision for modification or withdrawal is contained in Article XXVII of GATT 1994. This Article allows a Member to withhold or withdraw a concession which was made during general tariff conferences or during multilateral rounds of trade negotiations if the participating government with which the concession was negotiated does not eventually become a Member or, having become a Member, ceases to be one. There is no time limit for the invocation of the Article but the Member concerned has to consult with Members which have a substantial interest in the product concerned. This provision has been generally incorporated in the Protocols embodying the results

of tariff negotiations, including the Marrakesh Protocol on the Uruguay Round concessions.

C.   Other Provisions Relating to Tariff Negotiations and Renegotiations

Most-favoured-nation treatment

1.   Tariff negotiations under the General Agreement are to be held on a non-discriminatory basis as provided for in Article I, on general most-favoured-nation treatment. This article requires that in all matters connected with imports and exports, including customs duties and similar charges, international transfer of payments, method of levying such duties and charges, rules and formalities, internal taxes or charges and regulations affecting internal sale, purchase, transportation, distribution and use of imported products,

> "any advantage, favour, privilege or immunity granted by any contracting party to any product originating in, or destined for, any other country shall be accorded immediately and unconditionally to the like product originating in, or destined for, the territories of all other contracting parties".

2.   Thus, a WTO Member has not only to treat all other Members equally, but has to extend to each of them the best treatment it accords to any trading partner. An important element of the obligation is that the extension of any concession or favour to all Members has to be immediate and unconditional. All tariff concessions made by Members in the course of negotiations and renegotiations have to be extended to all other Members on a non-discriminatory basis. It follows also that all modifications and withdrawals of tariff concessions, including retaliatory withdrawals, must be applied on a non-discriminatory basis.

3.   Although the MFN clause barred the grant or maintenance of any tariff preference, an exception was made for the "historical" preferences which were listed in Article I and Annexes A to F of GATT 1947. The most extensive of the excepted preferences were those of the Commonwealth countries and of France. While these preferences were allowed to be maintained, an important advance was made in keeping with the spirit of the MFN clause, insofar as margins of preference were frozen at the levels indicated in the schedules of tariff concessions, or, where such a margin had not been indicated in the schedules, at the historical level that existed on the dates mentioned in the text of, or annexes to, GATT 1947.

4.   Article I exceptions were of considerable economic importance at the time GATT 1947 came into being, but their importance rapidly dwindled. Preferential margins were eroded as the MFN tariffs were reduced in successive negotiations and in most cases preferential tariffs were not. Moreover, other developments, such as the formation of the European Economic Community, led to the absorption of some of the preferences in such arrangements as the Lomé Convention, for which now waivers, and not the historical preferences, provide the legal basis. When the UK acceded to the EEC, the Commonwealth

preferences were largely withdrawn. Some residual preferences continue to exist even now, but their economic importance is very small. Still smaller are the lists of preferential concessions on which commitments continue in schedules of WTO Members.

Schedules of concessions

5.   After tariff negotiations have taken place, the results are incorporated in the schedules of concessions of the participant concerned. Each WTO Member has a schedule of concessions unlike in GATT 1947, when several contracting parties which had followed the route of succession under Article XXVI:5(c) did not have any schedules. The schedule of each Member is given a number in Roman numerals by order of accession. Under GATT 1947 at the outset the schedules had two parts: Part I for MFN concessions and Part II for preferential concessions. Two more parts have been added since then: Part III lists concessions on non-tariff measures and Part IV lists the specific commitments made during the Uruguay Round on domestic support and export subsidies in agriculture. The obligations in respect of concessions and commitments incorporated in the schedules are contained in Article II of the General Agreement. The fundamental aim of this article is to ensure the predictability and security of tariff commitments contained in the schedules. The most important implication of a tariff concession is that there is a commitment not to apply customs duty upon the importation of the product above the level indicated in the schedule. This tariff level is thus "bound" against an increase.

Other duties or charges (ODCs)

6.   Article II provides for the products listed in the Schedules, on their importation, to be "bound" against an increase not only in the ordinary customs duty but also in respect of all "other duties or charges of any kind" (ODCs) beyond those (i) imposed on the date of this Agreement, or (ii) directly or mandatorily required to be imposed thereafter by legislation in force in the importing country on that date. The level and the nature of the ODCs which a contracting party to GATT 1947 could levy on tariff items subject to concessions consistently with its obligations were not recorded in any international instrument. If and when a dispute were to arise on the issue, the contracting party concerned would have had to produce evidence from its national records to show that the ODCs were indeed in force at the particular level on the date of the Agreement or were "directly or mandatorily required to be imposed thereafter by legislation in force in the importing territory on that date". The Uruguay Round Understanding on the Interpretation of Article II:1(b) of GATT 1994 brought about a major change in respect of this provision. Now all ODCs have to be recorded in the Schedules and, where no such entry has been made in the relevant column of the Schedule, it is presumed that there are no ODCs on the tariff item. The Uruguay Round Understanding provides as follows:

> "In order to ensure transparency of the legal rights and obligations deriving from paragraph 1(b) of Article II, the nature and level of any

"other duties or charges" levied on bound items, as referred to in that provision, shall be recorded in the Schedules of concessions annexed to GATT 1994 against the tariff item to which they apply. It is understood that such recording does not change the legal character of "other duties or charges".

7.   The reference date in Article II of the General Agreement in respect of ODCs is "the date of this Agreement". For the purposes of the concessions negotiated in 1947, the date of the Agreement is 30 October 1947, as provided for in Article XXVI:1. For subsequent negotiations under GATT 1947, the reference date is the date of the Protocol to which the relevant schedules are annexed, be they accession negotiations or rounds of multilateral trade negotiations or other negotiations. Thus the date applicable to any concession for the purposes of Article II is the date of the instrument by which the concession was first incorporated into the General Agreement. The Uruguay Round Understanding specifies a particular date as the reference date for the concessions negotiated during the Round and makes the position clear about the future negotiations and renegotiations:

> "The date as of which "other duties or charges" are bound, for the purposes of Article II, shall be 15 April 1994. "Other duties or charges" shall therefore be recorded in the Schedules at the levels applying on this date. At each subsequent renegotiation of a concession or negotiation of a new concession the applicable date for the tariff item in question shall become the date of the incorporation of the new concession in the appropriate Schedule. However, the date of the instrument by which a concession on any particular tariff item was first incorporated into GATT 1947 or GATT 1994 shall also continue to be recorded in column 6 of the Loose-Leaf Schedules".

8.   It may be added that the new rule does not affect the position of ODCs with respect to pre-Uruguay Round concessions. The WTO Member retains the right as envisaged in Article II:1(b) with respect to such concessions. However, earlier concessions do have an implication for the level of ODCs to be recorded in future. Where a tariff item has previously been the subject of a concession, the Uruguay Round Understanding requires the level of ODCs recorded in the Schedule not to be higher than the level obtaining at the time of the first incorporation of the concession. A three-year time limit after the date of entry into force of the WTO Agreement, or after the date of deposit of the instrument incorporating the Schedule into GATT 1994, whichever is later, was given to any Member to challenge the existence of an ODC on the grounds that no such ODC existed at the time of the original binding, as well as the consistency of the recorded level with the previously bound level, but no such challenge was made.

9.   As a broad definition of "other duties or charges" it has been accepted that only those levies that discriminate against imports are covered, e.g. stamp duty, development tax, revenue duty etc. In GATT 1947 panels, import deposit schemes and charges on transfer of payments imposed by governments have also

been found to be covered by the limitation on imposition of ODCs in respect of the products on which tariff commitments have been made.

10. Article II of the General Agreement allows the introduction of terms, conditions or qualifications in the Schedules in respect of tariff commitments. Yet it has been recognized in practice that Article II creates for the Members "the possibility to incorporate into the legal framework of the General Agreement commitments additional to those already contained in the General Agreement and to qualify such additional commitments, not however to reduce their commitments under other provisions of the General Agreement".

Levies that do not impinge on bound concessions

11. Article II clearly itemizes the categories of levies on imports which do not impinge on bound concessions. Thus, notwithstanding bound concessions in the Schedules, contracting parties (Members) have the freedom to impose the levies mentioned below:

(a) a charge equivalent to an internal tax imposed consistently with the provisions of paragraph 2 of Article III regarding national treatment;

(b) any anti-dumping or countervailing duty applied consistently with the provisions of Article VI;

(c) fees or other charges commensurate with the cost of services rendered.

12. Article VIII of the General Agreement separately stipulates that all fees and charges imposed on or in connection with importation or exportation shall be limited to the approximate cost of the services rendered. Thus, if fees are imposed in respect of bound tariff items which are disproportionate to the services rendered, they will infringe the obligations under both Articles VIII and Article II.

13. It needs to be mentioned here that any additional duty imposed pursuant to the special safeguard provisions of the Agreement on Agriculture and price-based measures imposed for balance-of-payments reasons under the Understanding on the Balance-of-Payments provisions of GATT 1994, also do not affect Article II commitments.

Import monopolies

14. Tariff concessions incorporated in the schedules have an implication not only for customs duties and ODCs but also for the pricing practices of import monopolies. Article II provides that such monopolies shall not "operate so as to afford protection on the average in excess of the amount of protection provided for in that Schedule". Specific arrangements relating to the operation of monopolies can also be negotiated and inscribed in the Schedules. An interpretative note to Article II, paragraph 4, states that the paragraph will be applied in the light of the provisions of Article 31 of the Havana Charter. This provision envisaged that Members of the ITO would negotiate "arrangements

designed to limit or reduce any protection that might be afforded through the operation of the monopoly to domestic producers of the monopolized product". In fact, in the 1947 Geneva negotiations and the 1950 Torquay negotiations, the Benelux countries and France made concessions on monopoly duties, minimum imports by an import monopoly or domestic selling prices of products subject to a monopoly. In such cases, the specific entries in the Schedules with respect to the operations of the monopoly determine the extent of the commitment.

Domestic court ruling on classification

15.   Paragraph 5 of Article II provides for consultation and negotiations for compensatory adjustment in the event domestic courts or quasi-judicial authorities in a Member rule on a classification question in a manner which is at variance with the concession embodied in the Schedule. This paragraph is really a provision for renegotiation of commitments made already. However, an important difference from other renegotiation provisions which we have considered earlier is that here the renegotiation can be done after the change in tariff, as against the requirement in Article XXVIII for renegotiation to be completed before the modification or withdrawal of the concession.

Specific duties and depreciation of currency

16.   Tariffs can be bound in *ad valorem* or specific terms. In cases in which they are expressed in specific terms the real incidence of tariffs can be affected by a depreciation of the currency. In the days of fixed exchange rates Article IV of the original Articles of Agreement of the International Monetary Fund required each member of the Fund to state a par value for its currency in terms of gold or US dollars of a fixed gold value. A change in the par value of a member's currency could be made only after consultation with the Fund. Paragraph 6 of Article II of GATT 1947 provided that in cases in which the par value was reduced consistently with the Articles of Agreement of the International Monetary Fund (from such value prevailing on "the date of this Agreement") by more than 20 per cent, the specific duties could be adjusted to take account of such reduction, provided that the CONTRACTING PARTIES concurred that such adjustments would not impair the value of the concessions. The "date of this Agreement" here has the same connotations as the "date of this Agreement" with reference to Article II:1(b) described earlier. Pursuant to this provision certain contracting parties were authorized to make adjustments nine times between 1950 and 1975.

17.   After the system of fixed exchange rates was abandoned, Article IV of the IMF Articles was revised so as not to require the stating of par values but instead to stipulate that "each member undertakes to collaborate with the Fund and other members to assure orderly exchange arrangements and to promote a stable system of exchange rates". Some members of the Fund have floating exchange rates, while others maintain the exchange rate against one other currency, a basket of currencies or an international unit of account. To take into account this

change in the international monetary system, a decision was adopted by the CONTRACTING PARTIES in 1980 providing as follows:

"In the present monetary situation the CONTRACTING PARTIES shall apply the provisions of Article II:6(a) as set out below unless they consider that this would not be appropriate in the circumstances of the particular case, for example, because it would lead to an impairment of the value of a specific duty concession.....

"If a contracting party, in accordance with Article II:6(a) of the General Agreement, requests the CONTRACTING PARTIES to concur with the adjustment of bound specific duties to take into account the depreciation of its currency, the CONTRACTING PARTIES shall ask the International Monetary Fund to calculate the size of the depreciation of the currency and to determine the consistency of the depreciation with the Fund's Articles of Agreement....

"The CONTRACTING PARTIES shall be deemed to have authorized the contracting party to adjust its specific duties....if the International Monetary Fund advises the CONTRACTING PARTIES that the depreciation calculated as set out above....is in excess of 20 per cent and consistent with the Fund's Articles of Agreement and if, during the sixty days following the notification of the Fund's advice to the contracting parties, no contracting party claims that a specific duty adjustment to take into account the depreciation would impair the value of the concession...."[8]

Schedules of concessions an integral part of GATT 1994

18.   Article II makes the annexed Schedules of Concessions an integral part of Part I of the General Agreement, which consists of Articles I and II of the Agreement. One of the consequences of this in GATT 1947 was that amendments to Schedules required acceptance by all contracting parties, as required in Article XXX of GATT 1947. The position has not changed in the WTO Agreement as it is provided that, in respect of certain articles (including Articles I and II of GATT 1994), amendments shall take effect only upon acceptance by all Members. We shall examine later the pragmatic ways in which GATT contracting parties dealt with the requirement of unanimity for the amendment of Schedules.

---

[8]   GATT, BISD, Twenty-seventh Supplement, pp. 28-29.

CHAPTER II

TARIFF CONFERENCES AND ROUNDS OF MULTILATERAL TRADE NEGOTIATIONS

A.   Overview

1.   Eight tariff conferences and rounds of multilateral trade negotiations were held between 1947 and 1994 within the legal framework outlined in Chapter I. These were the Geneva Tariff Conference (1947), the Annecy Tariff Conference (1949), the Torquay Tariff Conference (1950-51), the Geneva Tariff Conference (1956), the Geneva Tariff Conference (1960-1961), also known as the Dillon Round, the Kennedy Round (1964-1967), the Tokyo Round (1973-1979) and the Uruguay Round (1986-94). The first four conferences, which are also referred to as rounds, are known by the place where they were held, the next two after individuals who had provided the inspiration for the negotiations (US Under Secretary of State, Douglas Dillon and the US President, J.F. Kennedy). The last two rounds have been known by the place where the Ministers adopted the Declaration launching the negotiations.

2.   The Geneva Tariff Conference (1947) was held during the course of preparations for the Charter for the International Trade Organization, when 23 members of the Preparatory Committee appointed by the Economic and Social Council of the United Nations accepted the invitation of the United States to negotiate concrete arrangements for the reduction of tariffs and trade barriers. The idea was for the principal trading nations to take action "to enter into reciprocal and mutually advantageous negotiations directed to the substantial reduction of tariffs and to the elimination of preferences". Once the negotiations had taken place, these members wanted to give effect to the results without waiting for the Organization to come into existence. For this purpose they drew up the General Agreement on Tariffs and Trade (GATT 1947). The Annecy Tariff Conference was convened to enable negotiations to take place between the existing contracting parties and 11 governments which had requested accession, of which nine eventually became contracting parties (Denmark, Dominican Republic, Finland, Greece, Haiti, Italy, Nicaragua, Sweden and Uruguay). At Torquay, negotiations took place not only between the contracting parties and the six governments which had applied for accession (Austria, Federal Republic of Germany, Korea, Peru, the Philippines and Turkey), but also among the contracting parties themselves for additional concessions. Two out of the six governments, viz. Korea and the Philippines, which negotiated for accession at Torquay, became contracting parties after fresh accession negotiations many years later.

3.   The Geneva Tariff Conference of 1956 was somewhat unique. Only 25 out of 39 contracting parties agreed to participate in the negotiations and concessions were made only by twenty-two. These negotiations were held under the procedures established by the CONTRACTING PARTIES for negotiations to be held at any time between two or more contracting parties. However, since all

the major trading nations participated in the negotiations and exchanged concessions, this tariff conference is normally listed as a round of multilateral negotiations.

4.   The Geneva Tariff Conference (1960-61), or the Dillon Round, was convened in the context of the formation of the European Economic Community with the initial six members. The first part of the Conference was devoted to conducting renegotiations under Article XXIV:6 with the EEC and the second to holding a general round of negotiations among contracting parties for new concessions. During the second part, governments negotiating accession were also given the opportunity to carry out tariff negotiations for their accession.

5.   The Kennedy Round was a major attempt to reduce tariffs on an across-the-board basis. A plurilateral agreement on anti-dumping practices was also negotiated. Attempts were made, albeit unsuccessfully, to negotiate broader agreements on agricultural protection going beyond tariffs. The focus, however, remained very much on tariff negotiations.

6.   In the Tokyo Round, while tariff negotiations were important, the negotiations on non-tariff measures were given equal, if not greater, importance. No tariff conference under GATT 1947 was confined purely to tariffs and even the early rounds envisaged negotiations on quotas and the protection afforded through the operation of import and export monopolies. But it was during the Tokyo Round that a successful attempt was made to negotiate agreements on a range of non-tariff measures. Understandings were also reached during the Round on such basic or "framework" issues as differential and more favourable treatment of developing countries, dispute settlement and balance-of-payments safeguards.

7.   In the Uruguay Round, negotiations on trade in services and trade-related aspects of intellectual property rights attracted greater attention at the outset than trade in goods. In the area of trade in goods, agricultural negotiations held centre stage throughout the round. Tariff negotiations relating to industrial products, although not regarded as the main achievement of the round, did contribute to the success of the negotiations as a whole.

B.   Modalities of Tariff Negotiations

The early rounds

1.   The rules and procedures adopted for the first three rounds of negotiations were guided by the provisions of the ITO Charter. The rules for the Geneva Tariff Conference mentioned that, since the results of the negotiations would need to be fitted into the framework of the International Trade Organization after the Charter had been adopted, the negotiations must proceed in accordance with the relevant provisions of the Charter as already provisionally formulated. The rules and procedures for these negotiations had the following common elements which were based on the provisions of the Charter:

(i)   The negotiations were to be conducted on a selective product-by-product basis;

(ii)   The requests for reduction of tariff on a product could be made in principle only in respect of products of which the requesting countries were individually or collectively the principal suppliers to the countries from which the concessions were asked;

(iii)   Each participating government had full flexibility on granting concessions on individual products; it was free not to grant concessions on individual products; or if it chose to grant a concession, it could reduce the duty or bind it at the existing or a specified higher level;

(iv)   The binding against increase of low duties or of duty-free treatment was in principle recognized as a concession equivalent in value to the substantial reduction of high duties or the elimination of preferences;

(v)   The negotiations were to proceed strictly on the basis of reciprocity and no government was to be required to grant unilateral concessions, or to grant concessions to other governments without receiving adequate concessions in return.

2.   During the early years of GATT 1947, the CONTRACTING PARTIES attached particular importance to the objective of the gradual elimination of preferences. The rules and procedures of the first three tariff conferences were designed to achieve this objective. For this purpose, the rules for the Annecy and Torquay negotiations reproduced paragraph (c) of Article 17 of the Havana Charter, as noted below :

1.   "In negotiations relating to any specific product with respect to which a preference applies,

(i)   when a reduction is negotiated only in the most-favoured-nation rate, such reduction shall operate automatically to reduce or eliminate the margin of preference applicable to that product;

(ii)   when a reduction is negotiated only in the preferential rate, the most-favoured-nation rate shall automatically be reduced to the extent of such reduction;

(iii)   when it is agreed that reductions will be negotiated in both the most-favoured-nation rate and the preferential rate, the reduction in each shall be that agreed by the parties to the negotiations; and

(iv)   no margin of preference shall be increased."[1]

---

[1]   GATT Doc. GATT/CP.2/26 and GATT, BISD, Vol. I, p. 104.

Discussions after the Torquay Conference: the problem of low-tariff countries

3.　　While the Geneva and Annecy negotiations were considered to be great successes, the results at Torquay were not as broad or as extensive as had been hoped initially. One of the problems arose from the difficulty encountered by low-tariff countries in entering into tariff negotiations. The issue is best summarized in the report of the ICITO published in January 1952 after the conclusion of the Torquay negotiations:

> "Another inhibiting factor was the problem presented by the disparities in the levels of tariffs. A number of European countries with a comparatively low level of tariff rates considered that they had entered the Torquay negotiations at a disadvantage. Having bound many of their rates of duty in 1947 and 1949, what could these low-tariff countries offer at Torquay in order to obtain further concessions from the countries with higher levels of tariffs? The rules adopted by the CONTRACTING PARTIES for their negotiations stipulate that the binding of a low duty or of duty-free treatment is to be recognized as a concession equivalent in value to the substantial reduction of high tariffs or the elimination of tariff preferences. Some thought that, in observance of this rule, the high-tariff countries should make further reductions in their duties in exchange for the prolongation of binding of low duties. But although the high-tariff countries were sometimes willing to offer concessions without expecting comparable reductions from countries with low tariffs, they were not prepared to grant what they considered to be unilateral and unrequited concessions. No general solution was found at Torquay, but the question will be further explored in the near future. Meanwhile, the area of negotiations between some of the European countries was restricted by this divergence of view."[2]

4.　　To resolve the above difficulties experienced during the Torquay negotiations, the Benelux countries put forward a proposal which involved the unilateral reduction of duties by high-tariff countries. Subsequently France suggested a plan which was to be applied by all contracting parties and which envisaged an agreement among governments to reduce their tariff levels by a fixed percentage. The French plan was refined and improved by a Sub-Group of 11 industrialized countries whose report[3] was adopted by the CONTRACTING PARTIES on 13 October 1953. The broad features of the improved plan, which came to be known as the GATT Plan, were the following:

> (i)　　Bilateral negotiations between contracting parties on a selective product-by-product basis were to be replaced by the adoption of a common plan for reduction of duties across-the-board; each participating country was to reduce by 30 per cent the average

---

[2]　　ICITO, GATT in Action: Third Report on the Operation of the General Agreement on Tariffs and Trade, 1952, pp. 9-10.

[3]　　GATT, BISD, Second Supplement, pp. 67-92.

incidence of its duties in each of the ten sectors into which import trade was divided; the reduction was to be achieved in three years through annual cuts of ten per cent each;

(ii) The balance for any particular contracting party was to be measured not by setting off specific concessions obtained against specific concessions granted but by setting off the overall concessions made by it under the common plan and those made by its trading partners;

(iii) The plan required efforts proportionate to each contracting party's tariff level; a demarcation line was calculated for this purpose on the basis of a weighted average of the weighted averages of the tariffs of ten European and North American countries, after exclusion of the revenue component of these duties; if, for any sector the average incidence of the duties of a participating country was lower than a demarcation line, the reduction to be effected was to be proportionately decreased; if the average incidence was equal to or lower than a floor (say 50 per cent) of the rate at the demarcation line, the participating country was to be exempted from the requirement to reduce the average incidence of its duties for that sector;

(iv) There was an obligation to reduce individual rates of duty which exceeded given levels; ceiling levels were prescribed for raw materials (5 per cent), semi-manufactures (15 per cent), finished manufactures (30 per cent) and agricultural products (27 per cent), and the individual rates of duty had to be brought down to the level of the ceiling;

(v) Each contracting party was free to vary the reduction to be made on individual items (except to the extent required in respect of rates above the stipulated ceiling rates), but the aggregate average reduction for each sector was to be the percentage required on the basis of the demarcation line;

(vi) Specific provisions were to apply to "countries and customs territories in the process of economic development"; the reduction of the average incidence was to be computed on the tariff as a whole and not by the sectors; there was to be a common demarcation line of say 10 per cent; the duties affecting products included in their programme of economic development were to be excluded from reduction of the average tariff incidence as well as reduction of high tariffs (above the ceiling level) for individual items.

1956 Geneva Tariff Conference

5.   Despite the broad support for the GATT plan for tariff reduction, when the next tariff conference was convened in 1956, there was no consensus on proceeding on that basis and, in adopting the rules and procedures[4] for the new round, the CONTRACTING PARTIES reverted to the selective product-by-product technique. These negotiations were held on the basis of Article XXIX of the revised General Agreement which was later to be re-numbered as Article XXVIII *bis*. The new Article provided for negotiations to be carried out either on a selective product-by-product basis or "by the application of such multilateral procedures as may be accepted by the contracting parties concerned". But the rules adopted for the negotiations mentioned only the selective product-by-product basis.

1960/61 Geneva Tariff Conference: (Dillon Round)

6.   The bilateral item-by-item negotiation procedures were also generally adopted in the rules for the 1960/61 Geneva Tariff Conference, which came to be known as the Dillon Round. The rules of the negotiations[5] mentioned that the negotiations would be held on the basis of the principles of Article XXVIII *bis*. Taking advantage of the reference in this article to "such multilateral procedures as may be accepted by the contracting parties concerned", the European Economic Community tabled an offer of a linear 20 per cent tariff reduction with certain exceptions. While the United Kingdom matched this offer, other contracting parties adhered to the selective product-by-product technique.

Kennedy Round (1964-67)

7.   During the Kennedy Round (1964-67), which was launched with the adoption by the Ministers of a Resolution[6] on 21 May 1963, two major departures were made in the negotiating modalities. First, it was agreed that the tariff negotiations among industrialized countries in respect of industrial products, would be based upon a plan of "substantial linear tariff reductions". Second, while the principle of reciprocity remained the general rule guiding the negotiations, it was agreed that "the developed countries cannot expect to receive reciprocity from the less-developed countries". Further details of the concept of non-reciprocity are given later in the section below on developing countries.

8.   Two main considerations led to the adoption of the linear approach. First, the item by item, request-offer method adopted in past negotiations, with its dependence on the extent to which the principal supplier was willing to reciprocate the reduction of duty in a particular product, had led to very small reductions which were in some cases worthless in commercial terms. Second,

---

[4]   GATT, BISD, Fourth Supplement, p. 81-82.

[5]   GATT, BISD, Eighth Supplement, p. 115.

[6]   GATT, BISD, Twelfth Supplement, pp. 47-49.

with the increase in the number of contracting parties the traditional method had become increasingly cumbersome and unwieldy.

9.   During the negotiations the participants agreed that the rate of 50 per cent would be used "as a working hypothesis for the determination of the general rate of linear reduction". Exceptions to the linear reduction were envisaged, but it was stipulated that there would be a bare minimum of exceptions "which would be subject to confrontation and justification". They had to be justified on the basis of "overriding national interests" and could not be based on sectoral interest or bargaining considerations. The process of confrontation and justification was carried out in a body attended by the governments participating in the negotiations on the basis of the linear offer.

10.   The Ministerial Resolution which had launched the Kennedy Round had envisaged that criteria would be developed during negotiations for "determining significant disparities in tariff levels and the special rules applicable for tariff reductions in these cases". The resolution had also recognized the problem of "certain countries with a very low average level of tariffs or with a special economic or trade structure such that equal linear tariff reductions may not provide an adequate balance of advantage". On the problem of tariff disparity, several proposals were made designed to secure larger reductions in products on which the tariff levels were high, but no consensus could be reached on the criteria. In the end the European Economic Community received satisfaction in the reciprocal balancing exercise in bilateral negotiations by applying a set of criteria that resulted in the reduction of its tariff by less than 50 per cent on items on which the existing duties were significantly lower in the EEC than in the United States and the United Kingdom. It was also agreed that Canada was a country with a special economic or trade structure and further that Australia, New Zealand and South Africa, by virtue of their very large dependence on exports of agricultural and other primary products, also fell in the same category. All four countries were therefore allowed to make item-by-item offers of the traditional type instead of adopting the approach for linear reduction. However, in the case of these countries, the expectation remained that they would grant concessions of equivalent value.

Tokyo Round (1973-79)

11.   The Ministerial Declaration[7] which launched the Tokyo Round (1973-79) envisaged that the negotiations should aim, *inter alia*, to "conduct negotiations on tariffs by employment of appropriate formulae of as general application as possible". In the negotiations, a number of proposals were made in respect of industrial tariffs as indicated below:

   (a)   Canada proposed that duties lower than 5 per cent should be abolished, those between 5 and 20 per cent reduced by 50 or 60

---

7   GATT, BISD, Twentieth Supplement, p. 19.

per cent, and those higher than 20 per cent brought down to 20 per cent;

(b)   United States suggested that there should be a linear reduction formula with an element of harmonization, subject to a maximum reduction of 60 per cent. The proposal was to cut tariffs by an amount equal to one and a half times the amount of the tariff plus 50 per cent, up to a maximum cut of 60 per cent. The formula proposed was $y = 1.5\,x + 50$ where y was the rate of reduction and x the initial rate of duty;

(c)   The EEC's harmonization formula was $y = x$ (4 times) where $y =$ rate of reduction and $x =$ initial rate of duty. With a base rate of 20 per cent, the result obtained is 10.28 per cent, as explained below:

1st stage (20% of 20% = 4%) 20% - 4% = 16%

2nd stage (16% of 16% = 2.56%) 16% - 2.56% = 13.44%

3rd stage (13.44% of 13.44% = 1.81%) 13.44% - 1.81% = 11.63%

4th stage (11.63% of 11.63% = 1.35%) 11.63% - 1.35% = 10.28%

(d)   Japan proposed a linear reduction formula of 70 per cent with a permanent harmonization element of 3.5 per cent *ad valorem*. Where the base rate is 20 per cent, a reduction by 70 per cent gives a rate of 6 per cent. Adding 3.5 per cent, the final rate comes to 9.5 per cent. The reduction obtained is about 50 per cent.

(e)   Switzerland suggested the following harmonization formula:

A = coefficient (14 or 16)

X = initial rate of duty

Z = resulting rate of duty

The application of each of the formulae mentioned above results in harmonization, i.e., the higher the duty, the larger the reduction.

12.   The Swiss formula was eventually accepted by most industrialized countries as a working hypothesis for reduction of tariffs on industrial products. The United States, Japan, Switzerland and Czechoslovakia made their offers on the basis of the coefficient of 14, whereas the European Community, the Nordic countries, Australia, Austria and Hungary used the coefficient of 16, which resulted in slightly lower reductions. Canada applied a different formula and New Zealand, South Africa and Iceland carried out negotiations according to the item-by-item technique. Negotiations among the main developed countries were concluded in June 1979 and it was only later that a number of developing countries engaged in serious negotiations and obtained additional concessions from Canada and the EEC. For negotiations on agricultural tariffs, the item-by-item technique continued to apply even in negotiations among the industrialized countries.

13.   The rules adopted for the negotiations on industrial tariffs did not contain any reference to exceptions. In actual fact, however, the governments which made their offers on the basis of the accepted formula exempted many product

groups from its application. They made either shallower cuts or excluded products altogether from reduction. Such exceptions or exclusions were then compensated by deeper than formula reductions on other products or groups of products.

Uruguay Round

14. The Punta del Este Ministerial Declaration[8] which launched the Uruguay Round did not stipulate whether the tariff negotiations would follow the linear or formula approach or would revert to the earlier practice of product-by-product approach. The following paragraph was included in the Declaration on the subject of tariffs:

> "Negotiations shall aim, by appropriate methods, to reduce or, as appropriate, eliminate tariffs, including the reduction or elimination of high tariffs and tariff escalation. Emphasis shall be given to the expansion of the scope of tariff concessions among all participants."

Main proposals for tariff reduction

15. When the discussion began in the negotiating group on tariffs, the modality of negotiations was the main question addressed. The following paragraphs summarize some of the key proposals that were made.

16. The United States advocated the adoption of a request-and-offer approach. It argued that, after the previous rounds, the tariff regimes of countries which had participated in the formula cuts had already been substantially liberalized and little overall protection remained to justify a linear approach. Further, modern data processing techniques made it possible to conduct request-offer negotiations efficiently. Moreover, such procedures were best suited to address tariff peaks and tariff escalation, the reduction of which was an objective of the negotiations.

17. The proposal made by the EC was designed to ensure that higher tariffs were subjected to deeper cuts in the industrialized countries and that there was effective participation by the developing countries. For industrialized and more advanced developing countries, the EC made the following proposal for reduction of duties:

-   base rate of 40% or higher: reduction to a ceiling of 20%
-   base rate of less than 40%: reduction on the following basis:

    - rates between 0% and 29%

    $$R = D + 20$$

    (where R is the percentage reduction and D the base rate of the customs duty);

    - rates between 30% and 40%

---

[8]   GATT, BISD, Thirty-third Supplement, p. 19.

$$R = 50$$

(flat rate reduction of 50%).

For other developing countries (other than the least-developed) the approach proposed was as follows:

- base rate of more than 35%: reduction to a ceiling of 35%
- base rate of 35% or less: possibility of bilateral negotiations with a view to reducing and harmonizing the rate of duty.

For the least-developed countries it was proposed that contributions would be made within the limits of their capabilities.

18.   Thus the EC proposed a formula approach with a modicum of a bilateral element. One of the matters on which the EC had initially taken a strong view was elimination of tariff rates below 3 per cent. While some participants regarded such tariffs as having only a nuisance value with little protective effect, the EC was opposed to their elimination as even low tariffs gave participants a certain negotiating leverage. In its final proposal, the EC expressed willingness to consider eliminating such tariffs on the condition that "no compensation or credit is claimed" for such action.

19.   In the beginning, Japan proposed the elimination of tariffs on all industrial products without exception. Subsequently, it proposed that developed countries eliminate a certain proportion of their tariffs. Tariffs which were not eliminated were to be subject to reductions under a harmonization formula such as the one used in the Tokyo Round.

20.   Canada suggested the adoption of the following formula:

$$R = 32 + \frac{D}{5}$$

where R is the rate of reduction and D is the base rate. In performing the calculation "D over 5" the result had to be rounded down to the next full number. The maximum figure for R was to be 38 per cent. The proposal also involved eliminating rates which fell below 3 per cent after applying the formula. Canada suggested also that the request and offer approach would supplement the tariff reduction formula approach with a view to providing the maximum possible reduction or elimination of tariffs and NTBs.

21.   Switzerland proposed the following harmonization formula, which was similar to the one used in the Tokyo Round:

$$Z = \frac{15x}{15 + x} \text{ where } Z = \text{final duty and } x = \text{initial duty.}$$

22.   Many developing countries expressed a preference for the formula approach while maintaining that they themselves needed to take into account their individual development, financial and trade needs. Brazil proposed a general formula which consisted of binding at zero level by developed countries of their tariffs on all products, to be applied on a preferential basis only to the developing countries for a period of ten years. After that period, the zero rate was to be extended to all countries. Some developing countries called for the need to

establish an approach for giving recognition to the liberalization measures already adopted by them.

Mid-Term Review

23.   At the mid-term review meeting at Montreal, agreement was reached not on whether a formula or request-offer approach had to be adopted but on a number of key points which guided the negotiations thereafter. The Ministers agreed on the following approach, subject to the understanding that the participation of developing countries in the tariff negotiations would be in accordance with the general principle governing the negotiations as laid down in the Punta del Este Declaration:

"(a)   A substantial reduction or, as appropriate, elimination of tariffs by all participants with a view to achieving lower and more uniform rates, including the reduction or elimination of high tariffs, tariff peaks, tariff escalation and low tariffs, with a target amount for overall reductions at least as ambitious as that achieved by the formula participants in the Tokyo Round.

(b)   A substantial increase in the scope of bindings, including bindings at ceiling levels, so as to provide greater security and predictability in international trade.

(c)   The need for an approach to be elaborated to give credit for bindings; it is also recognized that participants will receive appropriate recognition for liberalization measures adopted since 1 June 1986.

(d)   The phasing of tariff reductions over appropriate periods to be negotiated."[9]

Initial offers

24.   Further proposals after Montreal to reach agreement on a formula approach did not succeed and in the procedures approved in January 1990 it was agreed that the participants would submit proposals for the reduction, elimination and binding of tariffs on a line-by-line basis in accordance with the agreement reached at the mid-term review. This implied that it was left to each participant to determine the manner in which it would reach the overall target of reduction, which translated into a quantitative reduction of one-third (33 1/3)%). In making their offers the developed countries which had proposed a formula used either the formula proposed by themselves or those proposed by others. The EC and Finland, Sweden and Norway employed (the latter with some variations) the formula proposed by the EC, while Canada, Japan and Austria used the formula proposed by Canada, except that Austria did not subject the reduction to a

---

[9]   Uruguay Round Doc. MTN.TNC/7(MIN), p. 4.

maximum of 38 per cent as proposed by Canada. Australia adopted the following formula, where D = base rate and R = rate of reduction, with some exceptions:

where D> 15% $R = \dfrac{D\text{-}15 \times 100}{D}$

where 10% > D ≤15 $R = \dfrac{D\text{-}10 \times 100}{D}$

where D≤2 $R = 100\%$ (elimination).

25.   The United States stuck to its approach of following the request-offer, item-by-item technique. Its original submission on industrial tariffs was in two parts. It proposed tariff elimination in respect of a number of product groups if two conditions were met: (a) other participants provided duty-free treatment on the same products; and (b) non-tariff measures on such products, wherever relevant, were eliminated. The other part of its offer contained a list of products on which it was willing to grant concessions "only in response to requests from other participants, and in exchange for acceptable offers on both tariffs, and where relevant, non-tariff measures". In regard to its intentions for conducting market access negotiations, the United States stated that it would accept requests from its trading partners either on a "request/offer" basis or a "formula" basis. Item-by-item requests submitted by trading partners employing a "request/offer" approach were to be considered in their entirety, without regard to the requesting country's supplier status. For requests made on the basis of a "formula" approach, the United States said that it would limit its consideration to those items for which the requesting country was the principal supplier.

26.   In a subsequent submission made by the United States, the proposal for tariff elimination in product groups and sectors was considerably expanded. Specific tariff offers were made on other products except those where it was indicated that the US had reserved the item. The US offer explained that such reserves arose from two situations:

(a)   where the principal supplier of the item had not requested a concession from the United States until that time; or

(b)   where countries with which the United States was not negotiating in the Uruguay Round supplied a substantial share of imports to its market.

The US submission further stated that in either situation the US was willing to consider a tariff reduction on the item if the requesting country offered reciprocity "based on the most-favoured-nation value of the trade in the tariff line". An important point made in the US submission of offers was that countries failing to participate in the Uruguay Round market access negotiations should not receive the benefits from these negotiations. In order to achieve this objective, the United States stated its intention "to refine U.S. offers sufficiently to ensure that offers responded primarily to the interests of those trading partners having submitted specific requests and having made specific offers".

Tokyo Accord and after

27.   In subsequent negotiations the sectoral proposals for the elimination of tariffs ("zero for zero" as they came to be called) occupied a central place in the negotiations among developed countries. In some of these sectors there were also proposals for harmonization of tariffs whereby all participants would agree to bring down the duty rates to the same level. Such proposals were made for chemicals, textiles and clothing and non-ferrous metals. While the principal impulse for the sectoral proposals came from the United States, the EC put its weight behind reduction of tariff peaks. Disagreements among the major trading countries on these aspects were one of the reasons that delayed the conclusion of the Round. Industrial tariff negotiations resumed only after Canada, the EC, Japan and the US (known as the QUAD) reached an agreement on these issues at Tokyo in July 1993. A communication[10] from Japan dated 7 July 1993, circulated to all participants contained the following summary of the Tokyo accord:

"(a)   Tariff and non-tariff measure elimination: In the context of a far-reaching and balanced market access package, we have thus far identified a common list of product sectors for complete elimination of tariff and non-tariff measures (pharmaceuticals, construction equipment, medical equipment, steel - subject to the MSA, beer, and subject to certain agreed exceptions, furniture, farm equipment and spirits). We shall seek to add to this list as many sectors as possible.

(b)   Harmonization: We have identified chemical products for a harmonization of tariffs at low rates, including, in some cases, zero, and further negotiations may lead to the harmonization of tariffs in additional product areas.

(c)   For tariffs of 15 per cent and above, we will negotiate the maximum achievable package of tariff reductions, recognizing the objective of reaching 50 per cent reductions, subject to agreed exceptions and to other exporting countries agreeing to provide effective market access through tariff reductions and appropriate non-tariff disciplines.

(d)   Other tariff cuts: For products other than those subject to (a) and (c) above, we will negotiate tariff cuts by an average of at least one-third. We have also identified a number of sectors where tariffs could be reduced substantially beyond this level, in some cases, possibly beyond 50 per cent."

---

[10]   Uruguay Round Doc. MTN.TNC/W/113; MSA refers to the Multilateral Steel Agreement covering non-tariff measures also, which was sought initially by the participants in the zero-for-zero initiative on steel as a pre-condition for the elimination of tariffs. Negotiations for the MSA were not successful and the pre-condition was dropped.

28.   The negotiations among the developed countries thereafter concentrated heavily on the search for sectors for tariff elimination and harmonization. While a number of developing countries were approached to join the sectoral proposals only a few agreed to participate. However, even without a majority of the developing countries, it was ensured that the sectoral agreements had a sufficiently broad-based participation, as will be seen from the following estimates of trade coverage made on the basis of 1994 data:

Proposals for tariff elimination

Product sector	Participants	1994 exports percentage of world exports	1994 imports percentage of world imports
Agricultural equipment	Canada, EU (12), Hong Kong, Iceland, Japan, Korea, Norway, Singapore, Switzerland, US	88.24	74.94
Beer	Australia, Canada, EU (12), Hong Kong, Japan, US	79.76	85.97
Construction equipment	Canada, EU (12), Hong Kong, Japan, Korea, Norway, Singapore, Switzerland, US	84.84	64.00
Distilled spirits (Brown)	Canada, EU (12), Hong Kong, Iceland, Japan, Norway, US	86.63	78.17
Furniture	Canada, EU (12), Hong Kong, Japan, Korea, Norway, Singapore, Switzerland, US	72.44	85.53
Medical equipment	Canada, EU (12), Hong Kong, Iceland, Japan, Norway, Singapore, Switzerland, US	89.73	74.30
Paper	Canada, EU (12), Hong Kong, Japan, Korea, New Zealand, Singapore, US	71.16	71.63

Product sector	Participants	1994 exports percentage of world exports	1994 imports percentage of world imports
Pharmaceuticals	Australia, Canada, Czech Rep., EU(12), Iceland, Japan, New Zealand, Norway, Singapore, Slovak Rep., Switzerland, US	86.83	73.50
Steel	Canada, EU (12), Hong Kong, Japan, Korea, Norway, Singapore, US	72.54	63.77
Toys	Canada, EU (12), Finland, Japan, Korea, US	32.84	69.73

Proposal for Harmonization

Chemicals	Canada, Czech Republic, EU (12), Japan, Korea, Norway, Singapore, Slovak Republic, Switzerland, US	82.57	68.79

The harmonization proposal on chemicals envisaged elimination of duty in respect of HS Heading 2901-2902 and HS Chapter 30, reduction of duty to 5.5% in respect of Chapter 28 and HS 2903-2915 and to 6.5% in respect of HS Heading 2916-2942 and HS Chapters 31-39.

Source: WTO Secretariat.

29.   The negotiations on tariff peaks did result in considerable reduction but not elimination of rates above 15 per cent in the developed countries. The overall target for reduction by one-third in respect of industrial tariffs was reached by all developed countries and exceeded by some.

30.   As for the developing countries, one of the main objectives of the developed countries was to secure an increase in the scope of bindings. In respect of countries with interests in exports of textile and clothing products, the major trading countries sought to secure, with mixed success, reduction and binding of tariffs in the textile and clothing sector itself. In developing countries which made ceiling bindings, the effort of developed-country participants was to get the binding level closer to the applied level. (More details of the tariff offers of developing countries are given in Section E below.)

Tariff negotiations on tropical and natural resource-based products

31.   The negotiations on tariffs in respect of tropical products and natural-resource-based products proceeded on their own tracks in the separate

negotiating groups established by the Trade Negotiating Committee on the basis of separate mandates in the Punta del Este Ministerial Declaration that are reproduced below:

"Tropical products

Negotiations shall aim at the fullest liberalization of trade in tropical products, including in their processed and semi-processed forms, and shall cover both tariff and all non-tariff measures affecting trade in these products.

The CONTRACTING PARTIES recognize the importance of trade in tropical products to a large number of less-developed contracting parties and agree that negotiations in this area shall receive special attention, including the timing of the negotiations and the implementation of the results…"[11]

"Natural resource-based products

Negotiations shall aim to achieve the fullest liberalization of trade in natural resource-based products, including in their processed and semi-processed forms. The negotiations shall aim to reduce or eliminate tariff and non-tariff measures, including tariff escalation."[12]

In the negotiating group on tropical products, seven product groups were identified as tropical products, it being understood that the list was not exhaustive. These groups were: tropical beverages; spices, flowers and plaiting products; tobacco, rice and tropical roots; tropical fruits and nuts; natural rubber and tropical wood; jute and hard fibres. In respect of natural resource-based products, a proposal submitted by the Chairman in 1990 included fish and fish products, forestry and forestry products and non-ferrous metals and minerals in the basic definition, but there was no agreement on this list.

32.   In accordance with the Punta del Este mandate, the developed countries and a few developing countries made interim contributions on tropical products at the time of the mid-term review in December 1988.[13] Some of the contributions by the developed countries were on a preferential basis under the GSP. The following terms and conditions were attached to these contributions:

    (a)   Participants undertook to apply the reductions on a provisional basis, for the duration of the round. It was understood that if any participant found it necessary to withdraw any or all of its contributions, other participants could reassess their own contributions;

---

[11]   GATT, BISD, Thirty-third Supplement, p. 23.

[12]   Ibid.

[13]   Uruguay Round Doc. MTN.GNG/17 and Add.1; some further autonomous unilateral contributions were notified by participants after the issuance of this document.

    (b)   in relation to contributions made on an MFN basis, individual participants were to consider binding concessions at the end of the Round in the light of the overall results achieved.

33.   After the Montreal meeting, although work continued in the group on tropical products, the negotiations on these products were subsumed under the negotiations relating to tariffs on industrial products and the separate negotiations on agricultural products. In respect of natural resource-based products, the negotiations never really took off, although a great deal of technical work was done and the Chairman even made concrete proposals for the reduction of tariffs. All products regarded as natural resource-based products were dealt with in the group on tariffs.

Tariff negotiations on agriculture

34.   In agriculture, tariff negotiations were carried out as a part of the overall negotiations on market access, domestic subsidies and export subsidies. The following basic rules for agriculture negotiations are formally set out in the Uruguay Round Agreement on Agriculture:

    (i)   The coverage is given in terms of the Chapters, Codes and Headings of the Harmonized System. These are H.S. Chapters 1 to 24 less fish and fish products, H.S. Codes 2905.43 (mannitol), H.S. Code 2905.44 (sorbitol), H.S. Heading 33.01 (essential oils), H.S. Headings 35.01 to 35.05 (albuminoidal substances, modified starches, glues), H.S. Code 3809.10 (finished agents), H.S. Code 3823.60 (sorbitol n.e.p.), H.S. Headings 41.01 to 41.03 (hides and skins), H.S. Heading 43.01 (raw furskins), H.S. Headings 50.01 to 50.03 (raw silk and silk waste), H.S. Headings 51.01 to 51.03 (wool and animal hair), H.S. Headings 52.01 to 52.03 (raw cotton, waste and cotton carded or combed), H.S. Heading 53.01 (raw flax) and H.S. Heading 53.02 (raw hemp). It is specified that the product descriptions in round brackets are not necessarily exhaustive.

    (ii)   All border measures other than ordinary customs duties are required to be "tariffied" or to be converted into tariff equivalents, and maintenance of, resort to, or reversion to these measures are prohibited. A footnote to Article 4 of the Agreement on Agriculture lists these measures as including quantitative import restrictions, variable import levies, minimum import prices, discretionary import licensing, non-tariff measures maintained through state trading enterprises, voluntary export restraints, and similar border measures, whether or not the measures were maintained under country-specific derogations from the provisions of GATT 1947. However, the same footnote excludes measures maintained under balance-of-payments provisions or under other general, non-agriculture-specific provisions of GATT 1994 or of the Multilateral Trade Agreements in Annex 1A to the WTO Agreement.

(iii)   In agricultural products subject to tariffication, the Agriculture Agreement allows recourse to a special safeguard provision whereby Members may impose temporarily an additional duty on a product over the level at which the tariff is bound, if:

    (a)   the volume of imports of that product during any year exceeds a trigger level which is related to the existing market access opportunities as set out in the Agreement; or

    (b)   the price at which imports of that product falls below a trigger price equal to the average 1986 to 1988 reference price.

The additional duty in the event of imports exceeding the volumetric trigger is required not to exceed one-third of the ordinary customs duty. The additional duty in the event of a fall in the import price can be imposed in accordance with a scale graduated in proportion to the extent of fall in the price as provided in the Agreement.

(iv)   Section A of Annex 5 of the Agreement on Agriculture conditionally exempts from the tariffication requirement any primary agricultural product and its worked and/or prepared products if imports of such product during the base period (1986-88) are less than 3 per cent of the corresponding domestic consumption, no export subsidies have been provided and effective production-restricting measures are applied to the primary agricultural product. This exemption, which was designed to meet the concerns of Japan about rice, was not open-ended and had to be formally invoked before the Protocol embodying the results of the Uruguay Round was finalized. On the obligation side, the requirement is that the Member would have to establish minimum access opportunities amounting to 4 per cent of the base period domestic consumption for the first year of the implementation period. The quota has to be increased annually by 0.8 per cent of the domestic consumption so that, in the final year of the implementation period, it expands to 8 per cent of the domestic consumption. The Member concerned may choose not to apply the special treatment at any time during the period of implementation. As an incentive it is provided that where a Member ceases to avail itself of the special treatment it may only increase the minimum access opportunity by 0.4% per year (instead of 0.8%) during the remainder of the implementation period.

(v)   Section B of Annex B extends the above special treatment to developing countries in respect of any primary agricultural product that is the predominant staple in the traditional diet of the developing-country Member. A developing country Member availing itself of the special treatment has also to provide minimum access opportunities amounting to 1 per cent of the base period domestic consumption, increasing to 2 per cent in the fifth year and 4 per cent in the 10th year of the implementation period.

35.   As for the extent and manner of reduction of tariffs, the Agreement on Agriculture does not say anything. However, the Dunkel text,[14] which was proposed by the then Director-General and which became the basis of negotiations in this area without being formally adopted, had included an annex on modalities for market access negotiations which had the following elements:

(i)   The customs duties, including those resulting from tariffication, were to be reduced on a simple average basis by 36 per cent, with a minimum rate of reduction of 15 per cent for each tariff line to be implemented in six years. The base rate was to be the bound rate and for unbound rates the duties applied on 1 September 1986. For developing countries, the rate of reduction was fixed at two-thirds of the general rate, i.e., 24 per cent, with a minimum rate of reduction of 10 per cent. The implementation period for developing countries was 10 years. The least-developed countries were exempted from reduction commitments. In the case of products subject to unbound ordinary customs duties, developing countries had the additional flexibility of being able to offer ceiling bindings.

(ii)   Where there were no significant imports, minimum access opportunities had to be established. The minimum access opportunity was to be not less than 3 per cent of the domestic consumption in the base period (1986-88), increasing to 5 per cent by the end of the implementation period. Current access opportunities which, during the base period, were in excess of the minimum access requirement of 3 to 5 per cent had to be maintained and increased during the implementation period. For the purpose of minimum and current access opportunities, the participants were expected to bind an in-quota rate which had to be at a level at which trade flows could take place. This provision was made to safeguard against the possibility of the tariff levels resulting from tariffication being pitched so high as to prevent any trade from taking place.

(iii)   A separate annex in the Dunkel text laid down the procedures for the calculation of the tariff equivalent of non-tariff measures. This calculation had to be done by using the actual difference between internal and external prices. The external reference prices had to be determined in general on the basis of the actual average c.i.f. unit values for the importing country. Where average c.i.f. unit values were not available or appropriate, the external price had to be

---

[14]   Uruguay Round Doc. MTN.TNC/W/FA.

either (a) appropriate average c.i.f. unit values of a nearby country or (b) estimated from average f.o.b. unit values of one or more major exporters adjusted by adding an estimate of insurance, freight and other relevant costs to the importing country. The internal prices were generally to be a representative wholesale price on the domestic market or an estimate of that price where adequate data was not available. The external and internal prices had both to be calculated on the basis of the data for the years 1986 to 1988.

36.   In the implementation of these modalities, some latitude was tolerated by the Uruguay Round participants, specially in respect of tariffication and minimum access commitments. For many products in a number of countries, the tariff equivalents incorporated in the schedules were in fact much higher than the tariff equivalent during the base period calculated by some commentators. In relation to minimum access commitment, despite the MFN requirement, Members counted special arrangements as part of their minimum access commitments and allocated the minimum access to exporters having special arrangements. Thus the modalities for agriculture appear to have served only as broad guidelines and there was a considerable element of bilateral and plurilateral negotiations in the commitments that were finally accepted.

C.   Procedural Aspects of Rounds of Negotiations

The first five rounds

1.   Before Article XXVIII *bis* was introduced into GATT 1947, rounds of tariff negotiations were convened from time to time on an *ad hoc* basis. There was no requirement in GATT 1947 for the CONTRACTING PARTIES to convene conferences for such tariff-cutting exercises on a multilateral basis. The Dillon Round was the first to be convened after Article XXVIII *bis* had been introduced, enabling the CONTRACTING PARTIES to sponsor from time to time negotiations "on a reciprocal and mutually advantageous basis, directed to the substantial reduction of the general level of tariffs and other charges on imports and exports". However, in all the rounds up to the Dillon Round, since the approach adopted was that of product-by-product negotiations, the procedures followed were similar. Each round began with the adoption of a decision convening a tariff conference on a fixed future date. The decision required the contracting parties to exchange request lists and furnish the latest edition of their customs tariffs and their foreign trade statistics for a recent period well in advance of the first day of the conference and the offers had to be made on the first day. The negotiations were concluded generally over a period of six to seven months after the offers had been made. The Dillon Round was an exception and the negotiations took a year and a half to conclude. The following schedule stipulated for the Torquay negotiations was typical of early GATT rounds:

Not later than	22 November 1949	exchange of customs tariff, details of other import charges or taxes and of annual import statistics
Not later than	15 January 1950	exchange of lists of products on which concessions are intended to be requested
Not later than	15 June 1950	exchange of the final list of products on which tariff and other concessions are requested
Not later than (first day of meeting in Torquay)	28 September 1950	exchange of concessions offered, indicating the existing and proposed rate of duty on each item

2.   The rules of the Dillon Round stipulated not only the time frame of the negotiations but also the form in which the request and offer lists would be submitted. The request lists were to have information on the following:

(i)   Tariff item number

(ii)   Description of products

(iii)   Present rate of duty

(iv)   Requested rate of duty

The consolidated lists of offers were required to have information on the following:

(i)   The tariff item number

(ii)   Description of products

(iii)   Present rate of duty

(iv)   Requested rate of duty

(v)   Concession offered, and

(vi)   Countries to which the offer was made.

3.   Up to the Dillon Round, negotiations began only after the offers had been exchanged. These negotiations were essentially bilateral between pairs of delegations. A report[15] on the operation of GATT 1947 published by the ICITO in June 1950 mentions that 123 pairs of countries completed negotiations at Geneva and 147 at Annecy. The expectation was that 400 negotiations would take place at Torquay.

4.   The above account should not, however, give the impression that the negotiations were entirely bilateral in character. First, the request and offer lists were circulated to all participating governments. Second, these governments granted concessions not only on the basis of concessions received directly on

---

[15]   ICITO, Liberating World Trade: Second Report on the Operation of the General Agreement on Tariffs and Trade, 1950.

products for which their countries were principal suppliers but they also took into account the benefits derived by them on the basis of concessions exchanged between other pairs of countries. The following description of the process in the Geneva negotiations is given in another report published by the ICITO.

"The multilateral character of the Agreement enabled the negotiators to offer more extensive concessions than they might have been prepared to grant if the concessions were to be incorporated in separate bilateral agreements. Before the Geneva negotiations, a country would have aimed at striking a balance between the concessions granted to another country and the direct concessions obtained from it without taking into account indirect benefits which might accrue from other prospective trade agreements; it might even have been unwilling to grant an important concession if it had been obliged to extend that concession to third countries without compensation.

The multilateral method of negotiation thus maximized the scope and extent of the concessions granted. As a rule, the requests for concessions covered all products of interest to the negotiating countries; but for a product of which the principal supplier was not among the participating countries, the duty was generally reserved for negotiation on another occasion with that principal supplier; some duties thus reserved at Geneva have been negotiated with acceding governments at Annecy."[16]

5.   Adoption of the principal supplier rule was necessary because of the application of the most-favoured-nation rule concurrently with the principle of reciprocity. Concessions could not be granted to a small supplier unless reciprocal concessions had been received from the larger suppliers. In the event of a tariff concession being granted to the principal supplier, it was acceptable to some extent if the smaller supplier got a free ride. Instances of free ride were reduced when the participating governments agreed to take into account the indirect benefits in making their own offers. However, a free ride for the smallest suppliers could not be avoided.

Kennedy and Tokyo Rounds

6.   In the Kennedy and Tokyo Rounds, in which the linear or formula approaches were adopted in the Ministerial Decisions launching the rounds, the initial discussions related to bringing greater specificity to the approach. Once a decision had been taken (working hypotheses of 50 per cent in the Kennedy Round and the harmonization formula $Z = \dfrac{AX}{A + X}$ in the Tokyo Round) the participants were expected to submit their offers on the basis of the approach adopted. The next stage was the assessment by each participating country of the

---

[16]   ICITO, The Attack on Trade Barriers: A Progress Report on the Operation of the General Agreement on Tariffs and Trade from January 1948 to August 1949.

offers made by its trading partners. In such assessments the exceptions and exemptions were evaluated and each participating country sought from its trading partners additional concessions to make good the shortfalls in receiving reciprocity. For this purpose, request lists of product lines in which an improvement of the offer was sought were exchanged. Some participating countries took the stand that to redress the shortfalls they would withdraw or modify their own offers, and lists of such products were sent to the trading partners. In fact, during the Tokyo Round, some participating countries had made their initial offer on the basis of no exceptions and, thereafter, exceptions were made on the basis of evaluation of the offers of trading partners. The negotiating position of one of them was that it did not subscribe to the notion of compensation for exceptions, thereby implying that the only response to exceptions would be downward adjustment of its offers. A series of bilateral discussions were held in order to iron out the differences and to resolve the issue whether individual offers would be adjusted upwards or downwards in order to give satisfaction to the participating countries on the question of reciprocity. Multilateral discussions were also held to evaluate the offers. In the Kennedy Round, for instance, there was to be a process of "confrontation and justification" of departures from the working hypothesis of 50 per cent which participating countries were allowed to make for reasons of overriding national interest. Participating countries gave reasons for exceptions ranging from social and political considerations (declining and depressed industries, problems of small-scale enterprises, depressed areas, adverse effects for low-income people) to statutory requirements for exclusion (existing escape-clause action) and limits to negotiating authority granted by the legislature. While "confrontation and justification" took place in multilateral discussions, these debates had little influence on the course of the negotiations. One of the participants in the Kennedy Round has given the following assessment of the process of "confrontation and justification":

> "These sessions, lasting from January 19 through February 12, 1965, were an education in the detailed rationale, facts and figures, valid and spurious, for maintaining tariff protection. It was specially exhausting for those delegates with long lists to defend. But the contents of the lists did not change since they were now a subject of negotiation rather than debate".[17]

7.   The really meaningful discussions were those that took place bilaterally between the trading partners and particularly those between the major players. Thus a linear or formula approach did not obviate the need for bilateral negotiations: they only gave the participants an additional tool to employ in the bargaining process.

8.   The bilateral negotiations were in many cases preceded by a communication by the participating countries of the results of the assessment of

---

[17]   Ernest Preeg, Traders and Diplomats, pp. 87-88.

other offers made by them. In some cases, these communications contained detailed calculations showing how the shortfalls in reciprocity had been calculated (see the section on reciprocity below). Bilateral negotiations had to be held without the aid of a formula with those countries which had been exempted from adopting the working hypotheses (New Zealand, South Africa, Australia) and with developing countries to which the concept of non-reciprocity applied (see Section E below). In the bilateral negotiations, certain sectoral issues and conditionalities attached to specific offers were also discussed. For instance, in the Kennedy Round, the major industrial countries other than the US had made their offers on chemical products conditional on the resolution of issues relating to the American Selling Price in the US whereby certain chemical products were subject to customs valuation on the basis of the selling price in the United States. During the Tokyo Round, one country made the concession on newspaper and periodicals conditional on continued exemption for it from the manufacturing clause of US copyright legislation. Certain other concessions were made conditional on resolution of disputes. During the same round, the offers on textiles and steel were made by the US subject to the achievement of sectoral objectives (continuation of MFA and VERs on steel). There was a proposal for a snap-back clause on textiles and clothing products whereby the tariffs would be restored to pre-Tokyo Round levels should the MFA be terminated. This conditionality was retained by the United States in its Schedule. Other countries retained the right to review the situation in case the conditionality was given effect by the US. In some cases, besides global reciprocity countries sought reciprocity in individual sectors (automobiles, aircraft, aluminum, chemicals). In both the Kennedy and Tokyo Rounds bilateral negotiations also resulted in both the Kennedy and Tokyo Rounds in individual countries granting INRs on specific products to their negotiating partners in the process of balancing out for reciprocity.

9.   As a result of bilateral negotiations, participating countries submitted revisions of their offers at intervals - including both improvements and withdrawals. A condition attached by many was that further adjustments were possible in the light of possible deviations from concessions presented earlier by other trading partners. The offers became final only after they were rendered in the form of schedules and attached to the Protocols at the conclusion of the negotiations. At the end of bilateral negotiations, it was customary for countries to initial agreements on the list of products or specific approaches agreed. It was with the help of such initialed documents that these countries would verify the schedules before they were attached to the Protocols.

Uruguay Round

Industrial tariffs

10.   During the Uruguay Round, the initial work on tariffs on industrial products resulted in the submission of proposals for modalities. Proposals on modalities continued to be submitted after the agreement during the mid-term review for a target reduction at least as ambitious as the one achieved in the

Tokyo Round (i.e. one-third average reduction). In January 1990, participants gave up attempts on a common modality and agreed that each country would submit tariff proposals for reduction, elimination and binding on a line-by-line basis in accordance with the agreement reached at the mid-term review. After the submission of offers by a large number of participants, many of them, both developing and developed, exchanged request lists for improvement of offers. In accordance with the agreed procedures, each participant's tariff proposal was examined by the group of participants which had submitted proposals in order to determine whether it complied with the mid-term review agreement. To assist these reviews, analyses were provided by the Secretariat. These multilateral reviews supplemented the bilateral and plurilateral negotiations which constituted the core of the negotiations. In their original offers, in March 1990, while other developed countries had made specific proposals in most cases following a formula approach, the US had only listed the tariff lines in respect of which it was prepared to make offers on the basis of requests, apart from proposing sectors for tariff elimination. It was only in response to requests that the US made specific offers on most of the tariff lines. After the process of bilateral, plurilateral and multilateral discussions, most participating countries made revised offers in October 1990. Following the failure of the Brussels meeting, there was a pause in the negotiations.

11.   The tariff negotiations were reactivated after the submission of the Dunkel text, which contained a compromise on several outstanding areas of the negotiations. Participating countries were invited to submit their revised offers comprising both agricultural and industrial products in the form of schedules in March 1992. These schedules incorporated the results of the bilateral negotiations which had been undertaken by a number of countries centring on the proposals for the elimination and harmonization of tariffs in specific sectors. The bilateral negotiations were intensified after the accord among the QUAD countries at Tokyo in July 1993. As mentioned earlier, the main objective of the developed countries vis-à-vis the developing countries was to ensure that bindings covered the maximum proportion of the latter's import trade. The bilateral negotiations continued right up to the last day of substantive negotiations, namely 15 December 1993, and even beyond.

Agricultural tariffs

12.   The negotiations on agricultural tariffs (along with other specific commitments in the areas of domestic support and export subsidies) followed a somewhat different course. Country lists showing the extent of protection and support in respect of agricultural products were tabled prior to the Brussels Ministerial Meeting in December 1990, on the basis of formats established in line with the framework text proposed by the Chairman of the Negotiating Group on Agriculture. Mr. Dunkel's compromise text, submitted in December 1991, contained, *inter alia,* modalities for agricultural negotiations. Although the EC and a few others formally rejected the Dunkel text in early 1992, and the modalities proposed by him were never formally adopted, participants proceeded to table comprehensive schedules on tariffs, domestic support and export

subsidies from early 1992 onwards in line with the Dunkel text. The draft schedule of the EC in respect of export subsidies had to await the accord with the US in November 1992 (Blair House I). These schedules also had supporting tables to show the manner of calculation of the tariff equivalent of non-tariff measures (as also the Aggregate Measurement of Support for domestic support and export subsidies). Bilateral and plurilateral consultations and negotiations took place to understand better how the modalities had been observed for the calculation of tariff equivalent, minimum and current access, in-quota tariff rates, etc. and for improvement of access where possible. Since there was more than a modicum of tolerance in ensuring strict adherence to the modalities, the objective of bilateral and plurilateral negotiations was also to secure a situation in which no single participant deviated more than the others. A fresh dispute between the US and the EC erupted in 1993 and the agriculture negotiations were closed only after the two major economies made another deal in November 1993 on export subsidy (Blair House II).

Conclusion of tariff negotiations

13.   On 15 December 1993, on the strength of the submission made by all the major trading countries that they had concluded substantive negotiations with their main trading partners, in respect of both agricultural and non-agricultural products, the Chairman of the TNC declared that the Uruguay Round negotiations had been concluded. Since some negotiations were still continuing, the Chairman stipulated that, even if the negotiations were continued, there would be no withdrawals but only additional incremental commitments. As things turned out, not only were additional commitments made in the period before the Marrakesh meeting but there were withdrawals as well. The EC notified withdrawals in respect of non-ferrous metals and trucks on the ground that the United States had also retreated from the position at which its tariff offers stood on 15 December 1993. There were other withdrawals as well when the conditions stipulated in individual schedules were not fulfilled.

Verification of tariff schedules

14.   During the period from 15 February to the end of March 1994, meetings were held for verification of market access draft final schedules to enable participants to ensure that the agreed results of the market access negotiations were accurately reflected therein. The verification process held after the Uruguay Round was much more substantive and complex then the similar exercise conducted after the Tokyo Round. The following were the highlights of those meetings:

    (i)   To be a contracting party to GATT 1947, it was not always necessary for countries or customs territories to have a schedule of concessions. Many of them which had become contracting parties by succession under the procedures of Article XXVI:5(c) of GATT 1947 did not have a schedule at all. But, for the original membership of the WTO, it was a prerequisite for them to have a schedule of concessions and commitments annexed to GATT 1994 (besides a schedule of specific commitments annexed to GATS). Some of these contracting parties had not submitted any schedule before the substantive conclusion of the negotiations in December 1993, or had submitted it too late. While the proposed Ministerial Declaration on Measures in Favour of Least-Developed Countries gave additional time of one year from 15 April 1994 for these countries to submit schedules, there was no such dispensation for others. The period of verification allowed time for the participants that were late in submitting their draft schedules to carry out, where necessary, further negotiations with other participants and to submit the schedules for verification.

(ii)   In respect of industrial products, the participants were afforded the opportunity to ensure that the concession granted by their trading partners and noted in bilateral records of understanding appeared in the final schedule.

(iii)   The process also gave participants the opportunity to make final adjustments if the conditions attached by them in the conditional offer were not fulfilled or if their expectations were not otherwise fulfilled. It was in the course of the verification process that the EC announced its adjustments referred to earlier. For fear of unravelling, the EC clarified that it had sought to restrict the withdrawals to items for which the US was by far the largest supplier.

(iv)   During the verification process, the conditionalities attached by participants to their draft schedules were eliminated to a large extent. If some of them survived it was because the conditionality depended on matters which went beyond tariff negotiations, e.g., where the value of tariff concessions depended upon the negotiations in the area of government procurement. There were also some instances in which conditions were retained requiring trading partners to take certain policy actions (e.g., elimination of export restrictions on certain raw materials by exporters of wooden furniture).

(v)   The WTO Understanding on the Interpretation of Article II:1(b) of GATT 1994 required "other duties or charges" levied on bound tariff items to be recorded in the schedules of concessions, at the levels applying on 15 April 1994. During the verification process, participants obtained an assurance that this was the case. Where it was not, a correction was made to reflect the level actually levied on that date. Four Members, i.e. Cameroon, Côte d'Ivoire, Gabon and Senegal, were given additional time to specify their ODCs.

(vi)   The verification process was helped by the submission of analyses by the Secretariat showing, *inter alia,* the coverage of the agricultural and industrial schedules of participants, in terms of tariff lines and trade flows, the extent of trade-weighted reduction commitment on industrial products and simple average reduction on agricultural products. This helped participants to draw a conclusion on whether the agricultural tariff reduction modalities were complied with and whether the trade-weighted reduction target on industrial products had been reached.

(vii) During the verification process, participants also had an opportunity to make a last appeal to individual developing countries to improve the coverage of bindings or to lower the ceiling bindings or to improve their schedules on industrial products in other ways.

(viii) In respect of agricultural products, participants used the opportunity to raise questions on adherence to the modalities on such matters as the levels of in-quota tariffs and tariff quotas. The issues were resolved after further bilateral negotiations alongside the verification process.

15.   After verification, the schedules were attached to the Marrakesh Protocol to GATT 1994. The verification in respect of a large majority of the least-developed countries took place after the Marrakesh meeting. Special dispensation to complete the verification process (which implied also extended bilateral negotiations) was also given to other contracting parties to GATT 1947 which had submitted their draft schedules before the entry into force of the WTO Agreement but were not able to complete the negotiations in time to annex them to the Marrakesh Protocol. It was agreed that the approval of the schedules would be deemed to be approval of the terms of accession by the Members of the WTO under Article XII, paragraph 2 of the WTO Agreement.

D.   Reciprocity and its Measurement during Negotiations

1.   The notion that negotiations for the substantial reduction of tariffs are to be held on a mutually-advantageous and reciprocal basis, embodied in the Havana Charter and the preamble of GATT 1947, was reiterated in the rules of each round of negotiations even before it was incorporated in the substantive provision in Article XXVIII *bis* of GATT 1947. The Ministerial Declaration that launched the Kennedy Round mentioned the "principle of reciprocity" and the Tokyo Declaration provided that "the negotiations shall be conducted on the basis of the principles of mutual advantage, mutual commitment and overall reciprocity, while observing the most-favoured-nation clause, and consistently with the provisions of the General Agreement relating to such negotiations". The Punta del Este Declaration avoided a direct reference to reciprocity but clearly the principle was covered when it was stipulated that "(n)egotiations shall be conducted in a transparent manner, and consistent with the objectives and commitments agreed in this Declaration and with the principles of the General Agreement in order to ensure mutual advantage and increased benefit to all participants." The same declaration makes references to the launching, conduct

and implementation of the results of the negotiations "as a single undertaking" and "overall balance of the negotiations", both of the concepts being obviously connected with the notion of reciprocity on the higher plane of comprehensive negotiations.

2.   As mentioned earlier, neither the provisions of GATT 1994 nor the procedures of the eight rounds of tariff negotiations indicate how reciprocity is measured or defined. At the Review Session, Brazil had proposed a formula for measurement of concessions for determining reciprocity. On this "the Working Party noted that there was nothing in the Agreement, or in the rules for tariff negotiations which has been used in the past, to prevent governments from adopting any formula they might choose, and therefore considered that there was no need for the CONTRACTING PARTIES to make any recommendation in this matter".[18] No further attempt has been made to give greater definition to the manner in which reciprocity is to be measured and it has been left to each country to develop its own yardsticks.

3.   In the bilateral exchanges of tariff concessions during the first five rounds when negotiations were held on the basis of request-offer item-by-item technique, trade coverage and depth of tariff reduction were the two main criteria whereby reciprocal balance was established. These two criteria remained the basic consideration in measuring reciprocity during later negotiations as well. Sometimes they took the form of a single yardstick of the weighted average reduction of tariffs in bilateral trade. Things became more complicated with the adoption of a linear or formula approach and complementary techniques were used to establish reciprocity. Participating countries would compare the average reductions in the dutiable products or the trade coverage of 50 per cent reduction (in the Kennedy Round). Where the duty reduction was less than the working hypothesis of 50 per cent the offers were converted to the equivalent of 50 per cent before comparison. Thus, if the trade in a product was $10 million and the reduction 25 per cent, it would count as $5 million trade coverage on the basis of the 50 per cent reduction. Countries also took into account the extent to which the exception covered products of export interest to them.

4.   The following table drawn up by one of the participating governments in respect of its trade with a major trading partner during the Kennedy Round illustrates some of the parameters that were taken into consideration while measuring reciprocity:

---

[18]   GATT, BISD, Third Supplement, p. 22.

A-B Summary of Offers (1962 in million $)

	Non-Agricultural		Agricultural		Total	
	A	B	A	B	A	B
	Imports from B	Imports from A	Imports from B	Imports from A	Imports from B	Imports from A
Total Imports	2,457	2,927	220	1,171	2,677	4,098
Dutiable trade	2,167	1,976	178	355	2,365	2,331
Dutiable offered	2,081	1,706	167	38	2,248	1,744
Duty free trade	14	496	2	9	16	505
Binding of free offered	14	235	-	9	14	244
Greater than 50% cuts	9	2	-	-	9	2
50% cuts	1,921	1, 253	167	1	2,088	1,254
Less than 50% cuts	151	451	-	37	151	488
Average percentage cut dutiable	45.6%	35.9%	46.9%	1.7%	45.7%	30.7%
Total offered: 50% equivalents (including binding of duty free treatment	1,990	1,653	180	22	2,170	1,675

The attempt in the above summary was to show that A's offer had a positive balance in reciprocity terms as compared to B's offer on the basis of most yardsticks.

5.   In the case of another set of two countries, the following figures were given to illustrate the measurement of reciprocity:

	Imports of X from Y	Imports of Y from X
	1963 trade in million $	
Dutiable imports	1151,3	1547,7
Dutiable offered	1465,1	888,8
Percentage offered	94,7	77,7
Free available for concession (unbound)	6,7	373,1
Binding of free offered	100,0	90,0

6.   Another table used was in respect of offers on dutiable trade converted to the equivalent of 50 per cent reductions:

Imports (1963) in million $ by:	X	Y
Agricultural	19,5	184,8
Non-agricultural	1435,3	644,6
Over-all	1454,8	829,0

7.   One participant suggested during the negotiations in the Kennedy Round that a strong case could be made out for calculating the industrial balance on the basis of percentage of exceptions to the application of the working hypothesis. In other words, if country X had excepted 10 per cent of its industrial imports from the linear cut, but country Y only five per cent, the latter would be entitled to withdraw tariff concessions equivalent to another five per cent of its imports. For agricultural products, it was suggested that evaluation on the basis of a comparison of positive offers would be more appropriate.

8.   Although the above tables and references might suggest that statistical methods were used for measuring reciprocity, in fact the procedures adopted for internal assessment by governments of participating countries were much more complex. In determining reciprocity, participating countries took into account the existence of other factors such as quantitative restrictions which diminished the trade-creating possibilities of tariff reduction. The following extract from the final report by the USTR on the Kennedy Round Negotiations explains the various criteria used in measuring reciprocity:

"In order to simplify the presentation, the results of U.S. participation in the Kennedy Round tariff negotiations are presented in this report solely in terms of the value of trade covered by the concessions and the depth of the tariff reductions. However, in the course of the negotiations, numerous other factors were considered in evaluating the balance of concessions - the height of duties, the characteristics of individual products, demand and supply elasticities, and the size and nature of markets, including the reduction in the disadvantage to U.S. exports achieved through reductions in the tariffs applied to the exports of the United States and other non-member countries by the European Economic Community (EEC), the European Free-trade area (EFTA) and those countries in the British Commonwealth preferential system "[19]

9.   In the Kennedy and Tokyo Rounds, it was not only global reciprocity in bilateral trade that was sought by participating countries in tariff negotiations. Sometimes there were also sectoral objectives whereby countries sought reduction or harmonization of tariffs on specific products. Some participating

---

[19]   U.S. Office of Special Representative for Trade Negotiations, Report on United States Negotiations, 1967, Vol. I, p. iii.

countries reserved the right to proportion their concessions to the reciprocity that they obtained in the same sector. In the discussions on sectors in the Kennedy Round (aluminum; chemicals; cotton textiles; iron and steel; and pulp and paper), a proposal was made that countries participating in the sector group should strive to reduce their tariffs to certain target zones which would result in a harmonization of the tariffs of those countries. Thus global reciprocity in tariffs was complemented by reciprocity on specific products. On the other hand, during the Tokyo and Uruguay Rounds reciprocity in tariff negotiations was only a part of the equation in the larger and more comprehensive negotiations on non-tariff measures and (in the Uruguay Round) areas beyond trade in goods. Quantitative techniques for the measurement of reciprocity have become less important in tariff negotiations. Sectoral negotiations for the elimination or harmonization of tariffs and negotiations for the reduction of peak tariffs by the major trading countries implied that reciprocity had greater depth. In the sectoral negotiations, one of the conditions attached by the participants was that there would be broad-based participation by other producers and exporters. The extent to which such participation was ensured can be judged from the figures of percentage of world exports accounted for by the participants as already given in an earlier section. At the same time, in its application the principle of reciprocity has become more comprehensive. In agriculture, strict adherence to the tariff cutting formula of a reduction by a simple average of 36 per cent (subject to a minimum of 15 per cent on a particular product) was a way of achieving reciprocity. But this had to be accompanied by a reduction of production subsidies not enumerated in the green category and of export subsidies. Compulsory adherence to all the non-tariff measure agreements enhanced reciprocity and made it multi-dimensional.

E.   Developing Countries and the Concept of Non-Reciprocity

The first five rounds

1.   The developing countries participated in the earlier rounds of tariff negotiations on the basis of a reciprocal exchange of tariff concessions. The need of developing countries for special consideration was recognized for the first time when Article XXVIII *bis* was added during the Review Session. Paragraph 3 of this Article provides for negotiations to take into account, *inter alia,* - "the needs of less-developed countries for a flexible use of tariff protection to assist their economic development and the special needs of these countries to maintain tariffs for revenue purposes". When in 1959 a proposal was made that the negotiating rules for the Dillon Round should contain a provision on unilateral concessions, it was pointed out "that Article XXVIII *bis* recognized the special needs of less-developed countries and confidence was expressed that contracting

parties would bear this in mind in the course of the forthcoming negotiations".[20] In March 1961, the Executive Secretary of GATT submitted an Explanatory Memorandum to Committee III stating that Article XXVIII *bis*: 3 (b) could be interpreted to mean that the developing countries would not "always be held to strict reciprocity".[21] During the Dillon Round, while the concept of non-reciprocity was not explicitly recognized, the European Economic Community made a statement that the "Community is not considering requesting full reciprocity from less-developed countries during the second phase of the 1960-61 Tariff Conference".[22] Subsequently, in the Ministerial Declaration of 30 November 1961, it was stated that, "in view of the stage of economic development of the less-developed countries, a more flexible attitude should be taken with respect to the degree of reciprocity to be expected from these countries".[23] It was in the Ministerial Declaration launching the Kennedy Round that the concept of non-reciprocity was set forth for the first time in the rules adopted for the conduct of the negotiations. It was provided that "in the trade negotiations every effort shall be made to reduce barriers to exports of the less-developed countries, but that the developed countries cannot expect to receive reciprocity from the less-developed countries".[24] Efforts to elaborate the concept further were continued during the discussions in the Committee on Legal and Institutional Framework, the recommendations of which were later incorporated in Part IV of GATT. During the discussions in the Committee, it came to be recognized that it was really a question of less than full reciprocity on the part of the developing countries rather than none at all, as some of them were seeking. This implied that the developing countries could be expected to undertake not equivalent tariff commitments but commitments commensurate with their individual levels of development. It is this idea that is reflected in Article XXXVI, paragraph 8, and the addendum thereto, which states that "the less-developed contracting parties should not be expected, in the course of trade negotiations, to make contributions which are inconsistent with their individual development, financial and trade needs, taking into consideration past trade developments".

Kennedy and Tokyo Rounds

2.   During the Kennedy Round, instead of reciprocal concessions the developing countries were called upon to make at their own discretion a general contribution to the overall objective of trade liberalization. The Chairman of the Sub-Committee on Participation of Less-Developed Countries in the Kennedy Round reported to the Trade and Development Committee as follows:

[20]   GATT, BISD, Eighth Supplement, p. 110.

[21]   GATT, BISD, Tenth Supplement, p. 172.

[22]   GATT, BISD, Tenth Supplement, p. 172.

[23]   GATT, BISD, Tenth Supplement, p. 26.

[24]   GATT, BISD, Twelfth Supplement, p. 48.

"Ministers agreed that reciprocity would not be expected from developing countries. This decision has since been given formal legal expression by incorporation in Part IV of the General Agreement. There will, therefore, be no balancing of concessions granted on products of interest to developing countries by developed participants on the one hand and the contribution which developing participants would make to the objective of trade liberalization on the other and which it is agreed should be considered in the light of the development, financial and trade needs of developing countries themselves. It is, therefore, recognized that the developing countries themselves must decide what contribution they can make." [25]

3.   During the Tokyo Round the concept of non-reciprocity received a great deal of attention in the negotiations in the Framework Group in which developing countries made proposals for concretizing the concept. In the submissions made by Brazil, it was proposed that in trade negotiations the contributions by the developing countries should be directly linked to the additionality of benefits accruing to them from the negotiations; that evaluation of a concession should not be on the basis of trade coverage but on the relative impact of such a concession on the national economy and particularly on the trade flows; that the developing countries should be allowed to negotiate plurilaterally; that there should be a provision for a developing country to grant a single concession in exchange for several different concessions, and that the implementation of concessions by the developing countries should be staged or deferred. These proposals did not, however, find a place in the text of the Enabling Clause that resulted from these negotiations. On the other hand the concept of graduated reciprocity which was already embodied in Article XXXVI:8 was elaborated further in paragraph 7 of the Enabling Clause.[26] This paragraph provides that the developing countries having benefited generally from the application of a lower level of GATT obligations and specifically from the concept of non-reciprocity in trade negotiations should assume more obligations and make increased contributions and concessions on an autonomous basis as their trade situations improve and their economies develop. The Punta del Este Declaration virtually reproduced the language of Part IV of GATT and the Enabling Clause on non-reciprocity.

4.   How was the concept applied during the trade negotiations held after its recognition? First of all, in the Kennedy Round, the developing countries were not asked to participate in the linear reduction of industrial tariffs. The industrialized countries did not even formally submit request lists to the developing countries for negotiation of reduction of tariffs on products of interest to them. Some of them only gave the developing countries a list of suggestions for making contributions to the objective of liberalization of trade. These

---

[25]   GATT Doc. COM.TD/W/37, p. 3.

[26]   GATT, BISD, Twenty-sixth Supplement, pp. 203-205.

included not only suggestions for selective reduction of high tariffs, elimination of preferential margins and binding of a majority of tariffs at applied rates, but also action on such non-tariff measures as burdensome documentation requirements, special exchange rates, prior deposits for imports, state trading practices, consular fees, government procurement, import restrictions on capital goods, administration of import restrictions, labelling requirements, etc. It was also suggested to them that they should consider reduction of barriers to imports from other developing countries. In response, the more advanced developing countries reduced their tariffs or bound them at existing or higher levels on a selected number of items. They also claimed that action taken by them already for liberalizing quantitative import restrictions or import licensing or for elimination or reduction of import deposits or exemption from consular fees were contributions to trade liberalization. Some of them claimed that autonomous reduction of tariff rates (even though not bound) and elimination of Commonwealth tariff preferences in specific products or adoption of the Brussels Tariff Nomenclature should be counted as contributions. One contracting party stated that it had made a contribution by not having recourse to retaliation under Article XXIII of GATT even though the finding in the complaint made by it had been in its favour and the measures were continuing. Several developing countries stated that they would make contributions to trade liberalization by taking measures to enlarge trade exchanges among themselves through negotiations in which they were actively engaged. The developing countries were subjected to gentle exhortations during the Kennedy Round rather than tough negotiations.

5.   During the Tokyo Round, the mood *vis-à-vis* the developing countries was more demanding. In making their initial offers some developed countries declared that, although they subscribed to the concept of non-reciprocity, they would seek appropriate contributions from the more advanced developing countries. While, for tropical products, most developed countries did not demand any reciprocity before implementing their concessions on a GSP or MFN basis in advance of the conclusion of the negotiations, the United States did obtain a modicum of reciprocity from several developing countries. Bilateral agreements were exchanged between the United States and a number of developing countries whereby the latter listed the liberalization of import licensing and other measures such as import surcharges and made a commitment (although somewhat weak) to maintain them in exchange for advance implementation of tropical product offers by the United States.

6.   Only a few developing countries participated in the main tariff negotiations in the Tokyo Round, which ended with the signing of the Geneva Protocol on 30 June 1979. The Geneva (1979) Protocol was signed by all the developed contracting parties but by only four developing countries, namely Argentina, Jamaica, Romania and Yugoslavia. However, negotiations between some developed countries and the developing countries continued after the signing of the Geneva (1979) Protocol and the Protocol Supplementary to the Geneva (1979) Protocol was opened for signature towards the end of 1979. This Protocol was signed by Brazil, Chile, Côte d'Ivoire, Dominican Republic, Egypt,

Haiti, India, Indonesia, Israel, Korea, Malaysia, Pakistan, Peru, Singapore, Uruguay and Zaire among the developing countries. The EC and Canada, which had made additional concessions during the negotiations with the developing countries, also signed the Supplementary Protocol. Though the United States did not make additional tariff concessions to the developing countries after the signing of the Geneva (1979) Protocol, it did secure tariff concessions from selected developing countries in return for the concessions already incorporated by it in its Schedule attached to the Geneva (1979) Protocol. Additionally, it secured from them commitments in respect of quantitative restrictions and licensing requirements. Of particular interest is a bilateral agreement between the United States and a developing country which listed, not only the tariff concessions by the two sides but also the non-tariff measure liberalization made by the developing country concerned. The latter reserved the right to withdraw the non-tariff measures after intervals of three years but subject to consultation with the United States. The bilateral agreement mentions that, in the event of withdrawal by the developing country of the liberalized NTMs, the United States too would have the right to withdraw equivalent concessions to restore a balance. This was an attempt to bring non-tariff measures into the equation for exchange of tariff concessions.

Uruguay Round

7.   In the Uruguay Round, while the same rules on non-reciprocity were accepted in the ground rules as during the Tokyo Round, there was a sea-change in the attitude of the developing countries. Most of them had already undertaken wider economic reforms and decided to hasten the pace of integration into the world economy. They were, therefore, anxious to prove that they were very keen on full participation in the tariff negotiations. What made it easier for them was the fact that many of them had already lowered their tariffs by autonomous liberalization since the Tokyo Round and further after the commencement of the Uruguay Round negotiations. However, they did benefit from the application of the concept of non-reciprocity. First, in regard to industrial tariffs, it was generally not expected of them that they would reach the target amount for overall reductions "at least as ambitious as that achieved by the formula participants in the Tokyo Round". Second, in agricultural tariffs they were required to cut their tariffs only by two-thirds of the simple average reduction of 36 per cent set for others. The minimum reduction for them for any product line was set at 10 per cent as against 15 per cent for others. They were given the further benefit of implementation of reduction commitments in 10 years as against six years for others. The least-developed countries were not called upon to make any reduction in tariffs at all. In the case of products with unbound ordinary customs duties, the developing countries had the additional flexibility of offering ceiling bindings. On industrial tariffs a few of them were requested to join the sectoral zero-for-zero or harmonization initiatives, but in the end only three of them (Hong Kong, Korea and Singapore) joined these agreements. Nevertheless, the concessions made by the developing countries were quite substantial, specially when judged against the background of the commitments

undertaken by them in past rounds. Given below are the calculations made in the GATT Secretariat of pre- and post-Uruguay Round trade-weighted averages of tariffs of some of the developing countries on industrial products. The pre-Uruguay duties refer to 1994 bound duties or, for unbound tariff lines, to duties applicable as of September 1986. The post-Uruguay duties refer to the concessions listed in the schedules annexed to the Uruguay Round Protocol to GATT 1994. Import statistics used are generally those of 1988. Where the post-Uruguay trade-weighted average is higher than the pre-Uruguay Round average it is due to the use of ceiling bindings.

Trade-weighted averages of tariff

Country	Pre-Uruguay	Post-Uruguay
Argentina	38.2%	30.9%
Brazil	40.7%	27.0%
Chile	34.9%	24.9%
India	71.4%	32.4%
Indonesia	20.4%	36.9%
Korea	18.0%	8.3%
Malaysia	10.0%	9.1%
Mexico	46.1%	33.7%
Thailand	37.3%	28.0%
Turkey	25.1%	22.3%

Source: GATT Secretariat, The Results of the Uruguay Round of Multilateral Trade Negotiations, November 1994.

8.   Even more impressive was the increase in bindings by the developing countries. The following table, also drawn from the same GATT publication, gives the details:

Tariff bindings on industrial and agricultural products (percentages)

	Industrial products				Agricultural products			
	Percentage of tariff lines bound		Percentage of imports under bound rates		Percentage of tariff lines bound		Percentage of imports under bound rates	
	Pre-Uruguay	Post-Uruguay	Pre-Uruguay	Post-Uruguay	Pre-Uruguay	Post-Uruguay	Pre-Uruguay	Post-Uruguay
Total	43	83	68	87	35	100	63	100
Developed countries	78	99	94	99	58	100	81	100
Developing countries	21	73	13	61	17	100	22	100

Source: GATT Secretariat, The Results of the Uruguay Round of Multilateral Trade Negotiations, November 1994.

9.   The following table gives greater details of bindings in respect of industrial products for selected developing countries:

Scope of bindings in industrial products for selected developing countries

| Country | Industrial Products | | | |
| | Number of lines | | Percentage imports | |
	Pre-Uruguay	Post-Uruguay	Pre-Uruguay	Post-Uruguay
Argentina	5	100	21	100
Brazil	6	100	22	100
Chile	100	100	100	100
India	3	60	9	68
Indonesia	10	93	30	92
Korea	10	85	24	86
Malaysia	0	25	1	44
Mexico	100	100	100	100
Thailand	1	63	9	66
Turkey	34	37	38	39

Source: GATT Secretariat, The Results of the Uruguay Round of Multilateral Trade Negotiations, November 1994.

10.   It will thus be noted that, while the rules on non-reciprocity in trade negotiations between developing and developed countries have remained the same over the past three decades (and three rounds), the participation of the developing countries and the extent of their contributions have been increasing progressively and significantly.

Tropical Products

11.   Since tropical products are produced and exported by the developing countries, these products have received special attention in the negotiations among developing and developed countries in the last three rounds of negotiations. In the Kennedy Round, the offers made on tropical products were monitored separately in a Group set up for this purpose through a succession of periodic summaries brought out by the Secretariat. An indicative list of products was established by the Secretariat, but the participants treated all products on which requests had been made by the developing countries as tropical products irrespective of whether such products were included in the indicative list. A significant point in the offers made by the developed countries was that they demanded not reciprocal concessions in return but that their industrial trading partners also take similar action on such products. Some of the developed countries implemented their offers on tropical products with effect from January 1, 1967, in advance of the conclusion of the negotiations.

12.   In the Tokyo Round also a separate group was established on tropical products. While various proposals were made for dealing with these products ranging from across-the-board reductions in tariffs and other forms of protection

to elimination of tariff escalation based on degree of processing and negotiation of stabilization arrangements for particular tropical products, in the end a number of developed countries made offers of reduction of tariffs on a preferential (GSP) or MFN basis generally without asking for reciprocal concessions and they implemented the concessions in advance, midway through the negotiations.

13.   In the Uruguay Round, too, tropical products received separate attention and interim offers for tariff reduction on a preferential or MFN basis were made by the developed countries (and indeed by some developing countries) at the time of the mid-term review, and were implemented well ahead of the conclusion of the negotiations, again without seeking reciprocal concessions from the beneficiary countries. Thus, in each of the three last rounds of negotiations the concept of non-reciprocity was applied to tropical products.

Credit for autonomous liberalization

14.   It has already been mentioned that a major aspect of developing-country participation in the Uruguay Round was that many of them had already embarked on ambitious tariff and trade reform since the end of the Tokyo Round and the process of autonomous liberalization had continued after the commencement of the Uruguay Round. An important issue arose from the demand of the developing countries for being given credit for such autonomous liberalization. A widely-shared feeling was that credit in negotiating terms could be given for autonomous measures only if the tariff reduction was bound. The decision at Montreal that the base rate for unbound tariffs would be the normally applicable rates in September 1986 provided the basis to some extent for developing countries to be given credit for tariff reductions made since the commencement of the round, provided they bound those concessions. In December 1991 the Chairman of the Market Access Group made recommendations on guidelines for giving credit for ceiling bindings. The guidelines envisaged a general formula whereby for each 10 per cent of imports bound at 40 per cent there would be one per cent credit. For every 10 per cent of imports bound at ceiling levels below 40 per cent, additional credit was to be given in the proportion of one per cent for every 10 percentage points at which duties were bound below 40 per cent. Thus if a participating government bound 80 per cent of its imports at 40 per cent it received a credit of 8 per cent and if it bound 80 per cent of its imports at 30 per cent it received a credit of 16 per cent. In other words, in respect of a country which bound its tariffs at 30 per cent on 80 per cent of its imports, it was to be considered that it had reduced its tariffs by 16 per cent. In subsequent negotiations, the guidelines did not prove to be of any practical value as no targets for industrial tariff reduction were laid down for developing countries. Later there was an informal understanding shared by many participants that developing countries offering binding of industrial tariffs at 35 per cent across-the-board would be considered as having achieved the Montreal target.

F.   Base Date and Base Rate

1.   Since negotiations on tariffs have generally resulted in agreement on the extent of reduction, the base rate and base date were a particularly sensitive matter in the initial rounds of negotiations under GATT 1947 when countries were starting from a position of no existing tariff commitments under GATT. The rules of procedure for the first five rounds of negotiations contained the stipulation that the participating governments refrain from increasing tariffs and other protective measures inconsistently with the principles of the Havana Charter (and later the General Agreement) and with the objective of improving their bargaining position in preparation for the negotiations. In the rules for the Geneva negotiations in 1947, it was recognized that changes in the form of tariffs, or changes in tariffs owing to the depreciation or devaluation of the currency of the country maintaining the tariffs, which did not result in an increase of the protective incidence of the tariff, would not be considered as new tariff increases. In the rules for Annecy negotiations it was provided as follows:

> "In the event of a change in the form of tariff or a revision of rates of duties to take account of either a rise in prices or the devaluation of the currency of the country maintaining the tariff, the effects of such change or such revision would be a matter for consideration during the negotiations in order to determine, first, the change, if any, in the incidence of the duties of the country concerned and, secondly, whether the change is such as to afford a reasonable basis for negotiations."[27]

2.   For the Torquay negotiations, as a general rule, the basis for negotiations was to be the rates of duty in effect on November 15, 1949, but rules similar to those followed during the Annecy negotiations were also adopted for dealing with cases in which a revision of rates of duty had taken place. During the Kennedy Round the general rule was that "the duties used for reference purposes should reflect the results of the 1960/61 Tariff Conference (Dillon Round)". The base rate became an issue among the developed countries during the Tokyo Round because Australia and Japan used the GATT bound rates as the starting-point for offering reductions although the applied rates were much below these rates because of liberalization measures taken by them in recent years. No agreement could be reached on a common base date and the offers were made on the basis of base rates and dates chosen by individual participants, it being left to other participants to take the difference in base rates into account in their evaluation of offers.

3.   During the Uruguay Round, the base date and rate again became an issue, not for the products for which the tariffs were already bound but for those for which tariffs were not bound. The issue was important as a large number of developing countries had undertaken autonomous liberalization measures in the period after the Tokyo Round and they were anxious to ensure that they got

---

[27]   GATT Doc. GATT/CP.2/26, p. 3.

credit for such liberalization. The matter was settled at the Montreal meeting where it was decided that "the base rates for the negotiations will be the bound MFN rates and, for unbound rates, the normally applicable rates in September 1986". Since it was in September 1986 that the Uruguay Round was launched, the foundation was laid for the Uruguay Round participants, both developing and developed, to be given credit for any reduction made in unbound duties after the commencement of the Round. For agricultural products, the data for the years 1986 to 1988 had to be used for the calculation of the tariff equivalents.

G.   Staging of Tariff Reductions

1.   In the earlier rounds of negotiation, the tariff concessions normally became fully applicable immediately after the entry into effect of the Protocols. However, from the 1956 Geneva Conference onwards, staging of tariff reductions became an element in tariff negotiations. In the 1956 Geneva Conference, the US concessions were staged over two to three annual installments. In the Dillon Round, the presidential authority for the negotiations required the US to make the agreed reductions in a minimum of two and a maximum of four stages. With some countries, the US agreed to make the reductions in two stages. With a number of countries the US also agreed to put into effect the tariff concessions without awaiting the drawing-up of the protocol embodying the results of the negotiations.

2.   Since the Kennedy Round, staging of tariff concessions has become the general practice. The relevant protocol has generally embodied a norm for staging, leaving individual participants to deviate from the norm. Such deviations are naturally an element in the bargaining for reciprocity that takes place before the conclusion of the negotiations. In the Kennedy Round, the norm adopted was for the reduction to be implemented in five equal annual installments beginning on 1 January 1968. Where a participant began the reductions on 1 July 1968, or on a date between 1 January and 1 July 1968, the requirement was that it would make two-fifths of the reductions on that date and the remaining three installments on 1 January 1970, 1971 and 1972. Participants were, of course, free to make the entire concession effective on 1 January 1968 and to otherwise deviate from the norm, as agreed with their trading partners.

3.   In the Tokyo Round, a norm was similarly fixed, but this time the tariff reductions were to be implemented in eight equal annual reductions beginning on 1 January 1980 and becoming fully effective on 1 January 1887. As in the Kennedy Round, deviations were agreed for many participants, although some of them were later to announce acceleration in tariff reductions. Illustrations of some of the deviations as originally stipulated are given below:

    (a)   (i)   The European Community stipulated that, at the end of the initial phase of five years it would examine, having regard to the economic, social and monetary situation and the implementation by its partners of the various undertakings they had entered into, whether it was in a position to enter into the second phase of three years.

(ii)   Regarding the concessions for chemical products falling within Chapters 29, 32 and 39 of the CCT, the EC stated that the implementation would take place in the following manner:

- the first reduction, of one-eighth, would take effect on the date of entry into force for the US of the Agreement relating to the implementation of the Customs Valuation Agreement;

- the subsequent reductions would take effect in six annual stages.

(iii) The concessions for kraft paper and board were to be implemented, during the first phase, in two reductions, each of 0.5 points, on 1.1.83 and 1.1.84, and during the second phase, in two reductions, each of 0.5 points, on 1.1.86 and 1.1.87.

(b)   The United States Schedule contained the following lists indicating departures from the norm:

(i)   Concessions to be implemented in more than one stage but less than eight stages;

(ii)   Concessions to be implemented in eight stages but the implementation did not otherwise conform to the general staging rule;

(iii) Concessions to be implemented in more than eight but not more than ten stages;

(iv)   Staging for certain compound rates of duty.

(c)   Japan provided, *inter alia,* that for textile and steel products the commencement of reductions would be deferred to 1 January 1982 and thereafter the full reduction would be made in six equal installments.

4.   In the Uruguay Round once again a norm of five equal annual installments beginning on the date of entry into force of the WTO Agreement was provided in the Marrakesh Protocol in respect of industrial products and of six equal annual installments for developed countries and ten for developing countries in agricultural products. An important difference between the staging rules for these two sectors was that, whereas there was a possibility for deviations from the norm in respect of industrial products, there was no such possibility for agricultural products. Of course, there is no problem in accelerating the reduction. Where ceiling bindings were offered, these became applicable in general on 1 January 1995, or the date of entry into force of the WTO Agreement for the Member concerned.

5.   Important departures were made by the developed countries from the five-year rule in the sectoral agreements. While in some sectors implementation was agreed over longer periods, in others it was agreed to put the full reduction into effect immediately. The concessions on textiles and clothing were staged over longer periods by many participants and some developing countries linked the tariff concessions to the integration envisaged in the Agreement on Textiles and Clothing.

6.   While no deviations were possible in respect of agricultural tariffs, the EC commenced its reduction on 1 July 1996, taking advantage of the provision in the Agreement on Agriculture which defines "implementation period" as "the six-year period commencing in the year 1995" and the related provision which states that the "year" "in relation to the specific commitments of a Member refers to the calendar, financial or marketing year specified in the Schedule relating to that Member".

H.   Participation in Tariff Negotiations

1.   In the 1947 Geneva negotiations, 23 out of 24 members of the Preparatory Committee for the Charter for the International Trade Organization (not including the Soviet Union) accepted the invitation of the United States to negotiate concrete arrangements for the reduction of tariffs and trade barriers. In the subsequent negotiations at Annecy and Torquay, all contracting parties generally participated in the negotiations along with the governments applying for accession. There was a measure of optionality in participation for the contracting parties as participation was necessary only if they sought concessions in return and such concessions could be sought only by the principal suppliers. Even when a country participated in bilateral negotiations, in many cases where trade flows were insufficient, there was no exchange of concessions. In the 1956 Geneva negotiations, some developing countries did not participate at all, while other which participated did not make any offers. The same situation prevailed in the Dillon Round, in which only 23 out of 37 contracting parties made concessions.

2.   In the Kennedy and Tokyo Rounds, in which the linear or formula approach was followed, participation was in a sense obligatory. However, the concept of non-reciprocity applied to the developing countries and many of them did not undertake any tariff commitments. As compared with 76 contracting parties to GATT in 1967 only the following 31 countries and the EEC (6) granted tariff concessions in the Kennedy Round: Argentina, Australia, Austria, Brazil, Canada, Chile, Czechoslovakia, Denmark, Dominican Republic, Finland, Iceland, India, Ireland, Israel, Jamaica, Japan, Korea, Malawi, New Zealand, Norway, Peru, Portugal, South Africa, Spain, Sweden, Switzerland, Trinidad and Tobago, Turkey, United Kingdom, United States and Yugoslavia.

3.   In the Tokyo Round, although the number of contracting parties had risen to 85, only 36 countries and the EC (10) granted tariff concessions. The schedules of concessions of the following participants were annexed to the

Geneva (1979) Protocol, signed on 30 June 1979: Argentina, Austria, Canada, Czechoslovakia, EC, Finland, Hungary, Iceland, Jamaica, Japan, New Zealand, Norway, Romania, South Africa, Spain, Sweden, Switzerland, United States and Yugoslavia. However, negotiations were continued in later months of 1979 and the Protocol Supplementary to the Geneva (1979) Protocol signed on 22 November 1979 embodied the results of the further negotiations. This Protocol included the schedules of concessions of the following participants: Australia, Brazil, Canada (additional concessions), Chile, Côte d'Ivoire, Dominican Republic, Egypt, EC (additional concessions), Haiti, India, Indonesia, Israel, Korea, Malaysia, Pakistan, Peru, Singapore, Spain, Uruguay and Zaire.

4.   In the Uruguay Round, as mentioned earlier, it became obligatory for every Member to have a schedule of concessions on trade in goods. Due to this requirement, every government had to participate in the negotiations and grant concessions. The concessions of many developing country and least developed country Members were in the form of ceiling bindings.

I.   Institutional Aspects and Secretariat Support

1.   In the early rounds of negotiations, the practice followed was to establish a "Tariff Negotiations Working Party" at the opening of the conference. The Working Party was responsible for ascertaining the progress of negotiations and for making recommendations on questions of procedure and other matters connected with the conduct and conclusion of the negotiations. In the 1956 Geneva Negotiations and in the Dillon Round, a Tariff Negotiations Committee was established with broader functions: to exercise its good offices to maximize progress, to review consolidated offers, to be at the disposal of participants to arrange plurilateral or multilateral discussions, to consider any problems impeding or delaying the conclusion of the conference, and to draft the instrument or instruments embodying the results of the conference.

2.   During the Kennedy Round, when the Ministerial Resolution itself had decided upon a linear approach, the Trade Negotiations Committee was mandated to elaborate a trade negotiation plan with a view to reaching an agreement on the details of the plan for tariff reduction. It was given the overall function of supervising the conduct of trade negotiations.

3.   While the Trade Negotiations Committee was composed of representatives of all participating nations, the discussions on exception lists was held only among the participants which had made offers. Tariff and other market access problems in five product sectors, i.e. aluminum, iron and steel, cotton textiles, pulp and paper and chemicals were considered in smaller groups. Additional groups and sub-groups were set up in the negotiations to deal with agricultural products and non-tariff barriers (anti-dumping in particular).

4.   During the Tokyo Round, a Trade Negotiations Committee was similarly established to elaborate and put into effect detailed trade negotiating plans and establish appropriate negotiating procedures, and to supervise the progress of

negotiations. The Committee was not intended to be the place where substantive negotiations would take place and, for this purpose, five negotiating groups and several sub-groups were set up. The negotiating groups took up separately the negotiations on tropical products, tariffs, non-tariff measures, agriculture, sector approach and safeguards. The sub-groups were set up for non-tariff measures and agriculture.

5.   In the Uruguay Round, the Ministerial Declaration itself established the Trade Negotiations Committee to carry out the negotiations, a Group of Negotiations on Goods (GNG) and a Group of Negotiations on Services (GNS). The negotiating structure set up on 28 January 1987 for negotiations in the area of trade in goods consisted of 14 negotiating groups, including groups on tariffs, non-tariff measures, natural resource-based products, textiles and clothing, agriculture and tropical products, which related to market access. Towards the end of 1990, four of these negotiating groups, i.e. tariffs, non-tariff measures, natural resource-based products and tropical products, held joint meetings and thereafter they were merged into one market access group.

6.   In the initial rounds, the Secretariat's role in the conduct of negotiations was very modest, although the governments participating in negotiations looked to it for "appropriate assistance". The tariff and trade statistics as well as the request and offer lists were prepared by the participating governments themselves and the Secretariat merely helped to circulate them. As and when bilateral negotiations were concluded between pairs of participants, the jointly-agreed lists of concessions were transmitted to the Secretariat for record. At the conclusion of the negotiations, each participating government prepared for distribution through the Secretariat a consolidated list of concessions it had granted and a supplementary list showing the country or countries with which each concession was initially negotiated.

7.   However, by the time of the Tokyo Round, the Secretariat was providing considerable support for the tariff negotiations by preparing comprehensive, detailed and usable basic material on tariffs. The basic material on tariffs consisted of a tariff study giving the full facts on the tariff structure of each of the major trading countries together with trade statistics. For the EC and 10 developed countries, the GATT Secretariat established a basic file containing detailed information on duty rates, tariff bindings and the corresponding imports in recent years under each tariff line.

8.   The Secretariat support for tariff negotiations was broadened further in the Uruguay Round. Besides providing the basic statistical material on tariff rates and trade flows, the Secretariat was called upon to undertake evaluations of tariff offers. In 1990, the reviews of offers made by the participants to determine whether the Montreal targets had been achieved were held on the basis of analyses prepared by the Secretariat. Analytical work was also done by the Secretariat on each of the schedules before these were approved in the verification process. These analyses included calculation of trade-weighted average reduction in the case of industrial products and of simple average reduction in the case of agricultural products, checking whether all agricultural

products were bound and whether the minimum cut in the case of agricultural products complied with the requirements of the modalities. During the verification process, the Secretariat's role was further enhanced by requiring it to report on whether the ceiling bindings infringed existing bindings, the nature and application of other duties and charges and the completeness of agricultural supporting data.

J.   Results of Tariff Negotiations

1.   Only the overall results of tariff reduction and binding are considered here, as a more disaggregated analysis is outside the scope of this study.

2.   No reliable evaluation of the tariff reductions and other commitments made during the first five rounds of negotiations in GATT 1947 is available. However, studies were conducted in the Secretariat on the results of the negotiations during the Kennedy, Tokyo and Uruguay Rounds and the findings are summarized below.

3.   During the Kennedy Round, the principal industrialized countries made tariff reductions on 70 per cent of their dutiable imports, excluding cereals, meat and dairy products. Although the working hypothesis adopted for industrial products was for a linear cut of 50 per cent, because of numerous exceptions, an effective reduction of 35 per cent was obtained in industrialized countries for these products. The tariff reductions made by the developing countries were highly selective and would not have made a significant impact on their trade-weighted average tariff.

4.   During the Tokyo Round, the level of all industrial duties in industrialized countries (EC, US, Canada, Japan, Austria, Finland, Norway, Sweden and Switzerland) was reduced by one-third if measured on the basis of customs collection and by about 39 per cent if based on simple average rates. In these countries, the simple average declined from 10.4 to 6.4 per cent and the weighted average was reduced from 7.0 to 4.7 per cent (using import data from MFN origin in 1977, except that 1976 was used in the case of Austria, Canada and Norway). No comparable estimates are available for developing countries, again because of the selective nature of their bindings and reductions, but a GATT Secretariat study mentions that the coverage of their tariff reductions was $3.9 billion of their imports in 1976 and 1977. As for tariffs facing imports of developing countries, the average MFN reduction on industrial products was shallower than the overall cut, about one-quarter compared with one-third. This reflected the fact that important product groups in the exports of developing countries such as textiles, clothing, footwear and travel goods were subjected to lower than formula reduction.

5.   The main findings in the GATT Secretariat study of the results of the Uruguay Round in tariffs are given below:

   (a)   Developed countries agreed to reduce their tariffs on industrial goods from an average of 6.3 to 3.8 per cent, a reduction of 40 per cent;

(b)   The proportion of industrial products which would enter duty-free in the developed country markets would increase from 20 to 44 per cent;

(c)   The proportion of industrial products which would encounter tariffs above 15 per cent would decline from 7 to 5 per cent;

(d)   In the case of industrial products, the percentage of bound tariff lines rose from 78 to 99 per cent for developed countries, from 21 to 73 per cent for developing economies, and from 73 to 98 per cent for transition economies;

(e)   In agricultural products, all countries bound all their tariff lines, after - wherever applicable - converting their non-tariff measures into tariff equivalents. In a large number of cases, these were expressed in terms of specific duties with very high ad valorem equivalents. For unbound tariffs many developing countries offered ceiling bindings much above the current rates.

(f)   The developed countries reduced their tariffs on twelve groups of agricultural products by an overall simple average amount of 37 per cent, ranging from 26 per cent for dairy products to 48 per cent for cut flowers. The reduction on dutiable tropical products as a whole was 43 per cent, ranging from 37 per cent for "tropical nuts and fruits" to 52 per cent for "spices, flowers and plants";

(g)   The tariff cuts in the developed countries on industrial products, except petroleum, imported from the developing and least-developed countries were again lower as compared to the cut on imports from all sources, as shown in the following table:

Imports from	Trade-weighted tariff average		Percentage reduction
	Pre-Uruguay	Post-Uruguay	
All sources	6.3	3.8	40
Developing countries other than the least-developed	6.8	4.3	37
Least-developed countries	6.8	5.1	25

Source: GATT Secretariat, The Results of the Uruguay Round of Multilateral Trade Negotiations, November 1994.

The main factor responsible for the lower average reduction for imports from the developing countries was the lower reduction for textile and clothing as well as for fish and fish products.

(h)   The study measured changes in tariff escalation by the change in the absolute difference between the tariffs at the higher and the lower stages of processing and came to two conclusions. First, the developed country tariffs, averaged over all industrial products, were subject to escalation before the Uruguay Round cuts, and in most (but not all) instances would remain so after the cuts. Second, there had been greater absolute reductions in average tariffs at more advanced stages of production than at earlier stages of production.

6.   Studies done in the WTO, UNCTAD[28] and the OECD[29] show that, while the achievement during the last 50 years or so in industrial tariff reduction has been impressive, there is still considerable work to be done in future tariff negotiations. Among the aspects that might need attention in such negotiations, the following have been mentioned in particular:

In the developed countries:

(a)   The tariffication of non-tariff measures for agricultural products resulted in the introduction of very high outside-of-quota tariff rates, and in many instances of high inside-of-quota tariff rates;

(b)   In some countries, in the agricultural sector (and in some non-agricultural products) specific or mixed duties are used, leading to lack of transparency in the *ad valorem* incidence of tariffs;

(c)   In the industrial area, tariff peaks, defined as those above 15 per cent, continue to affect such sectors as textiles, clothing, footwear and motor vehicles.

In the developing countries:

(a)   High tariffs are prevalent in both agricultural and industrial sectors in a large number of countries. Some developing countries maintain much higher tariffs across-the-board than others at the same level of development. A similar divergence is noticeable in the level of bindings in industrial products;

(b)   In most developing countries, there is a large gap between the applied and bound rates. Since WTO Members have the freedom to raise duties to bound levels, the gap between the bound ceiling levels and the applied levels in both agricultural and industrial products is a source of uncertainty in international trade.

In both developing and developed countries:

Tariff escalation, although somewhat reduced in the past negotiations, continues to give additional protection to domestic producers.

---

[28]   UNCTAD, The Post-Uruguay Round Tariff Environment for Developing Country Exports, UNCTAD/WTO Joint Study, 1997.

[29]   OECD, Review of Tariffs Synthesis Report, 1999.

K.   Tariff Negotiations for Accession

1.   In the course of every tariff conference or round of multilateral trade negotiations, except the Geneva Tariff Conference of 1956, the negotiations encompassed accession negotiations with a number of countries. In fact, the Annecy Tariff Conference was convened only in connection with accession negotiations and in the Torquay Tariff Conference accession negotiations were a substantial component. The CONTRACTING PARTIES had also established as early as in 1949 "Procedures Governing Negotiations for Accession" outside of tariff conferences. In these procedures, and in practice, during the first five tariff conferences tariff negotiations were the principal - if not the sole - component of accession negotiations. The practice of establishing working parties to make an in-depth examination of the trade policies of the applicant countries developed much later, sometime in the mid-sixties. If working parties were established earlier in individual cases it was for a specific purpose such as examining the modalities of provisional accession.

2.   Not all countries in the process of accession which have participated in multilateral trade negotiations have concluded their tariff negotiations successfully during the rounds. Others which have had a negotiated schedule at the end of a round have not been able to accede until much later, sometimes after fresh tariff negotiations. A unique case was that of Bulgaria's participation in the Tokyo Round. While not successful in concluding its tariff negotiations pursuant to its request for accession, Bulgaria offered to give the benefit of the tariff concessions enumerated in the schedule tabled by it to all contracting parties to the GATT in accordance with the principles of Articles II, XIX, XXIV, XXVII, XXVIII and other relevant provisions of the General Agreement, provided, on their part, the contracting parties extended to Bulgaria reciprocal benefits in respect of tariff concessions enumerated in their Schedules.

Accession under GATT 1947

A review of the accession negotiations under GATT 1947 brings out the following features of the practice of contracting parties:

(i)   In the early days of GATT 1947, accession negotiations entailed an exchange of concessions and both the contracting parties and the applicant countries made concessions. Of course, the existing contracting parties' lists of new concessions were shorter as the applicant countries got the benefit of the concessions made earlier by the former. Since the Tokyo Round generally the practice has been that only the applicant country makes concessions. Even earlier some applicant countries did not request from contracting parties anything more than the benefit of existing concessions. This practice could be the consequence of the fact that, by the end of the Tokyo Round, the tariff concessions made by contracting parties had already become very comprehensive and the prevailing sentiment was to obtain concessions from acceding countries in return for concessions already made by the contracting parties in the past.

The outcome of tariff negotiations during accessions was initially in the form of bilateral lists of concessions. The concessions made by the acceding States were then embodied in the schedules which were annexed to the Protocol of Accession. As for the concessions made by the contracting parties, when accession negotiations were concluded in the context of multilateral trade negotiations, generally the practice was for the concessions to be reflected in the Protocols embodying the results of the multilateral trade negotiations and not in separate schedules annexed to the Protocol of Accession. In the Uruguay Round, some acceding states negotiated concessions which were directly incorporated in the schedules of the contracting parties annexed to the Marrakesh Protocol.

(ii)   The industrialized contracting parties have been the principal players in the accession negotiations of developing countries. Except in the first few years of the operation of GATT 1947, developing country contracting parties have seldom sought concessions from acceding developing countries.

(iii)   The tariff negotiations from the beginning up to the time when GATT 1947 was terminated remained bilateralized. The applicant country concluded bilateral tariff agreements with all or almost all the contracting parties with which it entered into negotiations.

(iv)   Since, in every case, there was a bilateral list of concessions, there was a record of the contracting parties with which the concessions were initially negotiated. However, a practice developed in the later phase of the operation of GATT 1947 for the acceding countries to specifically grant INRs on the tariff lines on the bilateral lists. In some cases INRs were specifically excluded in respect of a number of concessions on the lists.

(v)   The accession negotiations usually resulted in bilateral lists which were selective, comprising tariff lines in which the contracting party concerned was the principal supplier or had an interest as a substantial supplier or otherwise. The practice grew in the later phase of the operation of GATT 1947 for the contracting parties also to secure a ceiling binding for all or nearly all industrial products and in some cases for agricultural products as well.

(vi)   In the early phase of GATT 1947, the acceding country and the contracting party negotiating with the acceding country sent two notifications to the Secretariat, first that they had entered into negotiations with an exchange of offers, and second, that they had concluded the negotiations. Sometimes the Secretariat was also informed of the exchange of request lists. Later on, the practice was only to notify the Secretariat of the conclusion of negotiations, not their commencement.

(vii) In some cases, while negotiations were entered into they concluded on the note that the level of then existing trade was not such as to warrant an exchange of concessions.

(viii) Non-tariff measures figured increasingly in the bilateral negotiations in the accessions from the mid-80s onwards, and commitments were made by the acceding countries to become signatories to the Tokyo Round agreements on these measures. In some cases, specific commitments were made on the elimination of licensing in respect of tariff lines on which tariff concessions had been made. While the acceding country concerned retained the right to have recourse to existing GATT 1947 provisions (to impose quantitative restrictions), it also agreed that, if the use of such rights proved necessary, it would enter into negotiations to give compensation to contracting parties which would be affected.

(ix)   In the case of some accessions, contracting parties invoked the non-application clause (Article XXXV) and did not consent to the application of GATT 1947 between themselves and the newly-acceding countries. As a prerequisite of non-application is that negotiations should not have been entered into between the two contracting parties, those invoking the non-application clause had not entered into negotiations with the acceding country concerned. In one case, however, one contracting party, Brazil, notified that, not having completed its negotiations with Japan, it wished to invoke the provisions of Article XXXV of GATT. The notification went on to say that "(t)he Brazilian Government hopes that it will be able to suspend the application of the said Article as soon as negotiations with Japan have resulted in a mutually-advantageous agreement."[30]

The largest number of invocations of Article XXXV were against Japan at the time of its accession in 1955 when 14 contracting parties, including several important trading nations, i.e. France and the UK, resorted to the provision. The invocation was made on behalf - not only of their own but also - of their dependent territories. Four more invocations of Article XXXV were made against Japan subsequently at the time of accession of other contracting parties. When these invocations were later withdrawn, it was without entering into tariff negotiations. Upon withdrawal, however, these contracting parties got the opportunity to exchange concessions with Japan in subsequent multilateral trade negotiations such as the Kennedy Round and the Tokyo Round. New Zealand entered into bilateral tariff negotiations with Japan shortly after

[30] GATT Doc. L/405, p. 3.

withdrawal of its invocation of Article XXXV in March 1963. There was no case of non-application involving only Article II of GATT 1947 as permitted under Article XXXV.

(x)   In their accession negotiations, Romania and Poland did not make any tariff concessions. The Working Party on the accession of Poland had reported, *inter alia*, as follows:

"The Working Party noted that the foreign trade of Poland was conducted mainly by State Enterprises and that the Foreign Trade Plan rather than the customs tariff was the effective instrument of Poland's commercial policy. The present customs tariff was applicable only to a part of imports effected by private persons for their personal use in the nature of a purchase tax rather than a customs tariff. The Working Party agreed that due consideration had to be given to these facts in drawing up the legal instruments relating to Poland's accession to the General Agreement. The representative of Poland stressed that, as a result of possible changes in the economic system of Poland, a different situation might arise enabling Poland to renegotiate its position towards the provisions of the General Agreement.

"It was agreed that in view of the nature of the foreign trade system of Poland its main concession in the negotiations for its accession to the General Agreement would be commitments relating to an annual increase in the value of its imports from contracting parties."[31]

Consequently, Poland's schedule annexed to the Protocol for the Accession of Poland which entered into force on 18 October 1967 provided as follows:

"Schedule LXV - Poland

1.   Subject to paragraph 2 below, Poland shall, with effect from the date of this Protocol, undertake to increase the total value of its imports from the territories of contracting parties by not less than 7 per cent per annum.

2.   On 1 January 1971 and thereafter on the date specified in paragraph 1 of Article XXVIII of the General Agreement, Poland may, by negotiation and agreement with the CONTRACTING PARTIES, modify its commitments under paragraph 1 above. Should this negotiation not lead to agreement between Poland and the CONTRACTING PARTIES, Poland shall, nevertheless, be free to modify this commitment. Contracting Parties shall then be free to modify equivalent commitments."[32]

In the case of Romania, the same arguments applied and in the Working Party it was agreed that "because of the absence of a customs tariff in Romania, the main concession to be incorporated in its Schedule would be a firm intention

---

[31]   GATT, BISD, Fifteenth Supplement, p. 110.

[32]   GATT, BISD, Fifteenth Supplement, p. 52..

of increasing imports from contracting parties at a rate not smaller than the growth of total Romanian imports provided for in its Five-Year Plans."[33]

In the Tokyo Round, which was held after the accession of Poland and Romania, both contracting parties participated and made tariff offers. However, the tariff concessions made by only Romania were attached to the Geneva (1979) Protocol as Poland withdrew its offers, citing lack of interest by other contracting parties. By the time the Uruguay Round took place the economic systems of these two countries had changed and both of them had tariff schedules of the usual type attached to the Marrakesh Protocol.

(xi) When Bangladesh became independent it requested accession on the basis of the existing terms and conditions which applied to its territory including the schedules of tariff concessions. There were, therefore, no tariff negotiations and the schedule attached to the Protocol of its accession was based on the existing schedule of Pakistan.[34] A similar procedure was followed when Czechoslovakia was replaced by two successor States, the Czech Republic and the Slovak Republic. There were no tariff negotiations and the tariff schedules encompassing the concessions in the schedule of Czechoslovakia were annexed to each Protocol of Accession. In the case of Slovenia, however, the request for accession without negotiations was not accepted and negotiations were held to establish a new schedule.

(xii) In a number of cases provisional accession was granted to governments pending the completion of procedures for definitive accession. In only one case, that of Switzerland, was provisional accession preceded by tariff negotiation and Switzerland was temporarily granted GATT rights by the signatories to the Declaration on the Provisional Accession of the Swiss Confederation dated 22 November 1958. This Declaration provided, *inter alia,* that commercial relations between the participating contracting parties and the Swiss Confederation shall, subject to certain conditions, "be based upon the General Agreement as if the Swiss Confederation had acceded to the General Agreement in accordance with the relevant procedures and as if the schedules annexed to this Declaration were schedules annexed to the General Agreement...[35]

3.   The above description of the features of the practice of contracting parties applies to negotiations for accession under Article XXXIII of GATT 1947. As for accessions under paragraph 5 (c) of Article XXVI, no tariff negotiations were provided for and the government concerned became a contracting party on the

[33]   GATT, BISD, Eighteenth Supplement, p. 95.

[34]   GATT, BISD, Nineteenth Supplement, pp. 6-7.

[35]   GATT, BISD, Seventh Supplement, p. 19.

basis of a declaration by the "responsible contracting party" that the customs territory possessed or had acquired "full autonomy in the conduct of its external commercial relations and of the other matters provided for in this Agreement", as provided in the Article.

Accessions under the WTO

4.   The following are the features of the accessions to the WTO in respect of tariff commitments made by the acceding countries:

(i)   The trend in the last phase of the operation of GATT 1947 for the acceding countries to bind the tariffs on all or nearly all industrial products (besides agricultural products as required by the WTO Agreement on Agriculture) as well as granting concessions on a specific list of products has continued. While high tariffs have been accepted for agricultural products, the trend has been for the acceding developing countries to bind their industrial tariffs at much lower levels than was the case under GATT 1947. In some cases they have made commitments partially or substantially accepting the Uruguay Round sectoral agreements aiming at harmonization or elimination of tariffs.

(ii)   The practice of specifically granting initial negotiating rights even though such rights are inherent in bilaterally-agreed lists has continued. To guard against the practice of INRs being granted at different levels to different Members in respect of the same product, some Members have secured commitments that the level of tariff for each INR will not be higher than the rate at which it is extended to other Members.

(iii)   Commitments have been obtained envisaging that the bound rate on specific products will not be higher than the bound rate on competing products (e.g., rapeseed/colza/canola products *vis-à-vis* comparable soya products).

(iv)   In the bilateral agreements commitments have been made in respect of regional arrangements of which the acceding Member is a participant. In one case the commitment is to make serious attempts to obtain agreement from the partners in the regional arrangement to lower the existing common external tariff for specific products. In another case the commitment is to endeavour to limit to a minimum the effects of the negotiations in the regional arrangement on the tariff rates applied by the acceding Member at the time of accession. In one case the acceding Member declared its intentions (on a non-legally binding basis) to maintain its existing applied rates notwithstanding the ceiling bindings.

CHAPTER III

BILATERAL AND PLURILATERAL NEGOTIATIONS

A.   Bilateral and Plurilateral Tariff Negotiations under GATT 1947

1.   Reference has already been made in Chapter I to the procedures established by the CONTRACTING PARTIES for two or more contracting parties to hold tariff negotiations at times other than general tariff conferences. Ten negotiations were held under these procedures, nine of which were bilateral. One of them, held in 1956, was joined in by a large majority of the contracting parties and is, therefore, counted as one of the rounds of multilateral trade negotiations and has already been dealt with in the previous Chapter. Of the remaining nine, seven bilateral negotiations involved Germany and other contracting parties (South Africa, Austria (twice), Denmark, Norway, Sweden and Finland). Cuba and the US had bilateral negotiations under these procedures in 1957 and Japan and New Zealand in 1963. The bilateral negotiations between Japan and New Zealand were held shortly after the withdrawal by New Zealand of the invocation of Article XXXV against Japan in March 1962.

2.   Plurilateral tariff negotiations were also held in the context of the Tokyo Round. The Agreement on Trade in Civil Aircraft, negotiated during the Round among a group of mainly industrialized countries, involved tariff concessions and customs duties and other charges were eliminated from all civil aircraft, civil aircraft engines, other parts, components and sub-assemblies, as well as from all ground flight simulators and their parts and components. The signatories to the Agreement agreed in March 1984 to an expansion of the products covered by the Agreement.

B.   Bilateral and Plurilateral Negotiations under the WTO

1.   Since the entry into force of the WTO Agreement, there have been instances of concessions flowing from bilateral and plurilateral negotiations being bound by incorporation in the schedules of the participating countries concerned.

Information Technology Agreement

2.   The most far-reaching negotiations were those on information technology products. On 13 December 1996, during the course of the Singapore Ministerial Meeting, 28 Members of the WTO and States or separate customs territories in the process of acceding to the WTO adopted a Declaration[1] signifying their intention to eliminate the customs duties and other duties and charges on six categories of information technology products. These categories were computers,

---

[1]   WTO Doc. WT/MIN(96)16.

telecommunication products, semi-conductors, semi-conductor manufacturing equipment, software and scientific instruments. The modalities for reaching a final agreement by 1 April 1997 were spelt out in the Ministerial Declaration. A unique feature of these modalities was that the agreement was to become effective and the participants were to implement the decision to eliminate tariffs if "participants representing approximately 90 per cent of world trade in information technology products have by then notified their acceptance". When the matter was reviewed by the participants on 26 March 1997, the acceptances had risen to 39 participants accounting for 92.5 per cent of trade in these products. The Agreement therefore entered into effect on 1 April 1997. A number of other participants have joined the Agreement since then.

3.   Another unique feature of the Information Technology Agreement was that the starting-point for negotiations was not always tariff lines but a list of ITA products. The Ministerial Declaration contained an attachment A with a list of HS headings, but it also contained an attachment B giving a list of products. The modalities required the participants to implement the binding and elimination of duties by the following procedures:

(i)   In the case of the HS headings listed in Attachment A, by creating, where appropriate, sub-divisions in its Schedule at the national tariff line level; and

(ii)   in the case of the products in Attachment B, by attaching an Annex to its Schedule including all products in Attachment B, which is to specify the detailed HS headings for those products at either the national tariff line level or the HS 6-digit level.

4.   The ITA envisaged that customs duties would be eliminated in four stages starting on 1 July 1997 and ending on 1 January 2000. There was provision for extending the staging of reductions in limited circumstances. A few participants, including Costa Rica, Korea, Chinese Taipei, Thailand, Malaysia, Indonesia and India were given the benefit of extended staging for a limited number of products. In some cases, staging was permitted up to the year 2005. The Agreement also envisaged that, in future, the participants would review and enlarge the product coverage. Such a review was taken up in 1998, but disagreements over exclusion of certain consumer electronic items and over the proposed inclusion of certain items having a bearing on external and internal security stymied the negotiations.

5.   Although the initiative for the Agreement came from the QUAD members, the momentum of other governments wanting to join it was considerable, even though it was always clear that the concessions would be applied by the participants on an MFN basis. While some participants had low levels of existing tariffs on IT products, there were others which were maintaining moderately high levels of tariffs and in some areas very high levels of tariffs on these products. Since all tariffs were agreed to be reduced to zero, there would be a significant increase in market access worldwide for these products once the agreed elimination was implemented.

6.   The success of the sectoral approach in the case of the Information Technology Agreement raises some questions of policy regarding future negotiations. Generally speaking, it is widely acknowledged that only global tariff negotiations can yield far-reaching and substantial results in securing a reduction or elimination of tariffs, as in only such negotiations is there a possibility of sectoral trade-offs which are an essential ingredient for success. But individual sectors may have some unique features which may make it feasible for agreement to be reached on a stand-alone basis for some sectors. The information technology industry is a highly globalized one and there is keen competition to attract foreign direct investment in the industry. Duty-free treatment of inputs is one of the factors which make host countries attractive for foreign investors. In the circumstances, most governments were attracted to a worldwide agreement for the elimination of tariffs on information technology products, even outside the framework of global negotiations on tariffs.

7.   Another aspect of the Agreement which might call for comment is the provision whereby the Agreement became effective upon participants with a trade share of 90 per cent signifying their acceptance. At the time of the discussions at Singapore, the parallel was given of paragraph 6 of Article XXVI of GATT 1947, which stipulated that the GATT would enter into force definitively only after acceptance by contracting parties accounting for 85 per cent of the trade of all contracting parties. However, it can also be argued that the modality was not far different from the one adopted in sectoral negotiations for tariff harmonization and elimination during the Uruguay Round. In fact, as the figures given in an earlier section would show, in the sectoral agreements during the Uruguay Round, the participants were satisfied generally by the adherence of WTO Members with a share of exports which was in all cases less than the figure of 90 per cent stipulated in the Information Technology Agreement.

Pharmaceuticals

8.   It has been mentioned earlier that one of the areas in which the zero-for-zero initiative was successful in the Uruguay Round was pharmaceuticals. Duty elimination in this product group involved the items classified or classifiable in Harmonized System (HS) Chapter 30 and in H.S. Headings 2936, 2937, 2939 and 2941 (except for certain listed items) and four groups of pharmaceutical products and intermediate chemicals listed in the annexes to the record of discussions[2] among representatives of the governments participating in the agreement for tariff elimination on pharmaceuticals. Over 6000 products were covered. The record of discussions also mentioned that the WTO Members concerned would meet once every three years to review the product coverage with a view to including, by consensus, additional pharmaceutical products for tariff elimination. The first such review took place over the period 30 November 1995-11 July 1996 and resulted in 465 additional products being added to the list

---

[2]   GATT Doc. L/7430.

eligible for duty-free treatment. The second series of meetings took place during the period April 1998 to October 1998 and a further 639 products were added to the list.

Other liberalization commitments

9.   The United States and the EEC notified their decision to reduce duties on white spirits, one which (presumably) flowed from bilateral negotiations. There were also notifications of unilateral decisions on tariff commitments. For instance, Hong Kong, China took a decision to bind many of its tariffs at the applied level of zero duty. Pursuant to the provisions of Annex 5 to the Agreement on Agriculture, at the end of 1998 Japan tariffed the one product, i.e. rice, in which it had received special treatment and had maintained quantitative restrictions as a departure from the general obligation contained in paragraph 2 of Article 4 of the Agreement on Agriculture.

CHAPTER IV

PRACTICE AND PROCEDURES IN RENEGOTIATIONS

A.   Renegotiations during the period 1948-1957

Duration of schedules

1.   As Article XXVIII was substantially revised during the Review Session and the revised version came into effect in October 1957 we shall first consider the practice and procedures in renegotiations up to 1957.

2.   Article XXVIII as originally incorporated in GATT 1947 is reproduced below:

"1.   On or after January 1, 1951, any contracting party may, by negotiation and agreement with any other contracting party with which such treatment was initially negotiated, and subject to consultation with such other contracting parties as the CONTRACTING PARTIES determine to have a substantial interest in such treatment, modify, or cease to apply, the treatment which it has agreed to accord under Article II to any product described in the appropriate Schedule annexed to this Agreement. In such negotiations and agreement, which may include provision for compensatory adjustment with respect to other products, the contracting parties concerned shall endeavour to maintain a general level of reciprocal and mutually-advantageous concessions not less favourable to trade than that provided for in the present Agreement.

2 (a)   If agreement between the contracting parties primarily concerned cannot be reached, the contracting party which proposes to modify or cease to apply such treatment shall, nevertheless, be free to do so, and if such action is taken the contracting party with which such treatment was initially negotiated, and the other contracting parties determined under paragraph 1 of this Article to have a substantial interest, shall then be free, not later than six months after such action is taken, to withdraw, upon the expiration of thirty days from the day on which written notice of such withdrawal is received by the CONTRACTING PARTIES, substantially equivalent concessions initially negotiated with the contracting party taking such action.

(b)   If agreement between the contracting parties primarily concerned is reached but any other contracting party determined under paragraph 1 of this Article to have a substantial interest is not satisfied, such other contracting party shall be free, not later than six months after action under such agreement is taken, to withdraw, upon the expiration of thirty days from the day on which written notice of such withdrawal is received by the CONTRACTING PARTIES, substantially equivalent concessions initially negotiated with a contracting party taking action under such Agreement."

3.   The tariff commitments made in the 1947 Geneva negotiations had an initial validity of three years and in Article XXVIII as originally incorporated in GATT 1947 there was no provision for renegotiations for modification or withdrawal of these commitments before 1 January 1951. At Torquay it was decided[1] to extend the assured validity of the tariff commitments up to 1 January 1954 by an amendment of the text of paragraph 1 of Article XXVIII. Even before this amendment of Article XXVIII became effective in accordance with the requirement of Article XXX (by the acceptance of two-thirds of the governments which were at that time contracting parties), the Torquay Protocol provided for the extension of the commitment on the assured validity of the concessions by the contracting parties which signed either the Protocol or a Declaration which was separately adopted on "The Continued Application of the Schedules to the General Agreement on Tariffs and Trade".[2]

4.   On 24 October 1953, the CONTRACTING PARTIES adopted another Declaration[3] to provide that they would not invoke prior to 1 July 1955 the provisions of paragraph 1 of Article XXVIII. The adoption of a declaration without any accompanying amendment of the text of paragraph 1 of Article XXVIII was considered to be "the best means of giving effect to the desire of the majority of the contracting parties to prolong the assured life of their schedules beyond 31 December 1953.[4]

5.   By early 1955, the Review Session had already finalized its recommendations for amendment of a number of articles, including the amendment of Article XXVIII to its present form, which, *inter alia*, dispenses with the need to take a decision on the extension of validity of the schedules from time to time and instead provides for the possibility of renegotiations at three-year intervals beginning on 1 January 1958. On 10 March 1955, the CONTRACTING PARTIES adopted another Declaration[5] extending the assured validity of the schedules for a further period of two years and six months (up to 1 January 1958).

Renegotiations under paragraph 1 of Article XXVIII

6.   The first set of renegotiations already authorized under paragraph 1 of Article XXVIII of the original GATT 1947 were held during the Torquay Tariff Conference before the contracting parties agreed to prolong the life of the tariff commitments. These renegotiations were held in parallel with negotiations for new concessions among the contracting parties. The available records of the Torquay renegotiations show that renegotiations were held among 13 contracting parties, Australia, Brazil, Benelux (Metropolitan Territories, Belgian Congo and

---

[1]   GATT, The Torquay Protocol and the Torquay Schedule of Concessions, p.5.

[2]   GATT, BISD, Vol. II, p. 31.

[3]   GATT, BISD, Second Supplement, pp. 22-23.

[4]   GATT, BISD, Second Supplement, p. 61.

[5]   GATT, BISD, Third Supplement, pp. 30-32.

Ruanda-Urundi and Surinam), Chile, Cuba, Denmark, France, Haiti, Italy, New Zealand, South Africa, United Kingdom and Uruguay. The United States, while making a statement that it did not wish to invoke Article XXVIII during the Torquay negotiations, nevertheless carried out discussions for "certain adjustments" in respect of three products. Other details of the renegotiations are not available, but the results of these renegotiations were incorporated in the Torquay Protocol.

7.   The next series of renegotiations under paragraph 1 of Article XXVIII took place at the beginning of 1955, when further prolongation beyond 1 July 1955 of the assured life of the schedules became due for consideration. As many as 21 contracting parties notified their intention to invoke paragraph 1 of Article XXVIII before giving their support to the continuation of the assured life of the schedules. After 1955, the next renegotiations under this provision were in 1957, before the next period of validity of the schedules was to begin on 1 January 1958. Nine contracting parties took advantage of these negotiations.

8.   In the context of the renegotiations in 1957, the Secretariat made recommendations[6] for arrangements and procedures for the conduct of renegotiations. The procedures recommended by the Secretariat contained many of the elements which were included eventually in the procedures for renegotiations under Article XXVIII approved by the CONTRACTING PARTIES in 1980. It should also be recalled that Article XXVIII at that time envisaged negotiations and consultations only with contracting parties with which the concession was initially negotiated and with those having a substantial interest. The rights of contracting parties with a principal supplying interest were not separately recognized.

Authorization of requests for renegotiation on "sympathetic consideration"

9.   While renegotiations on a general basis took place before the extension of the assured validity of the schedules from time to time, a practice also developed for the CONTRACTING PARTIES to grant authorization on "sympathetic consideration" of requests to modify or withdraw tariff concessions. Even before the Torquay negotiations, four contracting parties, Brazil, Cuba, Pakistan and Ceylon (Sri Lanka), were granted such authorization. The Working Party on the "Continued Application of Schedules Annexed to the Agreement" on the basis of whose recommendation the Declaration of 24 October 1953 was adopted had cited earlier instances of such authorization and concluded that "(t)here was no reason to believe that contracting parties will be less ready in the future than they have been in the past to consider requests of this kind and to join in granting authority for the necessary negotiations, and the approval of this report would in itself be confirmation that the CONTRACTING PARTIES would give sympathetic consideration to such requests."[7]

---

[6]   GATT Doc. L/635.

[7]   GATT, BISD, Second Supplement, p.63.

10.   One of the additions to Article XXVIII emerging from the Review Session was the provision for special circumstance renegotiations which could be authorized by the CONTRACTING PARTIES under paragraph 4 of the revised Article. While the contracting parties were awaiting the entry into force of the Protocol amending various provisions of the General Agreement, including Article XXVIII, there was a desire to put paragraph 4 of the revised Article into effect immediately. Consequently, the Declaration[8] of 10 March 1955 whereby the CONTRACTING PARTIES extended the assured validity of the schedules for a further period of two years and six months also provided that, during that period or until the above-mentioned protocol entered into effect, whichever was earlier, contracting parties might enter into renegotiations under conditions and in accordance with procedures which were the same as those contained in paragraph 4 of the revised Article XXVIII.

11.   During the period 1948-57, before Article XXVIII in its current form entered into effect, there was recourse on 20 occasions to renegotiations under the customary practice of the CONTRACTING PARTIES showing "sympathetic consideration" for granting special authorization for renegotiations to contracting parties or under paragraph 4 of Article XXVIII, which was put into effect through the Declaration dated 10 March 1955 even before it had entered into force legally. These requests were made mostly on account of the urgent need for additional protection of specific industries or in a few cases on the ground of changes in classification of products.

12.   During the period before 1957, the renegotiations under paragraph 1 of Article XXVIII, those held pursuant to special authorization on "sympathetic consideration" as well as those under paragraph 4 of the Article were held quite smoothly. In general, the claims of "substantial interest" were recognized and the contracting parties with such interest were satisfied with the results of renegotiations. There were only a few cases in which claims of substantial interest were not recognized. There were no instances of retaliatory withdrawals. The renegotiations under paragraph 1 of Article XXVIII were generally completed over a short period and only in a few cases was an extension of time needed. After paragraph 4 of the Article was made operational through the Declaration, additional time was given to contracting parties under this provision to complete renegotiations which had been commenced earlier. Thus, a number of renegotiations which had begun under paragraph 1 of Article XXVIII were allowed to be continued under paragraph 4 of that Article.

Sui generis renegotiations by Brazil

13.   There was one *sui generis* case in which Brazil was granted a waiver from the obligations of Article II by a decision of the CONTRACTING PARTIES on 16 November 1956, to enable it to put into force its new customs tariff immediately as its programme for the reform of its final structure had resulted in

---

[8]   GATT, BISD, Third Supplement, pp.30-32.

a comprehensive tariff revision. Brazil was required to undertake negotiations in order to establish a new schedule within a year of the tariff revision. Pending the entry into force of the results of the negotiations, other contracting parties were allowed to suspend concessions initially negotiated with Brazil on the basis of "procedures analogous to those provided in Article XXVIII". Paragraphs 3 and 4 of the Decision are reproduced below *in extenso*:

"3. As soon as the negotiations referred to in paragraph 1 above have come to an end the Brazilian Government and other negotiating contracting parties shall submit to the CONTRACTING PARTIES a report on the results of the negotiations and on other action taken in pursuance of this Decision. The CONTRACTING PARTIES may make such recommendations to Brazil and to other contracting parties as they may deem appropriate. In particular, if any negotiating contracting party considers that the situation resulting from the negotiations and other action pursuant to this Decision does not constitute a mutually satisfactory adjustment, the CONTRACTING PARTIES shall authorize the suspension of the mutual obligations of that contracting party and of Brazil under the General Agreement.

4. Together with the report referred to in paragraph 3 above, the Brazilian Government and other negotiating contracting parties will submit to the CONTRACTING PARTIES the new Schedule III, and modifications in the schedules of other negotiating contracting parties resulting from such negotiations, provided that any contracting party determined by the CONTRACTING PARTIES to have a principal supplying interest or a substantial interest in any concession which would be modified or withdrawn as a result of such negotiations will be entitled to withdraw substantially equivalent concessions initially negotiated with the contracting party having modified or withdrawn such a concession. Such action will have to be taken not later than six months after such concession has been modified or withdrawn and after the CONTRACTING PARTIES having been duly notified."[9]

14.   The result of this authorization was full-fledged negotiations between Brazil on the one hand and 17 other contracting parties on the other, lasting about two years. A Tariff Negotiations Committee was established to conduct the negotiations and Brazil's trading partners reviewed past concessions made by them to Brazil. Request lists were exchanged by both sides and new sets of concessions agreed both by Brazil and by its trading partners.

15.   During the period 1948-57, apart from recourse to Article XXVIII for modification and withdrawal of concessions, there were also instances of recourse to Article XVIII:7 for renegotiation of bound concessions. Sri Lanka (then Ceylon) invoked the provision on four occasions, twice in 1955 and once each in 1956 and 1957, and Greece once in 1956.

---

[9]   GATT, BISD, Fifth Supplement, p.38.

B.   Renegotiations during the period 1958-1994 under Article XXVIII: 1, 4 and 5

1.   During this period, under GATT 1947, Article XXVIII in its present form was available to the contracting parties which had accepted the Protocol on the Review Session amendments after its entry into effect in October 1957 upon acceptance by two-thirds of the contracting parties. For other contracting parties which had not been able to complete the domestic legal formalities to accept those amendments, the revised Article XXVIII was made applicable by the adoption of a declaration on 30 November 1957 and again on 19 November 1960 on the continued application of schedules for three-year periods.

Main trends of renegotiations (1958-1994)

2.   During the period 1958 to 1994, the relative flexibility in the use of Article XXVIII:5 as compared to Article XXVIII:1 (where renegotiations could be done only in a slot of about six months before the commencement of successive three-year periods) and Article XXVIII:4 (where authorization had to be obtained and renegotiation had to be completed within defined time limits) induced a gradual shift to Article XXVIII:5. This is evident from the table given below:

Time period	Invocation of		
	Para. 1	**Para. 4**	**Para. 5**
1958-59	0	11	1
1960-69	27	21	11
1970-79	9	5	43
1980-89	2	2	54
1990-94	3	1	8

3.   The slide into desuetude of Article XXVIII:4 took place notwithstanding the fact that the authorization of renegotiations under this provision became progressively easier. In the early 1950s, when special authorization had to be given, the discussions among contracting parties were spread over two or three days. Even as early as in 1958, however, approval of requests for authorization under Article XXVIII:4 had become a routine matter and there was no detailed examination of "special circumstance" in the Intersessional Committee. Requests were granted even when the documents had not been circulated in advance in accordance with the rules of procedure. Again, the limitation of time in respect of Article XXVIII:1 renegotiations was not a big impediment and extension of time was easily given. But the relative freedom of Article XXVIII:5, under which negotiations could begin at any time and could be carried on over any period, made this paragraph very attractive to contracting parties. All that they had to do in order to be able to invoke Article XXVIII:5 at any time during a three-year period was to make a reservation to this effect at the beginning. Such a reservation was made by an increasing number of contracting parties during the period 1958-94, as will be seen from the following table:

Year

Nos.	58-60	61-63	64-66	67-69	70-72	73-75	76-78	79-81	82-84	85-87	88-90	91-93	94-96
	4	9	2	6	9	12	11	18	19	23	28	35	37

These reservations were made even if there was no intention at the time of the reservation to hold such negotiations, with a view to retaining the flexibility to invoke Article XXVIII:5 if the need arose to renegotiate a tariff concession.

Rules and procedures for renegotiations

4.   One development during the period was the adoption of rules and procedures for negotiations under Article XXVIII. In 1957, the CONTRACTING PARTIES had approved the rules and procedures for the renegotiations under Article XXVIII:1 planned before 1 January 1958. Suggestions for changes in these procedures were made by the Secretariat in the light of experience and new procedures[10] were approved by the Council in November 1980. An important point to be noted about these procedures is that they are in the nature of guidelines. The relevant parts of the minutes of the meeting of the Committee on Tariff Concessions are set out below:

> "The Chairman took up the question of the character of the document and recalled the comments made by the representative of Finland that the terms used in the text and particularly the word 'should' meant that the document should be interpreted as guidelines and that contracting parties entering into Article XXVIII negotiations were invited to follow those guidelines but should not consider them as binding obligations".[11]

5.   The main elements of the guidelines are described below:

What has to be done by the Member when initiating action to modify or withdraw a concession

6.   The Member invoking Article XXVIII:1 or 5 or seeking authority under Article XXVIII:4 must send a notification to the Secretariat indicating its intention and giving the following information:

(i)   List of items, with corresponding tariff line numbers, which are affected;

(ii)   Whether it is intended to modify or withdraw the concession;

(iii)   The Member, if any, with which the item was initially negotiated;

(iv)   The statistics of imports of the products involved, by country of origin, for the last three years for which statistics are available;

---

[10]   GATT, BISD, Twenty-seventh Supplement, pp.26-28.

[11]   GATT, Doc. TAR/M/3, p.9.

(v)   In the case of specific or mixed duties, both values and quantities have to be indicated.

7.   If the intention is to modify the concession, the Member concerned has been given the option to indicate the proposed modification in the first notification or to circulate it as soon as possible thereafter to the Members with INRs or with a principal or substantial supplying interest. At the same time as the first notification, and in the case of renegotiations under Article XXVIII:4 when the authorization has been granted, the Member seeking modification or withdrawal of a concession should communicate to other concerned Members the compensatory adjustments which it is prepared to offer.

What has to be done by Members claiming a principal or substantial supplying interest

8.   Within 90 days of the initial notification, other Members have to communicate in writing their claims of interest as a principal or substantial supplying Member and at the same time send a copy to the Secretariat. If the claims of interest are recognized by the Member seeking modification or withdrawal of a concession, such recognition constitutes a determination by the Ministerial Conference of interest as required in Article XXVIII:1. If a claim of interest is not recognized, the Member making the claim may refer the matter to the Ministerial Conference. It should be noted that the Member with INRs is not required to make a claim of interest.

What has to be done by the Member seeking to modify or withdraw a concession on completion of renegotiations

9.   Upon completion of each bilateral negotiation the Member seeking to modify or withdraw a concession is required to send to the Secretariat a joint letter attaching a report indicating (a) concessions to be withdrawn; (b) bound rates to be increased; (c) reduction of rates bound in the existing schedules and (d) new concessions not in existing schedules. On completion of all its negotiations, the Member concerned has to send a final report indicating the Members with which agreement has been reached and those with which agreement has not been reached and the names of Members with a substantial interest with which consultations have been held. Members are free to give effect to the proposed changes after the conclusion of the negotiations have been notified. Another notification has to be submitted to the Secretariat of the date on which the changes will come into effect.

Duties of the Secretariat

10.   The Secretariat is required to circulate as secret documents all notifications for initiating renegotiations, with the accompanying information as well as the reports on completion of bilateral negotiations and the final report on the conclusion of all negotiations/consultations. The report on the date on which the changes will come into force is also to be circulated, but not as a secret

document. The notifications to the Secretariat of claims of interest are only for the record.

Main features of renegotiations (1958-1994)

11.   The main features of the practice of contracting parties in the renegotiations under paragraphs 1, 4 and 5 of Article XXVIII are described below:

(i)   Tariff concessions were modified or withdrawn under Article XXVIII generally to afford additional protection to industry or agriculture. Other common reasons were rationalization or simplification of tariffs, introduction of new tariff nomenclature and conversion from specific to *ad valorem* tariffs;

(ii)   Extension of time to complete negotiations held under Article XXVIII:1 was granted as a routine matter if renegotiations could not be completed before 1 January. However, the practice developed later of dispensing with extensions and the contracting party concerned announcing that it would continue the renegotiations under Article XXVIII:5;

(iii) The renegotiations under Article XXVIII:4 were generally the most expeditious, although in some cases the process overlapped with a new cycle for renegotiations under Article XXVIII:1. In some cases, even when the renegotiations under Article XXVIII:1 were already in sight, special circumstance was claimed in response to domestic pressures and authorization obtained under Article XXVIII:4. The following extract from the summary record of the meeting of the Intersessional Committee held at the Palais des Nations on 20 April 1960, illustrates the above point:

"The representative of Australia pointed out that if the situation had permitted his Government to wait for a few months until the end of the present period of firm validity of concessions, it would have been able to renegotiate the concessions concerned in the normal way without the need for any special authority. However, there were urgent internal reasons which precluded delay. Perhaps the most important of these arose from the action taken by his Government in February 1960, as a result of which some 90 per cent of Australia's total imports were now exempt from import licensing. In some quarters in Australia there had been considerable criticism of this action. The Government wished to maintain the removal of controls while being able to afford a reasonable level of protection to domestic industry and it felt it important that it should be able to demonstrate to interested circles in Australia that the facilities provided in the GATT were meaningful and that countries could have recourse to Article XXVIII when circumstances justified it."[12]

In this instance the renegotiations were finally concluded only in July 1961. As regards Article XXVIII:5 renegotiations, in some cases the process was concluded within a few months while in others it took up to six years or more. Sometimes delays occurred due to inaction on the part of the trading partners of the contracting party modifying or withdrawing a concession.

(iv)   Three contracting parties, Australia, New Zealand and South Africa, were the most frequent users, followed by Canada.

(v)   The tariff rates resulting from Article XXVIII invocations were implemented generally after concluding the renegotiations with contracting parties with which the concession was initially negotiated or those with a principal supplying interest and consultations with those with a substantial interest. However, there were also a limited number of cases in which the new tariff rates were implemented after the renegotiations had been concluded with most but not all contracting parties concerned, or in which renegotiations had been in progress but no agreement had been reached or where the contracting party seeking to modify or withdraw the concession had reached the conclusion that no agreement was possible. In a few cases, the concession was suspended and the tariff raised or a tariff quota imposed even before the process of renegotiation had commenced. Some of these cases caused friction in trade relations and even led to retaliation or threatened retaliation. There has been less concern in cases in which the compensatory concessions offered have been simultaneously implemented and/or the renegotiations have been continued (and agreements reached at a later stage).

(vi)   Agreements were reached generally on the basis of compensatory concessions granted by the contracting party modifying or withdrawing a concession, but in some cases the package also envisaged the withdrawal of concessions by the contracting party affected. In one case, it was recognized that the trade coverage of the compensatory offer exceeded the trade coverage of the concessions withdrawn. It was, therefore, agreed that the credit for the balance of the trade coverage would be retained by the contracting party concerned to be drawn down in the event of future withdrawals of tariff bindings.

(vii)   In some cases of renegotiations commenced at the time of the conclusion of rounds of multilateral tariff negotiations, agreements were reached in the context of the tariff concessions exchanged during the rounds. Reference has already been made to the

---

[12]   GATT Doc. IC.SR.47, 29 April 1960.

renegotiations under Article XXVIII during the Torquay Tariff Conference. The Final Act of the Torquay Conference mentions that the negotiations encompassed "(n)egotiations between governments with a view to making adjustments in their concessions negotiated at Geneva or Annecy" besides negotiations for accession and negotiations for new or additional reciprocal tariff concessions. The Final Act also certifies that, in each case where a schedule of an existing contracting party annexed to the Torquay Protocol "provides treatment for any product less favourable than is provided for the same product in the existing schedule to the General Agreement, appropriate action has been taken to enable effect to be given to such a change".[13] While not as extensively as during the Torquay Conference, some renegotiations were also absorbed into subsequent tariff negotiations. The Final Act of the 1960-61 Tariff Conference (Dillon Round) mentions that the negotiations at that conference included renegotiations by contracting parties of existing concessions pursuant to Article XXVIII besides the renegotiations under Article XXIV:6 resulting from the establishment of the EEC.

On a limited basis some renegotiations were also concluded during the tariff negotiations in the Uruguay Round. Paragraph 7 of the Marrakesh Protocol is quoted below:

"In each case in which a schedule annexed to this Protocol results for any product in treatment less favourable than was provided for such product in the Schedules of GATT 1947 prior to the entry into force of the WTO Agreement, the Member to whom the Schedule relates shall be deemed to have taken appropriate action as would have been otherwise necessary under the relevant provisions of Article XXVIII of GATT 1947 or 1994. The provisions of the paragraph apply only to Egypt, Peru, South Africa and Uruguay."

In some cases of renegotiations involving agricultural products where renegotiations were blocked due to differences, agreement was reached in the context of the Uruguay Round Agreement on Agriculture.

(viii) The practice in the 1960s and the 1970s was for the contracting party seeking to modify or withdraw a concession under Article XXVIII to identify the contracting parties with which the concession was negotiated or those with a principal supplying interest and to seek negotiations with them. In later years, the practice developed for reliance to be placed entirely on the expression of interest in negotiations by other contracting parties.

---

[13] GATT, The Torquay Protocol and the Torquay Schedules of Concessions, p.5.

(ix)   Renegotiations were held and agreement reached with contracting parties with which the concession was negotiated even if that contracting party had ceased to be a significant supplier of the concerned product. As for contracting parties with a substantial interest, in some cases compensatory concessions were granted while in others consultations were held and the contracting party concerned was satisfied with the compensatory concessions granted to the contracting parties with which the concession was initially negotiated or those with a principal supplying interest.

(x)   The contracting parties seeking to modify or withdraw a concession under Article XXVIII invariably furnished the statistics in order to enable determination of the supplier status of other contracting parties. In most cases three years' data were given and the average for three years was used to determine supplier status.

(xi)   In one or two cases Article XXVIII renegotiations have been concluded on the basis of informal contacts with countries affected and without any formal agreement.

(xii)   In most cases Article XXVIII renegotiations have resulted in permanent changes in the tariff schedules. However, there were also cases in which renegotiations led to temporary increases in tariffs above the bound level or temporary suspensions of concessions accompanied by the imposition of limitations such as tariff quotas.

(xiii) In the 1950s and the 1960s, in several cases renegotiations under Article XXVIII followed safeguard action under Article XIX. This practice ceased in recent years because the availability of Article XXVIII:5 for renegotiations at any time proved to be a substitute for Article XIX action, particularly in the light of the practice of making temporary tariff increases under Article XXVIII.

(xiv)   In a few cases, recourse to Article XXVIII was the consequence of panel reports submitted in disputes under Article XXIII:2.

(xv)   During the Uruguay Round four contracting parties referred to in paragraph 7 of the Marrakesh Protocol (Egypt, South Africa, Peru and Uruguay) held renegotiations under Article XXVIII resulting in the establishment of full new schedules and the deletion of old schedules.

(xvi)   In specific cases there were unresolved differences of view on whether in determining the status of supplying contracting parties only the MFN trade or preferential trade should be taken into account and on how the supplier status should be determined in the case of a new product where three years' trade statistics were not available. These differences were settled in paragraphs 3 and 4 of the Uruguay Round Understanding on the Interpretation of Article XXVIII of GATT 1994.

(xvii)   Although in a number of cases contracting parties reserved their rights when other contracting parties went ahead with modification or withdrawal even before the renegotiations were complete, or where renegotiations were concluded without agreement with the principal supplier or without the substantial supplier being satisfied, and in other cases there were threats of retaliation before the renegotiations were satisfactorily completed, there were only three cases of retaliatory withdrawal of concession in renegotiations under Article XXVIII:1, 4 and 5 during the period 1958 to 1994. The rare use of the provision for retaliation in Article XXVIII:3 can be ascribed to the fact that renegotiations under the Article were generally successful. Other reasons were the general desire to avoid a chain of retaliatory withdrawals by other trading partners affected by the initial withdrawal. Since, under Article XXVIII:3 a concession must be withdrawn on an MFN basis (as compared to discriminatory retaliation under Article XXIII:2), there is an inherent difficulty in invoking the provision for retaliatory withdrawal. The details of the three cases are given below:

(a)   On 1 July 1965 the EEC notified its intention to modify the tariff concessions in respect of various types of cheese, including cheddar cheese. After agreement with one of the contracting parties on 29 June 1967, the EEC proceeded to effect the modification in the tariff rate on 1 August 1967 and renegotiations were continued with other contracting parties concerned. While agreements were eventually reached with Austria (28 March 1968), Finland (31 May 1968) and New Zealand (15 June 1970), no agreement could be reached with Australia and Canada. Canada did not retaliate, but Australia, which had a substantial supplier interest in respect of cheddar cheese, withdrew tariff concessions initially negotiated with the EEC on transistors and certain apparel items. This withdrawal took effect 30 days after the Australian notification dated 5 February 1968. As against the average imports from Australia into the EEC of cheddar cheese in 1963-65 of US$1,140,000, the trade coverage of withdrawn concessions was US$1,035,000 (average imports from the EEC into Australia).

(b)   In December 1974, the EEC notified its intention to modify concessions on unwrought lead and zinc by changing existing specific duties into *ad valorem* rates. In December 1975, it submitted its final report on the renegotiations indicating that, while agreement was reached with Australia, no agreement had been possible with Canada. The new rates of duty were made effective on 1 January

1976. On 4 June 1976, Canada notified its intention to invoke Article XXVIII:3 to withdraw bindings in the Canadian schedule on certain items which were initially negotiated with the EEC (canned meats, liqueurs, vermouths, aperitifs and cordial wines and wire of iron and steel). It claimed that the new rate of 3.5 per cent on unwrought zinc represented a substantial increase over the *ad valorem* equivalent of the old specific rate. The trade coverage (average imports of unwrought zinc into the EEC during the period 1973-75) was Can$35,332,000 against which the trade coverage of the concessions withdrawn by Canada was Can$30,216,000. The EEC had recourse to Article XXIII:2 on the Canadian action and the following conclusion was reached by the panel:

"The Panel was of the view that the withdrawal of concessions should have been less than the equivalent of the total export volume of zinc to the Community as account should have been taken of the rebinding of the Community duty. Also, the right of retaliation should be related to the actual damage suffered by Canada and consequently the withdrawals should have been based on the difference between the *ad valorem* equivalent of the specific rate calculated on imports from Canada only and the new *ad valorem* rate. Finally, account should have been taken of the fact that the *ad valorem* duty on lead had been fixed at a level lower than the incidence in respect of Community imports from Canada.... In the interest of maintaining the highest possible general level of concessions, the Panel finds that the Canadian retaliatory action should be withdrawn, i.e. the previous Canadian tariff bindings should be re-established as soon as the Community proceeds either to decrease their tariff on zinc or to make tariff concessions on other products of export interest to Canada of an equivalent value."[14]

(c)   On 11 June 1985, the United States notified that it had modified the concession on orange juice and indicated its willingness to enter into renegotiations under Article XXVIII. The duty on reconstituted orange juice was raised from 20 to 35 cents per US gallon. Despite mutually-agreed extension of the six-month time-period envisaged in Article XXVIII:3 for retaliatory withdrawal, no agreement could be reached. On 12 March 1986, Canada notified its decision to modify the concession on fresh vegetables, in respect of which the US had an initial negotiating right. The trade coverage of the item on which the concession was withdrawn was based on the three-year average as Can$4.5

---

[14]   GATT, BISD, Twenty-fifth Supplement, pp.48-49.

million against a decline of trade by US$4.8 million during the period January-October 1985 as compared to the previous year after the duty had been raised.

(xviii) The guidelines adopted in 1980 have been followed less than fully by the contracting parties to GATT 1947 and the Members of the WTO. Generally speaking, the contracting parties to GATT 1947 and WTO Members have given the particulars as required in the guidelines while initiating the renegotiations. Claims of interest have mostly been made within the ninety-day period, but where delays have taken place, contracting parties have not disregarded the claim. An important shortcoming has been that in many cases reports on the conclusion of bilateral negotiations as well as final reports have not been submitted. In the absence of such reports it is not possible to say whether the proposals for modification or withdrawal of concessions were given up or concluded successfully or absorbed in the framework of the rounds of multilateral trade negotiations. The Geneva (1967) Protocol concluding the Kennedy Round and the Geneva (1979) Protocol concluding the Tokyo Round do not mention Article XXVIII renegotiations at all, while the Marrakesh Protocol which concluded the Uruguay Round mentions the conclusion of renegotiations of only four Members.

C.   Other Renegotiations during the period 1958-1994

Specially-authorized renegotiations

1.   During the period 1958-1994, a practice emerged among contracting parties to seek from CONTRACTING PARTIES (acting under Article XXV:5) special authorization for renegotiations outside the framework provided for in paragraphs 1, 4 and 5 of Article XXVIII. There were more than 20 instances of such renegotiations being sought during the period for diverse reasons. Tariff reform, tariff rationalization or the establishment of new customs tariffs were the main reasons, but other reasons were also given, i.e. adoption of new tariff nomenclature, BTN, CCCN, or TSUS, structural adjustment programmes flowing from undertakings given to the IMF and the World Bank and transition from a centrally-planned to a market economy. A feature of these authorizations was that in each case a waiver was also given under Article XXV:5 of the General Agreement as the contracting parties concerned wanted to implement the new customs tariff involving a breach of existing tariff bindings even before conducting the renegotiations. Authorization for such renegotiations was usually given under the following terms and conditions:

(a)   Negotiations or consultations with interested contracting parties had to be entered into within six months of the modification and completed within a year or sometimes even earlier or before the next session of the CONTRACTING PARTIES;

(b)   While, on the one hand the application of the provision of Article II of the General Agreement was suspended "to the extent necessary to enable the Government of ... to apply the rates of duty resulting from the rationalization of its Tariff which may exceed those bound in Schedule....., pending completion of negotiations for the modification or withdrawal of concessions", on the other, freedom was given to other contracting parties "to suspend concessions initially negotiated with.... to the extent that they consider that adequate compensation.... is not offered within a reasonable time".

(c)   After the amendment of the General Agreement following the addition of Part IV, a paragraph was added to the decisions on waivers and special authorization for renegotiations making the concept of non-reciprocity enunciated in Article XXXVI:8 applicable to the renegotiations. However, in the waivers and special authorization granted in the late 1980s and early 1990s there was no reference to Article XXXVI:8.

2.   Most of the decisions on special authorization needed one or several extensions (in one case nine times) before the renegotiations could be completed. In one instance, the renegotiations were completed after 17 years of the modification of the schedule and in another case renegotiations went on for more than 20 years without being completed. A few contracting parties had recourse to waiver and special authorization more than once.

3.   The special authorization for renegotiations involving a waiver from the obligations of Article II granted during the 1960s, 1970s and early 1980s presaged similar decisions taken in the context of the implementation of the Harmonized Commodity Description and Coding System (Harmonized System) in the late 1980s and early 1990s. We shall deal with all aspects of the Harmonized System in the next chapter.

Renegotiations under Article XVIII:7 during 1958-94

4.   Article XVIII:7 was never very popular among the contracting parties to GATT 1947 as they preferred renegotiations by authorization on the basis of "a sympathetic consideration" of requests or under Article XXVIII:4 before Article XXVIII:5 made the whole process easier by permitting contracting parties to take up renegotiations at any time provided they had made a reservation at the commencement of each three-year period. The Analytical Index lists four invocations of this provision during the period 1958-94, but all records are not available in the Secretariat. A typical case was the invocation by Greece in 1965. It was linked to the establishment of steel works at Salonika and the new customs duty was to be made effective by a royal decree three months before the factory started production. Greece argued that the new industry would provide stimulus for secondary industries, absorb part of the unemployed labour

potential, yield savings in foreign exchange and, in general, contribute to raising national income. The plan was that the new duties would be reduced by 20 per cent every two years until they reached the level of 10 per cent.

Renegotiations under Article II: 5

5.　There was one instance in 1965 of renegotiations concluded under Article II:5. The case involved Canada and the European Communities and concerned compensatory adjustment in connection with the impairment of concessions on flash guns in the Canadian Schedule resulting from the decision of the Canadian Tariff Board of 17 May 1965 on the classification of electronic flash apparatus.

Withdrawal of tariff concessions under Article XXVII

6.　In the early period of the operation of GATT 1947, there were several instances in which a government having participated in the negotiations did not become a contracting party (e.g., Syria/Lebanon, Liberia, Philippines, Korea and Colombia) or having become a contracting party withdrew from the GATT (China). In the case of Palestine, the United Kingdom negotiated on behalf of the territory as it had the League of Nations mandate for the territory. The concessions negotiated on behalf of Palestine were contained in a separate section of the schedule of the UK. After the UK ceased to be responsible for the mandated territory of Palestine on 15 May 1948, the UK schedule of concessions was rectified by eliminating the concessions made on behalf of Palestine. This also led to action under Article XXVII.

7.　Fifteen contracting parties to GATT 1947 had had recourse to Article XXVII, some of them in several cases. Twelve withdrew concessions when China ceased to be a contracting party and one when the concessions made on behalf of Palestine were eliminated from the Schedule of the UK. Three contracting parties made withdrawals under Article XXVII when Syria/Lebanon did not become contracting parties and similar action was taken by seven in the case of the Philippines, two in the case of Liberia, four in the case of Colombia and one in the case of Korea. It should be pointed out that Colombia, Korea and the Philippines acceded to GATT in subsequent years after holding negotiations afresh.

Article XXIV:6 Renegotiations

Establishment of the European Economic Community

8.　The first invocation of Article XXIV:6 was made in the context of the formation of the European Economic Community, with the initial six members, established by the Treaty of Rome signed in March 1957. As already mentioned, the renegotiations under Article XXIV:6 were held during the Dillon Round. The Tariff Conference which had been convened on 1 September 1960 was mandated to devote the first part of the conference to carrying out renegotiations under Article XXIV:6 with the European Economic Community with a view to concluding such negotiations by Christmas 1960. The rules and procedures for the renegotiations as approved by the CONTRACTING PARTIES are reproduced below *in extenso,* so as to give the full picture:

> "1.   The Commission of the EEC agreed to submit towards the end of 1959 its common tariff, including rates for the large part if not all of the products contained in list G annexed to the Rome Treaty.
>
> 2.   The Community will submit by 1 May 1960 a list of the items bound by the Six under the GATT indicating opposite each item: the contracting party with which each item was initially negotiated; and (a) whether it considers the 'internal compensation', if any, to be inadequate; or (c) whether it considers the 'internal compensation' to exceed the compensation actually required.
>
> 3.   At the same time as the list of bound items, the Community will furnish statistical information on imports into the territories of the Six as a whole for 1958; statistical information relating to 1959 might have to be sent at a later date. The Community would, of course, supply supplementary data on request in the course of the negotiations.
>
> 4.   Contracting parties which so wish may submit to the Community as soon as possible after receipt of the May 1960 list, a notification of the items of which they are the initial negotiators or in which they consider themselves to have a principal supplying or substantial interest. At the same time, contracting parties may submit to the Community for its guidance lists of items on which they would wish to request compensation.
>
> 5.   At the opening of the Conference on 1 September 1960 the Community will make offers of compensation for all those modifications for which compensation was promised under 2(b) above in the list submitted on 1 May."[15]

9.   The Tariff Negotiations Committee established to oversee the entire negotiations adopted further "practical procedures" for Article XXIV:6 renegotiations and on 2 September 1960 the EEC submitted its list of offers. Documentation was also submitted setting out the Community's views on the adequacy, inadequacy or excess of internal compensation with respect to items bound under the GATT by the member States of the EEC, providing statistical data and indicating the principal supplier to the Community of each item in the common external tariff. Other contracting parties furnished generally the following lists in preparation for the renegotiations or consultations under the procedures of renegotiations:

> (i)   list of items on which the contracting party was prepared to accept the offer made by the EEC as the internal compensation was adequate;

---

[15]   GATT, BISD, Eighth Supplement, p. 119.

(ii)   list of items on which it wished to negotiate because it was the contracting party with which the concession was initially negotiated or which had a principal supplying interest;

(iii)   list of items in which it had a substantial interest and wished to be consulted.

10.   After the renegotiations or consultations that followed, the EEC concluded bilateral agreements with Australia, Austria, Canada, Ceylon (Sri Lanka), Chile, Czechoslovakia, Denmark, Finland, India, Indonesia, Japan, Norway, Pakistan, Peru, Rhodesia and Nyasaland, South Africa, Sweden, Switzerland, United Kingdom, United States and Uruguay. The agreement with the United States said that the agreement in the renegotiations excluded: (a) the tariff items relating to manufactured tobacco and certain petroleum products, and (b) the products falling within the purview of the European Coal and Steel Community. The products listed under (a) were to be the subject of further renegotiations under Article XXVIII and those falling under (b) were subsequently renegotiated under Article XXIV:6 during the Kennedy Round and were incorporated in the separate schedule of the European Coal and Steel Community. Agreement could not be reached with Brazil and Nigeria. Austria, Czechoslovakia, Sweden and Switzerland did not regard the compensation received by them as entirely satisfactory and consequently reserved their rights to invoke Article XXVIII:3 to make retaliatory withdrawals. On their part, the EEC and the member States affirmed their assessment that they had fully compensated the contracting party concerned and in the event of any withdrawal by the latter they too reserved the right to withdraw concessions to achieve reciprocal balance. In the case of Uruguay, which reserved the right to withdraw substantially equivalent concessions initially negotiated with the EEC on account of inadequacy of compensation in respect of fresh and frozen bovine meat, the EEC accepted the right of Uruguay to make such withdrawals.

11.   Important side-agreements signed between the EEC and the US related to quality wheat, corn, sorghum, ordinary wheat, rice and poultry. In these agreements the EEC agreed not to increase tariffs on quality wheat or make more restrictive the national import system on other products until the EEC Council of Ministers had decided to introduce the common agricultural policy. Upon the introduction of the common agricultural policy, the EEC undertook to hold renegotiations under Article XXVIII in respect of quality wheat and negotiations on the situation of exports of other products by the United States. Similar agreements were signed with Canada on quality and ordinary wheat and another agreement signed with Australia recognized its substantial interest in wheat and contained a commitment by the EEC to enter into consultations with Australia in the renegotiations under Article XXVIII:1 at a future date.

12.   The interpretation of negotiating rights under the above-mentioned bilateral agreements between Canada and the EEC in respect of quality wheat and ordinary wheat became the subject-matter of a dispute between the two contracting parties and was referred to an arbitrator in 1990 under the interim dispute settlement procedures agreed on at the time of the Mid-Term Review of

the Uruguay Round. The arbitrator's findings throw valuable light on negotiating rights and are therefore dealt with here briefly. The following questions were raised in the dispute:

(i)   Whether Canada could bring a claim based on a bilateral agreement under the multilateral procedures of the GATT;

(ii) What Article XXVIII rights did the agreements confer upon Canada; and

(iii) Whether by formally acknowledging the conclusion in 1962 of the Article XXIV:6 negotiations, Canada had lost her right to invoke the provisions of Article XXVIII:3 including the right to withdraw equivalent concessions.

13.   In respect of quality wheat the arbitrator gave the following award:

(i)   Since the bilateral agreement was attached to the formal letter attesting the conclusion of Article XXIV:6 negotiations and the EEC itself had in subsequent communications recognized the linkage of the agreement with Article XXIV:6 negotiations, the matter could be brought under the multilateral dispute settlement of the GATT;

(ii) Given the fact that the bilateral agreement referred specifically to Article XXVIII, and the EEC in 1983 and 1984 agreed to extend the negotiating rights of Canada, the latter retained the equivalent of all of its contractual GATT rights held as of 1 September 1960, as an INR holder and a principal supplier, including the right to withdraw concessions;

(iii) Since in 1962 it was not known what the import restrictions on wheat would be under the Common Agricultural Policy, and the parties were under considerable pressure to conclude the Article XXIV:6 negotiations, the very purpose of the bilateral agreement was to put Canada into a legal position equivalent to the one it would have been in if the time limits of Article XXVIII did not apply. It followed, therefore, that Canada maintained the right to withdraw equivalent concessions if the negotiations under the bilateral agreement were not successfully concluded.

14.   In respect of ordinary wheat, the arbitrator came to a different conclusion. The agreement itself was less precise and comprehensive. Besides, Canada had not followed up on the agreement as it had done in respect of quality wheat. The arbitrator concluded that "by silence for so long on the Agreement on Ordinary Wheat Canada has relinquished any rights under the General Agreement she might have possessed under it in 1962."

15.   A point should be made about the timing of the renegotiations under Article XXIV:6. The Sub-Group which was set up to examine the provisions of the Rome Treaty had recognized that "the negotiations required under paragraph 6 should be completed before the Members of the Community took the first step towards achieving a common tariff" at the beginning of 1962, although the

representative of the Six made a reservation that they were "not in a position to commit the institutions of the Community".[16] The renegotiations under Article XXIV:6 began on 1 September 1960 and were concluded with many trading partners by the middle of 1961. The member States notified the withdrawal of the earlier schedules on 17 August with the exception of the concessions concerning items falling within the scope of the European Coal and Steel Community which were listed in a separate communication. The agreement with the US was reached later, along with the agreements on new concessions under Article XXVIII *bis* during the Dillon Round on 7 March 1962 and with Canada on 29 March 1962. Negotiations with Australia were concluded in June 1962 and with Norway in November 1962. The Protocol Embodying the Results of the 1960-61 Tariff Conference was signed on 16 July 1962. It will be seen that the renegotiations under Article XXIV:6 were commenced and fully engaged well before the formation of the EEC and they were substantially complete around the time the first alignment towards the Common External Tariff (CET) commenced at the beginning of 1962.

Enlargement of the EEC to Nine Members

16.   The next major renegotiations under Article XXIV:6 took place at the time of the expansion of the EEC from six to nine member States. The Treaty establishing the Communities of Nine (Denmark, Ireland and UK in addition to the original six members) was ratified during the course of 1972 and on 11 January 1973 the EEC sent in a communication indicating its willingness to enter into Article XXIV:6 renegotiations. The relevant part of the communication is quoted below:

> "The ratification procedures have now been accomplished, and in accordance with that undertaking the European Communities propose that the contracting parties wishing to enter into tariff renegotiations in connection with the withdrawal of the schedules of concessions of the constituent territories of the enlarged customs union should consider for this purpose that the concessions at present bound in Schedules XL and XL *bis*, of the European Economic Community and of the European Coal and Steel Community respectively, are the concessions offered for application to the customs territory of the enlarged Community, subject to appropriate adjustments in the amounts of the tariff quotas indicated in those schedules of concessions. These adjustments are those required because of the accession of new member States which were formerly beneficiaries of the tariff quotas in question."[17]

17.   The EEC having opened the process of renegotiations with this offer, there were some suggestions to the European Communities in the Working Party on Accessions that the procedure for renegotiations under Article XXIV:6

---

[16]   GATT, BISD, Sixth Supplement, p. 74.

[17]   GATT Doc. L/3807.

adopted in the Dillon Round should be followed specially in regard to "internal compensation", and further, that a special Trade Negotiations Committee should be entrusted with the task of coordinating the negotiations. However, the conduct of the renegotiations was finally left entirely to the bilateral process. In addition to the voluminous documentation submitted to enable examination of the customs union under Article XXIV:5(a) of the General Agreement, the contracting parties were further aided in the process of the renegotiations by the Communities' submission of customs and statistical cards for individual tariff items. The customs cards contained tariff information for the item concerned as well as information on non-tariff barriers. The statistical cards covered information of the type supplied for the Dillon Round renegotiations.

18.   During the bilateral process that ensued, the EEC concluded agreements with Argentina (31 July 1974), Australia (19 July 1974), Brazil (18 July 1974), Canada (28 February 1975 - with the exception of cereals), India (31 January 1975), Poland (17 July 1974), Romania (31 July 1974), South Africa (12 July 1974), Sri Lanka (12 June 1974), United States (19 July 1974), Uruguay (31 July 1974) and Yugoslavia (29 July 1974), appended to each of which was a list of products on which the EEC granted concessions to the contracting party concerned. Some of the significant aspects of these bilateral agreements are noted below:

(i)   In the case of Canada, the agreement mentioned that the two sides had been unable to reach an agreement on cereals but that they had agreed to continue discussions with a view to finding through international negotiations agreed solutions to the problems of international trade in cereals.

(ii)   In view of the absence of a complete agreement in all their Article XXIV:6 negotiations, the EEC inserted in its schedule a general note reserving its "right of modifying the schedule of concessions to restore the balance of concessions if a contracting party, invoking the provisions of Article XXVIII:3, were to withdraw concessions following the Article XXVIII:6 renegotiations in connection with the enlargement of the Communities".

(iii)   Australia and the United States recorded their dissatisfaction with the compensation in respect of certain cereals and reserved their rights to resume the negotiations. They also reserved their rights under Article XXVIII to withdraw substantially equivalent concessions with respect to cereals or with respect to any future modification by the EEC to the draft schedule.

(iv)   The United States, the EEC and Australia proposed to the GATT Council that the time laid down in Article XXVIII:3 should not apply to these reservations. The Council agreed that "the six-month period referred to in Article XXVIII:3 would not apply to actions pursuant to these reservations and that such actions could be taken at any time upon expiration of 30 days from the day that written notice is given to the CONTRACTING PARTIES".[18]

   (v)   The agreements with the US and Canada specifically mentioned that the initial negotiating rights in the schedules of the EEC 6 would be carried forward into the new schedules. It should be mentioned that these INRs were in addition to the INRs that the US and Canada inherently had with respect to products figuring in the lists appended to the bilateral agreements.

19.   The schedules of the EEC 6, Denmark, Ireland and the UK were withdrawn on 1 August 1974 and the results of the renegotiations were contained in a draft new EEC schedule circulated on 6 August 1974. The first alignment in agriculture had taken place at the beginning of 1973 and in industrial tariffs on 1 April 1974. Thus, in the case of industrial tariffs, renegotiations began a year before the establishment of the CET, but they could be concluded only a few months after its establishment. In the case of agricultural tariffs, the negotiations began only after the establishment of the CET.

Enlargement of the EEC to 10 and then 12 Members

20.   Two other renegotiations under Article XXIV:6 took place before the establishment of the WTO: those relating to the accession of Greece in 1981 and of Spain and Portugal in 1986. In neither instance could the Article XXIV:6 renegotiations be concluded with all contracting parties concerned and, consequently, the results were not circulated. Some important aspects of Article XXIV:6 renegotiations in these two cases are outlined below:

   (i)   Greece became a member of the European Economic Community on 1 January 1981. On 8 May 1981, the EEC sent a communication stating its intention to replace Schedule XXV of Greece and Schedule LXXII and LXXII *bis* of the European Communities of Nine by a new schedule of concessions valid for the Communities of Ten. It proposed that contracting parties wishing to enter into tariff renegotiations "consider for this purpose that the concessions bound in Schedule LXXII and LXXII *bis* are essentially those to be offered as applicable in the customs territory of the enlarged Community".[19] Due to the inconclusive nature of the Article XXIV:6 renegotiations that followed, the replacement did not take place.

   (ii)   Portugal and Spain became members of the European Economic Community on 1 January 1986. On 4 February 1986 the EEC sent a communication[20] withdrawing Schedule XLV of Spain, Schedule

---

[18]   GATT Doc. C/M/99.

[19]   GATT Doc. TAR/16.

[20]   GATT Doc. L/5936/Add.2.

XLIV of Portugal and Schedule LXXII and LXXII *bis* of the European Community of 10. It also submitted the new Common Customs Tariff established by it as its offer under Article XXIV:6. The communication mentioned that, pending completion of the Article XXIV procedures and the creation of a new schedule for the Community of the 12, the new rates would be suspended and the duties laid down in the EC schedules would continue to apply to the Community of 10 while Spain and Portugal aligned their duties with the Common Customs Tariff.

(iii)   The United States sent a communication on 20 May 1986 notifying the suspension of certain concessions under Article XXVIII:3, and stating that the action was being taken as a variable levy had been applied since 1 March 1986 on certain agricultural products "notwithstanding the existence of any Spanish or Portuguese concessions and without prior examination of these actions in GATT or prior negotiation of compensation".[21] The communication mentioned that the action had immediate damaging effect in particular on the trade in two concessions made by Spain to the United States in previous negotiations, on corn and sorghum. The EEC contested the right of the United States to invoke Article XXVIII:3 at that stage as the renegotiations had not been concluded. It stated in a communication that its notifications regarding the accession of Portugal and Spain and for initiating negotiations under Article XXIV:6 "do not constitute a declaration of finalization of negotiations and that consequently, in its view, the six-month period provided for in paragraph 3 of Article XXVIII has not started."[22] Subsequently, a bilateral agreement was reached on 30 January 1987 concluding the negotiations under Article XXIV:6 and the United States restored the suspended concessions.[23]

(iv)   The bilateral agreement between the US and the EEC provided for the reduction of certain duty rates and the establishment of minimum access levels for corn and sorghum by the EEC on an autonomous basis until 31 December 1990. According to a communication[24] sent by the US, the agreement specified that both parties would initiate in July 1990 a "major review of the situation... with the objective of determining at that time what new action, if any, might be appropriate". Since the EEC did not agree to extend the compensation beyond 31 December 1990, the US

---

[21]   GATT Doc. L/5997.

[22]   GATT Doc. L/6009.

[23]   GATT Doc. L/5997, Add.2.

[24]   GATT Doc. L/6774.

again notified suspension of certain concessions with effect from midnight of 31 December 1990, arguing that "the time-limited Article XXVIII right could be construed, in this case, to expire on December 31, 1990, unless exercised". The EEC took the view that the bilateral agreement of January 1987 between the EEC and the US had concluded the negotiations under Article XXIV:6 and the compensation was part of a final settlement.[25] However, the two sides later agreed to extend the duty reductions and minimum access granted in the 1987 bilateral agreement first to 31 December 1991 and then again to 31 December 1992 and finally to 31 December 1993, when it was absorbed in the Uruguay Round package.

D. Renegotiations under the WTO Agreement (1995-1999)

Main features of renegotiations, except those under Article XXIV:6

1.   During this period, there were a number of instances of renegotiations under the provisions of paragraphs 1 and 5 of Article XXVIII and none under paragraph 4 of Article XXVIII or paragraph 7 of Article XVIII. The main features of the practices of WTO Members in these negotiations are given below:

(i)   There were only eight cases of renegotiations under paragraphs 1 and 5 of Article XXVIII, of which five were in 1995, two in 1996 and one in 1998. The frequency of recourse to Article XXVIII to modify or withdraw tariff concessions for protective purposes considerably decreased as compared to the period under GATT 1947.

(ii)   In most cases, the renegotiations relate to concessions on specific agricultural products. In one case the implementation of a new Customs Tariff on 1 January 1998 was the reason for seeking modification or withdrawal of concessions under Article XXVIII.

(iii)   In seven of the eight cases WTO Members had recourse to paragraph 5 of Article XXVIII, thus continuing the pattern established during the previous two decades under GATT 1947. In the only case under paragraph 1, although the invocation was in September 1996, presumably with the intention of changes coming into effect on 1.1.97, the negotiations continued and until the date of writing (1.10.99) no agreement had been notified.

(iv)   In one case the Article XXVIII:5 renegotiation begun under GATT 1947 was renotified and the conclusions reached took into account the results of negotiations and consultations held earlier under

---

[25]   GATT Doc. L/6785.

GATT 1947. In other cases Members only notified the agreement reached in renegotiations that had been commenced under GATT 1947. In one case, in January 1995, the notification was made under both GATT 1947 and GATT 1994.

(v)   The notifications on the intentions to modify or withdraw concessions contained information on INRs as well as import data and indicated the willingness of the notifying Member to enter into negotiations/consultations with interested Members. In one case the Member fixed a date (later extended) by which it would accept claims of interest. Other Members registered their claims of interest within a short period.

(vi)   While, in one case, the renegotiations commenced in 1995 were concluded quickly, and in another the agreement reached with the INR holder and principal supplier was notified, no progress was notified in any of the other cases till the time of writing (1.10.99).

Article XXIV:6 Renegotiations under the WTO

2.   On 15 December 1994 the EEC circulated for the information of the contracting parties to GATT 1947 the "Treaty concerning the accession of Austria, Finland, Sweden and Norway to the European Union", indicating that some further adjustment of the instruments concerning the accession of new Member States would be required to reflect Norway's decision not to accede and that the treaty would enter into force on 1 January 1995. It was also indicated that the EEC intended to withdraw the tariff schedules of Austria, Finland, Sweden and the EEC 12 and would be ready (from 1 January 1995) to enter into tariff negotiations provided for in Article XXIV:6. Pending completion of the Article XXIV procedures and the creation of a new schedule for the EEC 15, the communication stated that the tariff commitments of the EEC 12 would be fully respected. The acceding countries were, however, to align their duties with the Common Customs Tariff on 1 January 1995 except where a separate time-table was laid down in the Act of Accession.

3.   On 19 January 1995, the EEC informed the General Council that the ratification procedures for the accession of Austria, Finland and Sweden to the European Union had been completed and the Accession Treaty had entered into force on 1 January 1995. On 27 January 1995, the EEC furnished the basic data for discussion under Article XXIV:5 and negotiations under Article XXIV:6. They consisted of concordance tables of tariff concessions made by the newly-acceding Members along with that of the EEC 12 and trade data showing the value and quantity of total trade for three years with other GATT contracting parties for each tariff line together with a breakdown by country of origin.

4.   Following the commencement of the process under Article XXIV:6, 15 WTO Members expressed an interest in joining the negotiations, but the process followed thereafter was entirely bilateral. An important point was raised even before 1 January 1995 that the renegotiations under Article XXIV:6 should have been commenced and concluded before the establishment of the Common

External Tariff. Following an agreement with the US, the EEC adopted a decision on 29 December 1994, opening tariff quotas in the newly-acceding member States during the period 1 January to 30 June 1995, "to provide temporary relief to its trading partners for the most serious cases in which there is an increase in import duties".[26] Not satisfied with this action, Canada invoked Article XXVIII:3 and on 1 March 1995 gave a 30-day notice for the withdrawal of certain concessions initially negotiated with the EEC. Canada requested the EEC to provide interim compensation by reinstating the 1995 tariff rate that would have been in effect in Austria, Finland and Sweden had they not joined the EEC during the period 1 April to 1 July 1995, in respect of certain products of interest to it. The EEC stated in response that it had acted in the same manner on that occasion as in the case of earlier expansions of the Community and contested that Canada was in a situation which justified the exercise of rights under Article XXVIII:3. However, an agreement was reached and the EEC provided interim compensation to Canada by accelerating the tariff reduction on newsprint already committed in the Uruguay Round. The above agreements with the US and Canada on interim compensation on account of the establishment of the Common Customs Tariff even before the commencement and conclusion of Article XXIV:6 renegotiations were not notified to the WTO Members.

5.   While the renegotiations under Article XXIV:6 were being held, the EEC notified its agreement to the prolongation of all rights under Article XXVIII:3 of GATT 1994 beyond 30 June 1995 first until 31 December 1995 and then until 31 January 1996.

6.   On 28 February 1996, the EEC notified its new Schedule CXL, containing the tariff and other commitments "in the light of the Article XXIV:6 negotiations which have now been concluded with most of the EC partners.[27] The notification mentioned that, as all current negotiations under Article XXIV:6 had not been completed till then, the EEC reserved the right to modify the concessions. The US and Canada objected to this notification on the ground that the bilateral agreements with the EEC, although initialled, had not been formally signed. A number of agricultural exporting countries made the point that, even if agreement had been reached on the netting out of export commitments and aggregation of domestic subsidy commitments, Article XXIV:6 procedures could not be applied with respect to the commitments on domestic support and export subsidy commitments for the modification of which appropriate legal modalities of implementation had to be discussed and agreed. Argentina made the point that the notification was not in order when the negotiations and consultations under Article XXVIII had not been concluded.

7.   The bilateral agreements with the US and Canada were notified to the Secretariat by the end of July 1996, but other agreements were not notified. The

---

[26]   Official Journal of the European Communities, No. L356/5, Council Regulation (EC) No. 3361/94 of 29 December 1994.

[27]   WTO Doc. G/L/65/Rev.1.

EEC has continued to notify amendments in the schedule originally notified on 28 February 1996 in the light of further agreements and comments. At the date of writing (1.10.99) objections remained outstanding on the schedule of the EEC 15.

8.   In the other customs union agreements notified after the entry into force of the WTO Agreement, namely the MERCOSUR and the EEC-Turkey customs union agreements, the commencement of renegotiations under Article XXIV:6 had not been notified at the date of writing (1.10.99).

CHAPTER V

SCHEDULES OF TARIFF CONCESSIONS: RECTIFICATION, MODIFICATION, AND CONSOLIDATION

A.   Establishment of Schedules, their Rectification and Modification

Protocols of tariff concessions

1.   The results of tariff negotiations at Geneva in 1947 were incorporated in the schedules of concessions of each contracting party and were annexed to GATT 1947. Article II.7 of GATT 1947 provided that the schedules were an integral part of Part I of the Agreement, comprising Articles I and II. Since Article XXX of GATT 1947 specified that amendments to the provisions of Part I could become effective only upon acceptance by all the contracting parties, the implication of Article II.7 was that any change in the schedules of concessions needed acceptance by all the contracting parties. The position has not changed in GATT 1994 and the WTO Agreement.

2.   The schedules containing the concessions agreed during subsequent tariff conferences and rounds of negotiations were annexed to the protocols embodying the results of these conferences/rounds, namely the Annecy Protocol (1949), the Torquay Protocol (1951), the Sixth Protocol of Supplementary Concessions (1956), the Protocol Embodying Results of the Tariff Conference 1960-61, the Geneva (1967) Protocol, the Geneva (1979) Protocol and the Marrakesh Protocol to GATT 1994. In the case of the 1960-61 Tariff Conference and the Tokyo Round, there were supplementary protocols as well. The legal instrument of a protocol has also been used to formalize the results of the following categories of negotiations for new concessions:

(i)   Negotiations between two or more contracting parties outside of tariff conferences (the protocols being known as protocols of supplementary concessions);

(ii)   Accession negotiations; and

(iii)   *Sui generis* negotiations held by Brazil under a waiver for establishing a new schedule of concessions following tariff reform.

In the negotiations referred to in (ii) and (iii) above, not only the schedule of concessions made by the acceding government of Brazil but also the schedules of concessions made by other contracting parties were annexed to the protocols. As mentioned in Chapter II, the practice in accession negotiations before the Tokyo Round was for the existing contracting parties also to make concessions in the context of accession negotiations. During the early days of GATT all contracting parties signed the protocols embodying the results of the negotiations in tariff conferences, accessions or bilateral exchanges outside of tariff conferences. After 1959, however, they were signed only by those contracting parties whose schedules were annexed to the protocols. The schedules attached to the protocols were, consequently, binding only upon those contracting parties which had signed the protocols and had schedules annexed to them. They did not bind other contracting parties, which could have recourse to the provision in Article XXVIII:3(a) if previous concessions in which they had rights were nullified or impaired. As regards contracting parties which signed the protocols, the practice existed in GATT of affording other contracting parties the opportunity to verify whether the results of the negotiations had been correctly incorporated in the schedules that were to be annexed to the protocols. This was done by circulating draft schedules to other contracting parties for their verification before they were attached to schedules. The protocols were generally kept open for acceptance by signature or by depositing an instrument of acceptance for some time after they had been opened for signature. They entered into effect on a certain date in the future, thus giving time to those accepting the Protocols to carry out the necessary domestic procedures required for such acceptance.

Rectification and modification of schedules: Practice in the early years of GATT 1947

3.   How were other changes resulting from formal rectifications and from modifications consequent upon withdrawal under Article XXVII or renegotiations under Article XXVIII brought about in GATT schedules? The customary practice that developed in the early days of GATT 1947 included the following elements:

(i)   The proposals were circulated to the contracting parties for objections, if any, within a specified period;

(ii)   They were then examined by a working party;

(iii)   If no objections were received and if the working party found the request in order, the proposals were attached to a protocol.

4.   In the beginning the proposals for rectification were considered separately from those on modification, but later they were taken up together. There were in all five protocols of rectification, one protocol of modification and nine protocols of rectification and modification. The working parties played a decisive role in determining whether a proposal for rectification was appropriate or a proposal for modification was mature for inclusion in the next protocol. Thus the report of a Working Party adopted on 24 October 1953 contained the following recommendation:

"The Working Party also concerned itself with the proposal of the Greek Government to introduce a minimum *ad valorem* rate for certain specific rates and came to the conclusion that such changes could not be considered rectifications to be dealt with by the Working Party. It decided therefore to refer the question to the CONTRACTING PARTIES so that such changes could form the object of consultations and negotiations with the parties having an interest in those items. After the conclusion of the negotiations, the changes agreed upon could be embodied in a protocol of rectifications and modifications."[1]

5.   Another report of the Working Party which prepared the draft Fourth Protocol of Rectifications and Modifications stated as follows:

"One question could not be solved by the interested parties and was referred to the Working Party. Among the rectifications requested by the Austrian Government were those relating to Items 140 to 144 of the Austrian Tariff which were being made under the authority of the Note to these items included in the Austrian Schedule XXXII which granted the Austrian Government freedom to change the specific into *ad valorem* rates. The Austrian Government felt that it would not be impairing the value of the concessions if it retained beside the *ad valorem* duty the old specific rate as a minimum rate.

The Working Party took the view that such changes would constitute modifications of Austria's obligations and that it could not recommend their acceptance as rectifications. Such modifications could only be inserted in a protocol of rectifications and modifications after negotiations authorized by the CONTRACTING PARTIES in accordance with the proper procedures. The Austrian delegation, therefore, did not further insist on the insertion in the Fourth Protocol of Rectifications and Modifications of the specific minimum rates in Items 140 to 144."[2]

6.   The practice in respect of these protocols was to require the signature of all the contracting parties and there were long delays before they could enter into effect. The working party which drew up the Fourth Protocol of Rectifications observed as follows:

"The Working Party considered that the continuance of the present state of affairs, where rectification or modification protocols of this nature do not enter into force except after extended delays, was a serious impediment to the effective operation of the General Agreement. It felt, therefore, that it was necessary for the orderly functioning of the General Agreement that individual contracting parties should take action promptly on such protocols; it did not feel that compliance with this necessity should prove unduly onerous in that the procedure for securing agreement on rectifications and modifications gave an opportunity to all interested contracting parties to express their views before the rectifications and modifications were agreed upon and included in a protocol. The action thereafter required from contracting parties was accordingly of only a formal nature and for which no extended period of delay should be necessary."[3]

---

[1]   GATT, BISD, Second Supplement, p. 66.

[2]   GATT, BISD, Third Supplement, p. 130.

[3]   GATT, BISD, Vol. II, p. 142.

Introduction of the system of certification

7.   The situation did not improve despite the above observations and the last five protocols of rectification and modification entered into force ten years or more after they had been opened for signature. To overcome this problem, a proposal was made at the Review Session in 1955 to amend Article XXX by adding a paragraph which would have provided as follows:

> "3. Any amendment to the schedules annexed to this Agreement, which records rectifications of a purely formal character or modifications resulting from action taken under paragraph 6 of Article II, Article XVIII, Article XXIV, Article XXVII or Article XXVIII, shall become effective on the thirtieth day following certification to this effect by the CONTRACTING PARTIES; provided that prior to such certification, all contracting parties have been notified of the proposed amendment and no objection has been raised, within thirty days of such notification by a contracting party, on the ground that the proposed amendments are not within the terms of this paragraph."[4]

8.   Pending acceptance by the contracting parties of the above amendment of Article XXX, the CONTRACTING PARTIES adopted the procedure of certification and discontinued the practice of preparing protocols of rectifications and modifications, as noted below:

> "The CONTRACTING PARTIES agreed on 17 November 1959 that, as the Protocol Amending Part I and Articles XXIX and XXX of the General Agreement, which introduces in Article XXX a procedure for the certification of rectifications and modifications to the Schedules to the General Agreement, had not yet entered into force, the procedure of certification should nevertheless be adopted and the practice of preparing protocols of rectifications and modifications discontinued. The rectifications and modifications will be incorporated in certificates, as provided for in the revised text of Article XXX, but the certificates will enter into force only when the revised text of Article XXX has been accepted by all contracting parties."[5]

9.   Pursuant to the above decision, the CONTRACTING PARTIES adopted three certifications which were to become effective on the date of entry into force of the amendment to Article XXX. When the Protocol Amending Part I, and Articles XXIX and XXX did not enter into force by 31 December 1967, a decision was taken to abandon the Protocol. However, the CONTRACTING PARTIES decided to establish the certification procedures for modification and rectification through a decision[6] on 19 November 1968. The first certification[7]

---

[4]   GATT, Final Act adopted at the Ninth Session.

[5]   GATT, BISD, Eighth Supplement, p. 25.

[6]   GATT, BISD, Sixteenth Supplement, pp. 16-17.

[7]   GATT, BISD, Seventeenth Supplement, pp. 12-13.

under the 1968 decision reconfirmed the three certifications adopted conditionally under the 1959 decision, apart from incorporating new proposals for rectification and modification. In all, four collective certifications were adopted under the 1968 decision before a decision[8] was taken in 1980 to revise the procedures for rectification and modification. This decision, which is still in force, is analyzed below.

10.   The 1980 decision (like the 1968 one) covers changes in the authentic texts of the schedules of two types:

   (i)   Modifications resulting from actions/negotiations under Articles II, XVIII, XXIV, XXVII or XXVIII. It is clear that action under Article II refers to both paragraphs 5 and 6 of that article and under Article XVIII they refer to paragraph 7 of that article.

   (ii)   Rectifications involving amendments or rearrangements introduced in the national customs tariffs in respect of bound items or other rectifications of a purely formal character which do not alter the scope of the concessions.

11.   The procedure prescribed is that the Member concerned has to communicate to the Director-General a draft of changes within three months of completing the action for modification referred to in (i) above and in the case of rectification, where possible within three months but not later than six months after the amendments or rearrangements have been introduced in the national customs tariff, and for other rectifications "as soon as circumstances permit".

12.   The Director-General proceeds to notify the proposed changes to all Members and the draft becomes a certification if no objection is raised by a Member within three months. The grounds on which objections can be made are the following:

   (i)   In the case of modifications, the draft does not reflect the modifications resulting from actions under the relevant articles; and

   (ii)   In the case of proposed rectifications, the claim that they do not alter the scope of concessions is disputed.

13.   The 1980 decision also provided for the use of these procedures for the establishment of consolidated schedules (with which we deal in the next section). It also provided for these procedures to apply for the establishment of new schedules under paragraph 5(c) of Article XXVI of GATT 1947 (which is now no longer in force). An important aspect of the decision on the procedures for certification has to be highlighted here. As in the case of protocols to which the list of modifications and rectifications were attached, the certifications do not have any effect on the entry into force of the proposed modification or rectification. The idea is to formally incorporate in the schedules of Members modifications and rectifications which, in most cases, have already entered into

---

[8]   GATT, BISD, Twenty-seventh Supplement, pp. 25-26.

force. The 1980 procedures stipulate that "(w)henever practicable Certifications shall record the date of entry into force of each modification and the effective date of each rectification." In the case of modifications, the procedures to bring about changes in the legal obligations of the Members have already to be followed as a prerequisite for action to bring about changes in the authentic text. Thus, in the case of renegotiations under Article XXVIII, for instance, the procedures for these renegotiations should have already been complied with, before a request for modification of the schedule is made.

Introduction of individual certification

14.   The practice when the procedure for modification and rectification involved the adoption of protocols was, generally, for a number of modifications and rectifications to be attached to each protocol. This practice continued when the procedure of certification was adopted in 1968. The procedure followed was that the notifications received from individual contracting parties for modification or rectification were circulated to all contracting parties, indicating that if no objection was notified to the Secretariat within three months, the change in the tariff schedule would be deemed to be approved and would be included in the next certification of changes to schedules. When a sufficient number of notifications had been approved, a collective draft certification was prepared and circulated by the Secretariat to all contracting parties. This draft collective certification entered into force if, during a further three months after circulation, no objections were received. At the same time as the CONTRACTING PARTIES adopted the 1980 decision on procedures for modification and rectification, they also adopted a decision for the introduction of a loose-leaf system for the schedules of tariff concessions. We shall deal with this decision in detail in the next section. However, for the purposes of this section, it is necessary to note that the idea was that the schedules of tariff concessions would be published in the form of a loose-leaf system which could be continuously kept up to date when rectifications, modifications, withdrawals and new concessions were made. The system of collective certification was, therefore, to be given up and every schedule, as well as any subsequent change, was to be certified individually. The new procedure was quicker as it involved circulation of notifications for objections only once and not twice for three months each, as was done earlier. When delays occurred in the full operationalization of the decision on the introduction of the loose-leaf system, two more collective certifications were published in 1981 and 1987 respectively. After the Sixth Certification of Changes to Schedules to the General Agreement on Tariffs and Trade was published on 28 November 1987, the practice of collective certifications was abandoned.

15.   Since schedules of concessions are integral parts of the General Agreement, changes in them result in changes in the treaty obligations of Members. Because of this it is specified in all protocols and certifications that they will be registered in accordance with the provisions of Article 102 of the Charter of the United Nations.

16.   Two aspects of the practice in GATT 1947/WTO in regard to modification and rectification procedures must be mentioned here. First, although the 1980 decision mentions modifications resulting from actions only under Articles II, XVIII, XXIV, XXVII and XXVIII, in practice contracting parties/Members have also resorted to these procedures to incorporate the results of new commitments made unilaterally or entered into in the course of bilateral or plurilateral negotiations. Thus, these procedures were used in respect of the 1984 decision of the signatories to the Agreement on Civil Aircraft for expanding the products covered by the Agreement, and after the entry into force of the WTO Agreement for incorporating in the schedules unilateral commitments and the commitments made pursuant to the Information Technology Agreement, as well as the plurilateral agreement on pharmaceuticals and the bilateral agreement on white spirits. Second, contracting parties to GATT 1947 did not always follow up completion of renegotiations under Article XXVIII by making a request for consequential modification of schedules under these procedures.

B.   Consolidation of Schedules

Practice in the early years of GATT 1947

1.   Although every Member has one schedule of concessions, from the description of the process of establishment, modification and rectification of schedules given in section A above, it will be apparent that the tariff commitments of a contracting party to GATT 1947 were contained in several legal instruments. For a better grasp of the situation, it is necessary to look at the note entitled "Situation of Schedules"[9] prepared by the Secretariat. In this note, a list was given of all instruments constituting the schedule of each contracting party at the end of the Tokyo Round. By way of illustration, the list of instruments constituting Schedule V of Canada at that time is reproduced below:

"Canada Schedule V

Part I - MFN

-    Geneva 1947

     amended in PR1/48, PR3/49, PR4/50, PR5/55, PRM6/57. PRM7/57, Brazilian Protocol 1958

-    Annecy 1949

     amended in PR4/50, PR5/55, PRM6/57, PRM7/57

-    Torquay 1951

     amended in PRM/5, PRM6/57, PRM7/57

---

[9]   GATT Doc. TAR/W/7 dated 18 June 1980.

- Japanese Protocol 1955
- Geneva 1956

    amended in Third Certification of Rectifications and Modalities 1967
- Geneva 1962
- Israeli Protocol 1962
- Portuguese Protocol 1962
- Spanish Protocol 1963
- Kennedy Round 1964-67

    amended in First Certification of Changes 1969
- Geneva (1979) Protocol
- Protocol Supplementary to Geneva (1979) Protocol

Part II - Preferential

- Geneva 1947

    amended in PRM5/55, PRM6/57, PRM7/57
- Annecy 1949

    amended in PR4/50, PRM5/55, PRM6/57
- Torquay 1951

    amended in PRM5/55, PRM6/57, PRM7/57
- Geneva 1956
- Kennedy Round 1964-67

See also document SECRET/180 + Add 1, SECRET/244 + Add 1-4 (XXVIII:5), SECRET/183 + Add.1 (XXVIII:4), SECRET/193 (II:5) and SECRET/244/Add.4 (XXVIII:3) containing information on bilateral negotiations, the results of which have not yet been incorporated in an official schedule."[10]

2.   Since the very early days of the operation of GATT 1947, the contracting parties have been worried about the lack of transparency resulting from the fact that the schedules of concessions are scattered over several legal instruments. As early as 15 December 1950, on the basis of the report of a Working Party, the CONTRACTING PARTIES decided on the preparation of the "consolidated text of the Geneva, Annecy and Torquay schedules". It was agreed that the consolidated lists should include an indication of the country or countries with which each concession was initially negotiated and of the document in which the concession appeared. Immediately after the conclusion of the Torquay Conference the consolidated schedules were prepared and distributed to the contracting parties for their comments. After they had been finalized, doubts arose about the question of giving them legal status. The Working Party which

---

[10]   GATT Doc. TAR/W/7 dated 18 June 1980, pp. 4-5.

considered this question foresaw practical difficulties as "to authenticate the Consolidated Schedules would involve very extensive rechecking by governments of their own and others' Schedules and thus much time, work and expense".[11] The same Working Party also saw objections from the legal point of view inasmuch as some contracting parties would have constitutional difficulties in resubmitting the results of the negotiations to their legislatures in a different form. If the earlier protocols were withdrawn, difficulty was envisaged in ascertaining the exact scope of the original concession in the event of disputes. The Working Party concluded as follows:

> "... it would be preferable to retain the Consolidated Schedules in their form as a working document. In cases of disputes, or when the precise extent and wording of a concession was in question, reference would be made to the authentic texts. For normal working purposes, however, the consolidated texts would be used. In order that they might retain their value, the secretariat should be instructed to issue new complete pages to take account of any changes to the Schedules resulting from Protocols of rectifications, modifications, new concessions or any withdrawals or other alterations notified by contracting parties to the secretariat. Delegations should, therefore, be requested to accompany such notifications with details of the corresponding changes required to the Consolidated Schedules."[12]

3.   In 1955 there was a fresh move to draw up consolidated schedules to cover all changes up to the end of 1956 tariff negotiations. Contracting parties were asked to submit their new consolidated schedule by 1 July 1956 or at the latest by 1 January 1957. The time limit was later extended to 31 December 1957. By the end of 1957 as many as 17 contracting parties had submitted their draft consolidated schedules. The procedure prescribed for approval was that, if no comments were received within 90 days, the draft consolidated schedule was to be considered as approved. If objections were received, the contracting party concerned had to consult and settle all the points raised and submit to the Secretariat a list of changes which were to be made in the original draft. The Secretariat had to distribute the list of changes to the contracting parties and, if no objections were received within 30 days, the consolidated schedule was to be deemed to have been approved.

4.   The question of giving legal status to consolidated schedules was again raised in 1957. In 1958 the CONTRACTING PARTIES approved the recommendation of the Working Party on Schedules to give legal status to the consolidated schedules subject to the following conditions and procedures:

> "(a)   any contracting party, wishing to prepare a consolidated schedule to replace its separate schedules annexed to the various Protocols, may do so, provided a draft consolidated schedule is submitted to

---

[11]   GATT, BISD, First Supplement, p. 66.

[12]   GATT, BISD, First Supplement, p. 66.

        the CONTRACTING PARTIES for approval under the normal rectification procedures;

(b)   such a contracting party should give due notice of its intention and should submit copies early enough before the usual protocol of rectifications and modifications is prepared, to allow for adequate checking by all contracting parties;

(c)   the contracting party to which the draft consolidated schedule relates, should be expected to accept the understanding that earlier schedules and - as has always been the case in the past - negotiating records, would be considered as proper sources of interpreting concessions contained in legal consolidated schedules."[13]

5.   The Working Party dealt with the problem regarding the date applicable to each concession for the purposes of Article II:1(b) of the Agreement, the aim of which was to establish the date as of which "other duties and charges" were bound. The CONTRACTING PARTIES agreed to the recommendation of the Working Party "that the date applicable to any concession in a consolidated schedule should be, for the purposes of Article II, the date of the instrument by which the concession was first incorporated into the General Agreement".[14]

6.   Following the above decision consolidated schedules of a number of contracting parties were established in the certifications dated 15 January 1963, 29 April 1964 and 5 May 1967, which were adopted pending acceptance of the protocol for the amendment of Article XXX. While the possibility was created in the decision of the CONTRACTING PARTIES for the consolidated schedules of individual contracting parties to be given legal status, the option was retained also for other contracting parties to have unofficial consolidated schedules.

7.   In 1968, when the CONTRACTING PARTIES adopted a decision to follow the certification procedure for modification and rectification to schedules, paragraph 5 of the decision also provided for these procedures to be followed for the establishment of consolidated schedules. Pursuant to this paragraph, consolidated schedules were established in respect of Turkey (First Certification dated 12 July 1969), South Africa, Israel and Malawi (Second Certification dated 9 January 1974), New Zealand, Finland and Sweden (Third Certification dated 23 October 1974) and Cuba (Part I only), Japan and Portugal (Fourth Certification dated 20 April 1979). In some cases these consolidated schedules were updated versions of the schedules approved during the period 1963-67. These consolidated schedules were listed against these contracting parties in the note by the Secretariat dated 18 June 1980 describing the "Situation of

---

[13]   GATT, BISD, Seventh Supplement, pp. 115-116.

[14]   GATT, BISD, Seventh Supplement, p. 116.

Schedules".[15] The note also mentioned that the unofficial consolidated schedules of a number of other contracting parties were available in the Secretariat.

1980 Decision on the introduction of a loose-leaf system

8.   After the Tokyo Round, the CONTRACTING PARTIES approved a new proposal by the Director-General on the introduction of a loose-leaf system for the schedules of tariff concessions. The proposal[16], which was adopted on 26 March 1980, had the following elements:

(a)   Henceforth, the schedules of tariff concessions were to be published in the form of a loose-leaf system which could continuously be kept up to date when rectifications, modifications, withdrawals and new concessions were made. In order to establish the loose-leaf system, contracting parties submit consolidated schedules of tariff concessions as soon as possible and not later than 30 September 1980.

(b)   The schedules have the following information:

1.   Tariff item number

2.   Description of product

3.   Rate of duty

4.   Present concession established in

5.   Initial negotiating rights on the concession

6.   Concession first incorporated in a GATT schedule

7.   INRs on earlier occasions

8.   Annotations.

(c)   The existing understanding concerning consolidated schedules that earlier schedules and negotiating records should be considered as proper sources in interpreting concessions in consolidated schedules applied, *inter alia*, to INRs regarding earlier bindings. Once the previous INRs had been indicated as required in column 7 above, and the loose-leaf schedules had been established, that understanding would cease to be valid in respect of this element.

(d)   In view of the fact that the incorporation of previous INRs into the schedules would necessitate time-consuming research in old negotiating records, a further period of one year up to 30 September 1981 was allowed for indicating this information in the loose-leaf schedules. It was also proposed that earlier schedules and negotiating records would remain proper sources for interpreting concessions until 1 January 1987.

---

[15]   GATT Doc. TAR/W/7.

[16]   GATT, BISD, Twenty-seventh Supplement, pp. 22-24.

(e)   In column 6, the instrument by which the concession was first incorporated into a GATT schedule was to be indicated to enable a determination of the date as of which "other duties and charges" on importation are bound.

9.   The task of drawing up consolidated loose-leaf schedules of tariff concessions was taken up in earnest in 1980 and 1981. In subsequent years, however, the exercise was overtaken by the more ambitious endeavour of drawing up the consolidated schedules in the nomenclature of the Harmonized System, which we shall deal with in the next section. Efforts continued, however, in the Committee on Tariff Concessions up to 1990 to obtain and approve consolidated pre-Harmonized System schedules. In the report[17] of the Committee presented to the Council on 7 November 1990, it was mentioned that out of 65 contracting parties having a GATT schedule (EEC schedule = 12 member States), 45 schedules had been circulated in accordance with the requirements of the loose-leaf system, and 21 of them had already been approved.

1996 Decision on consolidated loose-leaf schedules

10.   After the entry into force of the WTO Agreement, a new initiative was taken to establish consolidated loose-leaf schedules on goods and the General Council adopted a decision[18] on 29 November 1996. The following are the significant elements of this decision:

(i)   The consolidated loose-leaf schedules are to be binding instruments replacing all previous schedules for all purposes except with respect to historical INRs.

(ii)   All the information contained in previous consolidated loose-leaf schedules is to be indicated with the addition of information on staging and on "other duties and charges" (ODCs). Thus the new consolidated schedules have to contain information in the following columns:

(a)   Tariff item number

(b)   Description of product

(c)   Rate of duty (base and bound rates)

(d)   Present concession established

(e)   Initial negotiating rights on the concession

(f)   Concession first incorporated in a GATT schedule

(g)   INRs on earlier occasions

(h)   Other duties and charges.

---

[17]   GATT, BISD, Thirty-seventh Supplement, p. 75.

[18]   WTO Doc. G/L/138.

(iii)   In respect of INRs, the decision states as follows:

"Each Member shall include in its schedule all INRs at the current bound rate. Other Members may request the inclusion of any INR that had been granted to them. Historical INRs different from the current bound rate not specifically identified shall remain valid where a Member modifies its concession at a rate different from the rate at which the INR was granted."

This statement, together with the stipulation that the consolidated schedule will replace all previous schedules for all purposes except with respect to historical INRs, seems to give to Members an option not to fill in historical INRs at all.

(iv)   The decision mentions that the 1980 "Procedures for Modification and Rectification of Schedules of Tariff Concessions" will apply with respect to modification and rectification of loose-leaf schedules. It does not mention whether the same procedures will be applied for the establishment of these schedules as foreseen in paragraph 5 of the 1980 Procedures. Presumably that is the intention.

(v)   Members have been discussing the possibility of establishing a new procedure for verification of schedules whereby Members would be assisted in the task by the Secretariat undertaking electronic verification. It is not clear from the record of discussions whether the idea is to first establish the consolidated schedules and then use the electronic version to verify future changes in the schedules or to introduce electronic verification for the establishment of the new consolidated loose-leaf schedules themselves. The decision states that until a methodology for verification is agreed upon existing procedures (presumably the 1980 Procedures) will continue to apply.

(vi)   No date has been set for the submission of new consolidated loose-leaf schedules.

11.   Implementation of the 29 November 1996 decision has not yet taken off. As we shall see in the next section, Members are submitting consolidated loose-leaf schedules in the context of the 1996 revision of the Harmonized System in accordance with the 1991 Decision on "Procedures to Implement Changes in the Harmonized System" and the 1980 Decision on "Introduction of a loose-leaf system for the schedules of tariff concessions". In the practice established in the 1980s, these consolidated schedules generally do not contain information on INRs (current and historical) and on the date of first incorporation of a concession in a GATT schedule. These consolidated schedules do not, therefore, fulfil the requirement of the 29 November 1996 Decision.

C.   Harmonized Commodity Description and Coding System

Introduction

1.   Contracting parties to GATT 1947 had used different nomenclatures in their customs tariffs before adopting the Convention on the Harmonized Commodity Description and Coding System (hereinafter referred to as the Harmonized System) drawn up by the Customs Cooperation Council in Brussels. While some convergence took place with the adoption by a number of them of the Brussels Tariff Nomenclature (BTN) and later Customs Cooperation Council Nomenclature (CCCN), there remained wide divergences in the nomenclatures used by the contracting parties in their customs tariffs and GATT schedules. The difficulty of contracting parties participating in tariff negotiations and renegotiations was compounded by the fact that most of them maintained data on imports and exports in the Standard International Trade Classification (SITC) developed in the United Nations, which was different from the nomenclatures used for customs tariff purposes. A unique feature of the Harmonized System was that it was to be used as the basis for customs tariff as well as international trade statistics nomenclatures. It was widely recognized that, in addition to the benefits for trade facilitation and analysis of trade statistics, adoption of the Harmonized System would help ensure greater uniformity among countries in customs classification and enhance their ability to monitor and protect the value of tariff concessions in GATT.

1983 Decision on GATT concessions under the Harmonized System

2.   Contracting parties to GATT also recognized that the introduction of the Harmonized System would imply considerable changes in the GATT schedules of tariff concessions. By their decision[19] dated 12 July 1983, the CONTRACTING PARTIES laid down detailed procedures for the transposition of GATT schedules to the Harmonized System nomenclature. The important elements of this decision are described below:

(i)   The main principle to be observed was that the existing GATT bindings should be maintained unchanged. The decision stipulated that "(t)he alteration of existing bindings should only be envisaged where their maintenance would result in undue complexity in the national tariffs and should not involve a significant or arbitrary increase of customs duties collected on a particular product."

(ii)   It was recognized that in some cases where the introduction of the Harmonized System resulted in tariff lines with different bound rates being combined or bound rates being combined with unbound rates, renegotiations under Article XXVIII would be necessary. To the extent that the value of existing concessions was

---

[19]   GATT, BISD, Thirtieth Supplement, pp. 17-21.

not impaired, the conversion of existing nomenclatures to the Harmonized System could be done through the rectification procedures.

(iii)   Special procedures were prescribed for undertaking the exercise for rectification and renegotiations under Article XXVIII. Each contracting party adopting the Harmonized System was to supply the following information to the Secretariat for circulation:

(a)   An up-to-date consolidated schedule of concessions in the existing nomenclature in loose-leaf form;

(b)   A proposed consolidated schedule of concessions in the nomenclature of the Harmonized System containing information on the new tariff schedule number, a complete product description, the proposed rate of duty for the item and the proposed INR(s) for the item. If practicable, this document had also to contain information on historical INRs and other information required for loose-leaf schedules. In other words, information had to be provided in all the columns as specified in the March 1980 decision on the introduction of the consolidated loose-leaf schedules;

(c)   A concordance table from the existing to the proposed consolidated schedules of concessions. For each item in the existing schedule, this document was required to indicate (1) the item number and an abbreviated product description; (2) the corresponding item(s) in the concordance table from the proposed to the existing consolidated schedules; (3) the existing and proposed rates of duty; (4) the initial negotiating right status for the existing item; (5) the percentage of total imports in the existing item which had been allocated to each of the proposed items; and (6) the value of trade allocated to each of the proposed new items for the most recent three years for which import statistics were available. Information on items (5) and (6) was not required to be supplied if there was no change in either the proposed rate of duty or the initial negotiating right status from the existing tariff line;

(d)   A concordance table from the proposed to the existing consolidated schedules of concessions giving broadly the same information as required for the concordance table from the existing to the proposed consolidated schedules of concessions;

(e)   A list of items proposed for certification;

(f)   A list of items proposed for renegotiations.

The decision recommended that, where it became unavoidable to combine headings or part of headings in implementing the Harmonized System, contracting parties could consider the following alternatives:

(a)   Applying the lowest rate of any previous heading to the whole of the new heading;

(b)   Applying the rate previously applied to the heading or headings with the majority of trade;

(c)   Applying the trade-weighted average rate of duty for the new heading;

(d)   Applying the arithmetic average of the previous rates of duty, where no basis existed for establishing reasonably accurate trade allocations.

3.   An account is given below of the main features of the process of implementation of the decision to transpose GATT schedules to the Harmonized System nomenclature:

(i)   There were a number of departures from the guidelines for renegotiations under Article XXVIII. For instance, some contracting parties, instead of submitting claims of interest within 90 days, made blanket reservations and then followed up with individual requests. The results of bilateral negotiations, although provided to the Secretariat, were not circulated to other contracting parties. Certain new practices were also introduced to facilitate the process of renegotiations. Some contracting parties exchanged information on "bilateral balances" showing the trade coverage of items in bilateral trade in which the bound duties were increased or decreased.

(ii)   Difficulties arose in practice in filling up the information in columns 6 and 7, concerning the first incorporation of the concession in the schedule and previous INRs respectively. Even before the commencement of the process for transposition of GATT schedules to the Harmonized System nomenclature, in connection with the introduction of the loose-leaf system, a Secretariat note[20] circulated in June 1982 had acknowledged that the complete listing of previous INRs in respect of concessions given in different nomenclatures and at different rates could be very complicated and in some cases could cover several pages in respect of one tariff line. It therefore proposed that INRs could be condensed into one INR at a mutually-agreed level through bilateral negotiations. However, if the INR holder so requested, the country submitting the schedule would have to fill column 7 in full detail. While the suggestion seemed to have been accepted in

---

[20]   GATT Doc. TAR/W/30.

principle, the consolidated schedules that were submitted both with pre-Harmonized System and Harmonized System nomenclatures continued to suffer from lack of information on previous INRs. Regarding the date of first incorporation of the concession to be furnished in column 6, some delegations suggested in the Committee on Tariff Concessions that the date to be indicated should be the date at which a concession or a part of a concession (earliest constituent component) was granted. However, other delegations requested more time to reflect on the proposal as the matter had come up for negotiations in the GATT Articles Group of the Uruguay Round and consequently no agreement could be reached on the content of column 6. The schedules in most cases did not have information on column 6 either. Again, the final schedules attached to various protocols did not have entries in column 5 on current INRs in most cases.

(iii)   The contracting parties accepted the following observations made by the Secretariat in a note dated 14 January 1987:

"It is recognized that participants will find it difficult within the time-frame envisaged for the implementation of the Harmonized System to include in their consolidated draft schedules which are to be annexed to the Harmonized System Protocol, information under column 6 (concession first incorporated in a GATT schedule) and column 7 (INRs on earlier concessions), of the loose-leaf model....Since the inclusion of this information is mandatory under the Decision of the GATT Council of 26 March 1980 (BISD 27S/22) on the introduction of the loose-leaf system, a schedule which is annexed to the Harmonized System Protocol and which contains information relating only to columns 1-5 would be considered a legally valid consolidated - but incomplete - schedule of concessions. In order to comply with the requirements of the above-mentioned decision, the missing information (relating to columns 6 and 7) would have to be submitted at a later stage. At that time, it will be necessary to certify the completed consolidated schedule...."[21]

(iv)   In the March 1980 decision on the introduction of the consolidated loose-leaf schedules, it had been provided that earlier schedules and negotiating records would remain proper sources for interpreting tariff concessions until 1 January 1987. In view of the delays in the submission of the consolidated schedules pursuant to the 1980 decision and further complications relating to Article XXVIII negotiations in connection with the introduction of the Harmonized System, the GATT Council reviewed the March 1980 decision in this respect. It was decided[22] to replace the words "until

---

[21]   GATT Doc. TAR/W/65.

[22]   GATT, BISD, Thirty-third Supplement, pp. 135-136.

1 January 1987" by the words "until a date to be established by the Council".

(v)   While it was agreed in the 1983 decision that alteration of existing bindings would be envisaged only if their maintenance would result in undue complexity in the national tariffs and that such alteration should not involve a significant or arbitrary increase of customs duties collected on a particular product, in actual practice many contracting parties, developed and developing, did raise their bound duties, in some cases significantly, in the process of the transposition of the GATT schedules to the Harmonized System nomenclature. In some cases these resulted in loud complaints[23] in the Committee on Tariff Concessions.

(vi)   In the Committee on Tariff Concessions, it was debated whether the protocol or certification approach would be the best means to incorporate in the GATT schedules changes resulting from the transposition of concessions to the Harmonized System nomenclature. The protocol approach was preferred in view of the greater flexibility it afforded. Three protocols were opened for acceptance in 1987 and one each in 1988, 1989, 1992, 1993 and 1994, in order to enable the contracting parties to annex their schedules to the protocols as and when they were ready.

(vii)   A large majority of GATT contracting parties decided to apply the Harmonized System in their customs tariff. While some followed the prescribed procedures ending with the annexing of their consolidated schedules in the Harmonized System to the Protocols before implementation, and others obtained waivers to enable them to implement the System before completing the GATT procedures (including renegotiations), some others implemented it without having followed those procedures. As of 14 October 1994, 28 contracting parties and the European Communities had their Harmonized System schedules attached to various protocols.

(viii) In view of the fact that the transposition to the Harmonized System nomenclature resulted in the tariff schedules of a large number of contracting parties being put on a completely new basis, a fresh decision[24] was adopted on the question of floating INRs on the lines of the ones taken by the CONTRACTING PARTIES at the end of the Kennedy and Tokyo Rounds.

---

[23]   GATT Doc. TAR/M/24.

[24]   GATT, BISD, Thirty-fifth Supplement, p. 336.

1991 Revision of the Harmonized System

4.   In July 1989 the Customs Cooperation Council adopted a Recommendation concerning the Amendment of the Harmonized Commodity Description and Coding System which was to come into effect on 1 January 1992. Most of the changes were of a technical or editorial nature, but in about a dozen cases the amendments involved substantive changes resulting from the transfer of a product from one 6-digit heading to another. For the implementation of the revision of the Harmonized System the CONTRACTING PARTIES adopted a decision[25] on 8 October 1991 simplifying the earlier procedures. This decision required contracting parties to submit a notification which included the pages of their loose-leaf schedules containing the proposed changes. These pages had to show clearly those items in which, in the view of the contracting party in question, the proposed changes did not alter the scope of the concession and those in which they did. For the items in which the proposed changes altered the scope of the concession, the following information had to be furnished:

(i)   A concordance table between the existing and the proposed schedule;

(ii)   A concordance table between the proposed and the existing schedule;

(iii)   An indication of the contracting party or parties with which the existing concession was initially negotiated;

(iv)   Import statistics by country of origin, for the most recent three-year period for which statistics were available.

5.   The procedures for modification and rectification had to be followed and the changes in the GATT schedules certified if no objection was raised within 90 days in respect of changes which did not alter the scope of the concession and if no consultation or negotiation was requested within the same period in respect of changes which altered the scope of concessions. If an objection was raised or a request for negotiation or consultation was made, the procedures for negotiations under Article XXVIII had to be followed. In the case of changes claimed as not altering the scope of a concession, if an objection was raised the contracting party concerned had to submit the full documentation, as required for changes in which the scope of a concession was altered.

6.   The implementation of the 1991 decision in respect of the 1992 revision of the Harmonized System was quite smooth. Eleven contracting parties notified changes in their schedules relating to the 1992 revision and ten of the notifications were certified.

---

[25]   GATT, BISD, Thirty-ninth Supplement, pp. 300-301.

1996 Revision of the Harmonized System

7.   The next revision of the Harmonized System approved by the Customs Cooperation Council at Brussels for implementation with effect from 1 January 1996 was more extensive than the 1992 revision. Since the 1991 decision on the procedures for incorporating in GATT schedules the 1992 changes in the Harmonized System was meant for "any changes which may be introduced in the future", these procedures were applied for the 1996 revision also. The process for introducing into the Schedule of Goods the changes in the 1996 revision of the Harmonized System began in 1995, after the entry into force of the WTO Agreement.

8.   Although the 1991 decision requires contracting parties (Members) to submit a notification which includes only the pages of their loose-leaf schedules containing proposed changes, the practice has varied among Members in respect of changes resulting from the 1996 revision of the Harmonized System. A number of Members have submitted the full consolidated loose-leaf schedules, including the items where there have been changes following the 1996 revision of the Harmonized System. Others have submitted only the list of items affected by the 1996 revision.

9.   A Secretariat note[26] dated 13 October 1994 stated that the final objective was that "delegations prepare a consolidated schedule in loose-leaf format" as agreed in the 1980 decision on the introduction of a loose-leaf system for the schedules of tariff concessions. Detailed guidelines were given in the note for the preparation of a new schedule in loose-leaf format while incorporating the changes in the 1996 revision of the Harmonized System. The format suggested was that of the 1980 decision regarding the introduction of the loose-leaf system with the addition of a new column on ODCs. The Members which have submitted consolidated loose-leaf schedules in accordance with these guidelines have in most cases not filled in columns 5 (current INRs), 6 (date of first incorporation) and 7 (INRs on earlier concessions) and the pattern set in the original transposition to the Harmonized System has been maintained.

10.   Long delays have taken place in completing the procedures for changes in schedules stemming from the 1996 revision of the Harmonized System. In the beginning the process was blocked in a large number of cases because of general reservations made by some Members. These Members took the position that the 1991 procedures were not adequate for the implementation of the 1996 revision and it was necessary for the Members to furnish the fuller documentation as required in the 1983 decision. Other Members asserted that the 1991 decision needed to be followed for the 1996 revision and amendment of the currently applicable procedures could be considered only for future changes in the Harmonized System. There could not be an agreement in this regard, but the Members which had made general reservations proceeded later to specify their reservations and the process was unblocked after the Council for Trade in Goods

---

[26]   GATT Doc. TAR/W/93.

took a decision which provided that, if the objections on the documentation already submitted were not specified by a certain date, they would be deemed to have lapsed.

11.   As in the past, Members which could not complete the required procedures before the date of implementation of the 1996 revision of the Harmonized System needed a waiver under paragraph 3 of Article IX of the WTO Agreement and a waiver[27] was granted to them initially up to 30 June 1996 and they were required to complete the negotiations and consultations by that date. The time limit has had to be extended a number of times and on 1.10.99 it was being proposed that the time limit be extended to 30 April 2000. A requirement in these decisions has been that Members should have submitted the documentation or, if special circumstances applied, should have requested technical assistance from the Secretariat for the completion of such documentation. As in the past, the waiver decisions authorize other Members to suspend concessions initially negotiated with the Members concerned to the extent that they consider that adequate compensation is not offered by the Member concerned.

12.   By 1 October 1999, 41 Members (counting the EEC as one) had submitted the documentation relating to the 1996 revision of the Harmonized System and out of these 10 had been certified and in seven the document was being prepared for certification. In respect of the remaining 24, the process has remained blocked, in some cases by more than two years, because of objections.

13.   Not all Members which have submitted the documentation but which have not completed the procedures have been seeking waivers or continuation of earlier waivers. Some Members which are covered by waivers have not submitted the documentation. A very large number of Members have neither submitted the documentation nor applied for waivers. It must be pointed out here that some of these Members, particularly those which have made ceiling bindings, may not need waivers and there might not even be a requirement for them to transpose their concessions on goods to the 1996 version of the Harmonized System.

D.   Integrated Data Base

1.   A data base on tariffs and trade has existed in the Secretariat since the early 1970s. The first data base, known as the GATT Tariff Study, containing information on customs tariff and imports in respect of 10 industrialized countries and the European Communities, was developed after the Kennedy Round to allow for an analysis of the tariff situation in those markets. During the Tokyo Round, the data base was used by the eleven GATT contracting parties participating in the exercise to facilitate the negotiations. The participants authorized the Secretariat to provide developing countries with summary

---

[27]   WTO Doc. G/MA/W/4/Rev.1.

information derived from the data base concerning products of export interest to them.

2.   In 1987, the exercise was widened to cover all contracting parties when the CONTRACTING PARTIES adopted a decision[28] on 10 November 1987 requiring the Secretariat to begin work on setting up an integrated data base (IDB) consisting initially of information at the tariff line level on three elements, namely imports, tariffs and quantitative restrictions. It was agreed that, for the purposes of the integrated data base, contracting parties would submit annually to the Secretariat tariff data for unbound items and import data for all bound and unbound items, in addition to the existing notification requirements on quantitative restrictions and bound tariffs. The data base thus set up was of great use during the Uruguay Round, in which it enabled the Secretariat to provide the analyses on the basis of which the participants evaluated the results of the Round in the area of tariffs on both agricultural and industrial products. The IDB also helped the Secretariat to provide analytical inputs into the exercise for verification of the tariff schedules of the participants so as to enable them to determine whether the Montreal target for reduction of industrial tariffs by one-third and the Agriculture Agreement requirement of reduction by a simple average of 35 per cent (24 per cent for developing countries) had been met.

3.   After the entry into force of the WTO Agreement, the operation of the IDB was reviewed. It was decided to downsize the IDB and make it operational with basic information on tariffs and imports before broadening its scope by including non-tariff measures. By a decision[29] dated 16 July 1997 the General Council required Members to supply to the Secretariat, on an annual basis, the information for the IDB. MFN tariffs, both current bound duties and applied duties, have to be furnished on an obligatory basis and preferential tariffs on an optional basis. Information on imports has to be furnished origin-wise, without indicating if the imports were admitted on a preferential or MFN basis.

4.   As regards dissemination of information contained in the IDB, in June 1997 the Committee on Market Access adopted a document which provided as follows:

> "The IDB contains information already in the public domain - customs tariffs published in the national tariff schedules, concessions available in the WTO list of concessions and import statistics available from national statistical authorities. This IDB information has been available to all WTO Members and to international organizations for their internal use. This is the present policy followed by the Secretariat in the dissemination of the IDB on the CD-ROM, but it may need to be reviewed."[30]

---

[28]   GATT, BISD, Thirty-fourth Supplement, pp. 66-67.

[29]   WTO Doc. WT/L/225.

[30]   WTO Doc. G/MA/IDB/1/Rev.1.

5.   Some Members have been concerned about the level of compliance by Members in the IDB notification requirement and suggested partial restriction of access to non-complying Members. However, in June 1999 it was agreed as follows:

"In light of the need to assure the broadest possible participation of Members in the IDB and full compliance with the 16 July 1997 Decision of the General Council (WT/L/225) concerning supply of information to the IDB, Members agreed that the Market Access Committee would undertake prior to 1 June 2000 a review of the operation of the IDB and of IDB-related technical assistance activities. If, at the time of the review, participation of Members in the IDB falls substantially below the current level of participation, access to the IDB data will be temporarily suspended until adequate participation is secured again, unless other steps considered appropriate by Members are agreed."[31]

6.   IDB information is distributed not only through the IDB CD-ROM but also on-line. While the IDB CD-ROM permits the viewing and printing of tariff-line and summary data, on-line tariff level data can be further analyzed using PC desktop software. This facility can be of great use during tariff negotiations and renegotiations.

---

[31]   WTO Doc. G/MA/IDB/3.

133

CHAPTER VI

CONCLUSIONS AND RECOMMENDATIONS

Plurilateral Negotiations on Sectors: An Additional Tool for Liberalization

1.   While global comprehensive rounds of trade negotiations are the best means of obtaining ambitious results in tariff liberalization, sectoral liberalization on a plurilateral basis is an additional tool which can be employed during the rounds as well as in the interval between rounds. Sectoral liberalization, whether during or between rounds, can be undertaken plurilaterally by Members having the predominant share of world exports (say 80 per cent), as was done in the Uruguay Round and in the Information Technology Agreement. There is precedent and there are rules governing plurilateral negotiations between rounds. Such negotiations can help to maintain the momentum for liberalization of world trade when more comprehensive negotiations are not taking place. Needless to say, the results should be applied on an MFN basis and all Members wishing to participate in the negotiations should be allowed to do so.

Surveillance of Future Renegotiations

2.   In order to help in expediting renegotiations and to ensure that the results of such negotiations are reported and incorporated in the schedules, the Committee on Market Access should maintain surveillance on all future renegotiations under the various articles of GATT 1994. For this purpose, periodic information should be required to be furnished by Members on the stage reached in each of the negotiations. The Secretariat can compile such information on the basis of data available to it.

Standing Body for Modification and Rectification

3.   At present, requests for rectification can be blocked by objections received from any Member on a proposal made by another Member they may remain so for years. Consideration should be given to establishing a standing body of Members that may, where an objection has been raised, review all proposals for rectification with a view to devising appropriate solutions.

Preparation of Updated Note on Situation of Schedules

4.   In order to facilitate the task of preparation of the consolidated loose-leaf schedules, to replace all previous schedules as decided by the General Council on 29 November 1996, the Secretariat should be requested to prepare an update of the note in document TAR/W/7 dated 18 June 1980 on "Situation of Schedules" and to list all the instruments constituting the schedules on goods of

Members. In the past, efforts to prepare consolidated loose-leaf schedules have succeeded only partially as information has been missing in several columns. Even the 29 November 1996 decision states that the new consolidated loose-leaf schedule will replace all previous schedules for all purposes except historical INRs. Thus, the past instruments will remain valid as a source of information for historical INRs even if Members are successful in filling in all the columns of the new consolidated loose-leaf schedules. The task of preparing the list of all past instruments constituting the schedule on goods deserves, therefore, to be given top priority.

Completion of Transposition to the Harmonized System

5.   Priority should also be given to the transposition of pre- and post-Uruguay Round schedules to the nomenclature of the Harmonized System as revised up to 1996. This should be substantially accomplished before a date is set for the submission of new consolidated loose-leaf schedules in accordance with the decision of 29 November 1996.

Tracking Information on Past Renegotiations

6.   The Secretariat should also be authorized to track down information on all renegotiations taken up under Article XXVIII where final reports have not been furnished in order to see whether the renegotiations were abandoned or concluded with withdrawals or modifications which were absorbed in the results of negotiations in the rounds. The task should be limited to the incomplete renegotiations mentioned in the Secretariat note dated 18 June 1980 on "Situation of Schedules" referred to in paragraph 4 above and the renegotiations undertaken thereafter.

Review of Need to Provide for Floating INRs in Respect of Uruguay Round Concessions

7.   Unlike in the Kennedy Round and the Tokyo Round, no decision was adopted in the Uruguay Round on floating INRs. In the absence of records of bilateral negotiations and on account of the fact that INRs were generally not granted specifically in the context of these negotiations, INRs are virtually non-existent in respect of the concessions agreed during the Uruguay Round. In view of the implications of this for the operation of Article XXVIII:3 of GATT 1994, consideration should be given to the adoption of a decision on floating INRs, in respect of the schedules attached to the Marrakesh Protocol. It might be even better to envisage a decision on floating INRs applying, not only to the schedules attached to the Marrakesh Protocol, but also to all future tariff concessions.

Update of 1980 Procedures for Modification and Rectification

8.   The 1980 Procedures for Modification and Rectification of Schedules of Tariff Concessions should be updated and the practice of applying these procedures to modifications resulting from unilateral decisions and bilateral and plurilateral negotiations should be codified.

APPENDICES

APPENDIX A

KEY PROVISIONS IN THE HAVANA CHARTER
GATT 1994 AND THE WTO AGREEMENT AND RELATED UNDERSTANDINGS

Havana Charter

Article 17

GATT 1994

Article I

Article II

Article XVIII

Article XXIV

Article XXVII

Article XXVIII

Article XXVIII *bis*

Article XXXV

Article XXXVI

Tokyo Round Decision on Differential and More Favourable Treatment, Reciprocity and Fuller Participation of Developing Countries

WTO Agreement

Understanding on Interpretation Article II:1(b) of GATT 1994

Understanding on Interpretation of Article XXVIII of GATT 1994

HAVANA CHARTER

Article 17

Reduction of Tariffs and Elimination of Preferences

1.   Each Member shall, upon the request of any other Member or Members, and subject to procedural arrangements established by the Organization, enter into and carry out with such other Member or Members negotiations directed to the substantial reduction of the general levels of tariffs and other charges on imports and exports, and to the elimination of the preferences referred to in paragraph 2 of Article 16 on a reciprocal and mutually advantageous basis.

2.   The negotiations provided for in paragraph 1 shall proceed in accordance with the following rules:

(a)   Such negotiations shall be conducted on a selective product-by-product basis which will afford adequate opportunity to take into account the needs of individual countries and individual industries. Members shall be free not to grant concessions on particular products and, in the granting of a concession, they may reduce the duty, bind it at its then existing level, or undertake not to raise it above a specified higher level.

(b)   No Member shall be required to grant unilateral concessions, or to grant concessions to other Members without receiving adequate concessions in return. Account shall be taken of the value to any Member of obtaining in its own right and by direct obligation the indirect concessions which it would otherwise enjoy only by virtue of Article 16.

(c)   in negotiations relating to any specific product with respect to which a preference applies,

(i)   when a reduction is negotiated only in the most-favoured-nation rate, such reduction shall operate automatically to reduce or eliminate the margin of preference applicable to that product;

(ii)   when a reduction is negotiated only in the preferential rate, the most-favoured-nation rate shall automatically be reduced to the extent of such reduction;

(iii)   when it is agreed that reductions will be negotiated in both the most-favoured-nation rate and the preferential rate, the reduction in each shall be that agreed by the parties to the negotiations;

(iv)   no margin of preference shall be increased

(d)   The binding against increase of low duties or of duty-free treatment shall in principle be recognized as a concession equivalent in value to the substantial reduction of high duties or the elimination of tariff preferences.

(e)   Prior international obligations shall not be invoked to frustrate the requirement under paragraph 1 to negotiate with respect to preferences, it being understood that agreements which result from such negotiations and which conflict with such obligations shall not require the modification or termination of such obligations except (i) with the consent of the parties to such obligations, or, in the absence of such consent, (ii) by modification or termination of such obligations in accordance with their terms.

3.   The negotiations leading to the General Agreement on Tariffs and Trade, concluded at Geneva on October 30, 1947, shall be deemed to be negotiations pursuant to this Article. The concessions agreed upon as a result of all other negotiations completed by a Member pursuant to this Article shall be incorporated in the General Agreement on terms to be agreed with the parties thereto. If any Member enters into any agreement relating to tariffs or preferences which is not concluded pursuant to this Article, the negotiations leading to such agreement shall nevertheless conform to the requirements of paragraph 2 (c).

4.   (a)   The provisions of Article 16 shall not prevent the operation of paragraph 5 (b) of Article XXV of the General Agreement on Tariffs and Trade, as amended at the First Session of the CONTRACTING PARTIES.

(b)   If a Member has failed to become a contracting party to the General Agreement within two years from the entry into force of this Charter with respect to such Member, the provisions of Article 16 shall cease to require, at the end of that period, the application to the trade of such Member country of the concessions granted, in the appropriate Schedule annexed to the General Agreement, by another Member which has requested the first Member to negotiate with a view to becoming a contracting party to the General Agreement but has not successfully concluded negotiations; *Provided* that the Organization may, by a majority of the votes cast, require the continued application of such concessions to the trade of any Member country which has been unreasonably prevented from becoming a contracting party to the General Agreement pursuant to negotiations in accordance with the provisions of this Article.

(c)   If a Member which is a contracting party to the General Agreement proposes to withhold tariff concessions from the trade of a Member country which is not a contracting party, it shall give notice in writing to the Organization and to the affected Member. The latter Member may request the Organization to require the continuance of such concessions, and if such a request has been made the tariff concessions shall not be withheld pending a decision by the Organization under the provisions of sub-paragraph (b) of this paragraph.

(d)   In any determination whether a Member has been unreasonably prevented from becoming a contracting party to the General Agreement, and in any determination under the provisions of Chapter VIII whether a Member has failed without sufficient justification to fulfil its obligations under paragraph 1 of this Article, the Organization shall have regard to all relevant circumstances, including the developmental, reconstruction and other needs, and the general fiscal structures, of the Member countries concerned and to the provisions of the Charter as a whole.

(e)   If such concessions are in fact withheld, so as to result in the application to the trade of a Member country of duties higher than would otherwise have been applicable, such Member shall then be free, within sixty days after such action becomes effective, to give written notice of withdrawal from the Organization. The withdrawal shall become effective upon the expiration of sixty days from the day on which such notice is received by the Director-General.

THE GENERAL AGREEMENT ON TARIFFS AND TRADE

Article I
General Most-Favoured-Nation Treatment

1.   With respect to customs duties and charges of any kind imposed on or in connection with importation or exportation or imposed on the international transfer of payments for imports or exports, and with respect to the method of levying such duties and charges, and with respect to all rules and formalities in connection with importation and exportation, and with respect to all matters referred to in paragraphs 2 and 4 of Article III,* any advantage, favour, privilege or immunity granted by any contracting party to any product originating in or destined for any other country shall be accorded immediately and unconditionally to the like product originating in or destined for the territories of all other contracting parties.

2.   The provisions of paragraph 1 of this Article shall not require the elimination of any preferences in respect of import duties or charges which do not exceed the levels provided for in paragraph 4 of this Article and which fall within the following descriptions:

(*a*)   Preferences in force exclusively between two or more of the territories listed in Annex A, subject to the conditions set forth therein;

(*b*)   Preferences in force exclusively between two or more territories which on July 1, 1939, were connected by common sovereignty or relations of protection or suzerainty and which are listed in Annexes B, C and D, subject to the conditions set forth therein;

(*c*)   Preferences in force exclusively between the United States of America and the Republic of Cuba;

(*d*)   Preferences in force exclusively between neighbouring countries listed in Annexes E and F.

3.   The provisions of paragraph 1 shall not apply to preferences between the countries formerly a part of the Ottoman Empire and detached from it on July 24, 1923, provided such preferences are approved under paragraph 5 [1] of Article XXV, which shall be applied in this respect in the light of paragraph 1 of Article XXIX.

4.   The margin of preference* on any product in respect of which a preference is permitted under paragraph 2 of this Article but is not specifically set forth as a maximum margin of preference in the appropriate Schedule annexed to this Agreement shall not exceed:

(*a*)   in respect of duties or charges on any product described in such Schedule, the difference between the most-favoured-nation and

---

[1]   The authentic text erroneously reads "subparagraph 5 (a)".

preferential rates provided for therein; if no preferential rate is provided for, the preferential rate shall for the purposes of this paragraph be taken to be that in force on April 10, 1947, and, if no most-favoured-nation rate is provided for, the margin shall not exceed the difference between the most-favoured-nation and preferential rates existing on April 10, 1947;

(b) in respect of duties or charges on any product not described in the appropriate Schedule, the difference between the most-favoured-nation and preferential rates existing on April 10, 1947.

In the case of the contracting parties named in Annex G, the date of April 10, 1947, referred to in subparagraph (a) and (b) of this paragraph shall be replaced by the respective dates set forth in that Annex.

ANNEX A

LIST OF TERRITORIES REFERRED TO IN
PARAGRAPH 2 (a) OF ARTICLE I

United Kingdom of Great Britain and Northern Ireland

Dependent territories of the United Kingdom of Great Britain and Northern Ireland

Canada

Commonwealth of Australia

Dependent territories of the Commonwealth of Australia

New Zealand

Dependent territories of New Zealand

Union of South Africa including South West Africa

Ireland

India (as on April 10, 1947)

Newfoundland

Southern Rhodesia

Burma

Ceylon

Certain of the territories listed above have two or more preferential rates in force for certain products. Any such territory may, by agreement with the other contracting parties which are principal suppliers of such products at the most-favoured-nation rate, substitute for such preferential rates a single preferential rate which shall not on the whole be less favourable to suppliers at the most-favoured-nation rate than the preferences in force prior to such substitution.

The imposition of an equivalent margin of tariff preference to replace a margin of preference in an internal tax existing on April 10, 1947 exclusively between two or more of the territories listed in this Annex or to replace the preferential quantitative arrangements described in the following paragraph, shall not be deemed to constitute an increase in a margin of tariff preference.

The preferential arrangements referred to in paragraph 5 (*b*) of Article XIV are those existing in the United Kingdom on 10 April 1947, under contractual agreements with the Governments of Canada, Australia and New Zealand, in respect of chilled and frozen beef and veal, frozen mutton and lamb, chilled and frozen pork and bacon. It is the intention, without prejudice to any action taken under subparagraph (*h*)[2] of Article XX, that these arrangements shall be eliminated or replaced by tariff preferences, and that negotiations to this end shall take place as soon as practicable among the countries substantially concerned or involved.

The film hire tax in force in New Zealand on 10 April 1947, shall, for the purposes of this Agreement, be treated as a customs duty under Article I. The renters' film quota in force in New Zealand on April 10, 1947, shall, for the purposes of this Agreement, be treated as a screen quota under Article IV.

The Dominions of India and Pakistan have not been mentioned separately in the above list since they had not come into existence as such on the base date of April 10, 1947.

ANNEX B

LIST OF TERRITORIES OF THE FRENCH UNION REFERRED TO IN PARAGRAPH 2 (b) OF ARTICLE I

France

French Equatorial Africa (Treaty Basin of the Congo[3] and other territories)

French West Africa

Cameroons under French Trusteeship[1]

French Somali Coast and Dependencies

French Establishments in Oceania

French Establishments in the Condominium of the New Hebrides[1]

Indo-China

Madagascar and Dependencies

Morocco (French zone)[1]

New Caledonia and Dependencies

Saint-Pierre and Miquelon

Togo under French Trusteeship[1]

Tunisia

---

[2] The authentic text erroneously reads "part I (*h*)".

[3] For imports into Metropolitan France and Territories of the French Union.

ANNEX C

LIST OF TERRITORIES REFERRED TO IN PARAGRAPH 2 (*b*) OF ARTICLE I AS RESPECTS THE CUSTOMS UNION OF BELGIUM, LUXEMBURG AND THE NETHERLANDS

The Economic Union of Belgium and Luxemburg

Belgian Congo

Ruanda Urundi

Netherlands

New Guinea

Surinam

Netherlands Antilles

Republic of Indonesia

For imports into the territories constituting the Customs Union only.

ANNEX D

LIST OF TERRITORIES REFERRED TO IN PARAGRAPH 2 (b) OF ARTICLE I AS RESPECTS THE UNITED STATES OF AMERICA

United States of America (customs territory)

Dependent territories of the United States of America

Republic of the Philippines

The imposition of an equivalent margin of tariff preference to replace a margin of preference in an internal tax existing on 10 April, 1947, exclusively between two or more of the territories listed in this Annex shall not be deemed to constitute an increase in a margin of tariff preference.

ANNEX E

LIST OF TERRITORIES COVERED BY PREFERENTIAL ARRANGEMENTS BETWEEN CHILE AND NEIGHBOURING COUNTRIES REFERRED TO IN PARAGRAPH 2 (*d*) OF ARTICLE I

Preferences in force exclusively between Chile on the one hand, and

1.   Argentina
2.   Bolivia
3.   Peru

on the other hand.

ANNEX F

LIST OF TERRITORIES COVERED BY PREFERENTIAL ARRANGEMENTS BETWEEN LEBANON AND SYRIA AND NEIGHBOURING COUNTRIES REFERRED TO IN PARAGRAPH 2 (*d*) OF ARTICLE I

Preferences in force exclusively between the Lebano-Syrian Customs Union, on the one hand, and

1. Palestine
2. Transjordan

on the other hand.

ANNEX G

DATES ESTABLISHING MAXIMUM MARGINS OF PREFERENCE REFERRED TO IN PARAGRAPH 4[4] OF ARTICLE I

Australia	October 15, 1946
Canada	July 1, 1939
France	January 1, 1939
Lebano-Syrian Customs Union	November 30, 1938
Union of South Africa	July 1, 1938
Southern Rhodesia	May 1, 1941

ANNEX I

NOTES AND SUPPLEMENTARY PROVISIONS

Ad Article I

Paragraph 1

The obligations incorporated in paragraph 1 of Article I by reference to paragraphs 2 and 4 of Article III and those incorporated in paragraph 2 (*b*) of Article II by reference to Article VI shall be considered as falling within Part II for the purposes of the Protocol of Provisional Application.

The cross-references, in the paragraph immediately above and in paragraph 1 of Article I, to paragraphs 2 and 4 of Article III shall only apply after Article III has been modified by the entry into force of the amendment provided

---

[4]   The authentic text erroneously reads "Paragraph 3".

for in the Protocol Modifying Part II and Article XXVI of the General Agreement on Tariffs and Trade, dated September 14, 1948.[5]

Paragraph 4

The term "margin of preference" means the absolute difference between the most-favoured-nation rate of duty and the preferential rate of duty for the like product, and not the proportionate relation between those rates. As examples:

(1)   If the most-favoured-nation rate were 36 per cent *ad valorem* and the preferential rate were 24 per cent *ad valorem*, the margin of preference would be 12 per cent *ad valorem*, and not one-third of the most-favoured-nation rate;

(2)   If the most-favoured-nation rate were 36 per cent *ad valorem* and the preferential rate were expressed as two-thirds of the most-favoured-nation rate, the margin of preference would be 12 per cent *ad valorem*;

(3)   If the most-favoured-nation rate were 2 francs per kilogramme and the preferential rate were 1.50 francs per kilogramme, the margin of preference would be 0.50 franc per kilogramme.

The following kinds of customs action, taken in accordance with established uniform procedures, would not be contrary to a general binding of margins of preference:

(i)   The re-application to an imported product of a tariff classification or rate of duty, properly applicable to such product, in cases in which the application of such classification or rate to such product was temporarily suspended or inoperative on April 10, 1947; and

(ii)   The classification of a particular product under a tariff item other than that under which importations of that product were classified on April 10, 1947, in cases in which the tariff law clearly contemplates that such product may be classified under more than one tariff item.

---

[5]   This Protocol entered into force on 14 December 1948.

Article II

Schedules of Concessions

1. (*a*) Each contracting party shall accord to the commerce of the other contracting parties treatment no less favourable than that provided for in the appropriate Part of the appropriate Schedule annexed to this Agreement.

(*b*) The products described in Part I of the Schedule relating to any contracting party, which are the products of territories of other contracting parties, shall, on their importation into the territory to which the Schedule relates, and subject to the terms, conditions or qualifications set forth in that Schedule, be exempt from ordinary customs duties in excess of those set forth and provided therein. Such products shall also be exempt from all other duties or charges of any kind imposed on or in connection with the importation in excess of those imposed on the date of this Agreement or those directly and mandatorily required to be imposed thereafter by legislation in force in the importing territory on that date.

(*c*) The products described in Part II of the Schedule relating to any contracting party which are the products of territories entitled under Article I to receive preferential treatment upon importation into the territory to which the Schedule relates shall, on their importation into such territory, and subject to the terms, conditions or qualifications set forth in that Schedule, be exempt from ordinary customs duties in excess of those set forth and provided for in Part II of that Schedule. Such products shall also be exempt from all other duties or charges of any kind imposed on or in connection with importation in excess of those imposed on the date of this Agreement or those directly or mandatorily required to be imposed thereafter by legislation in force in the importing territory on that date. Nothing in this Article shall prevent any contracting party from maintaining its requirements existing on the date of this Agreement as to the eligibility of goods for entry at preferential rates of duty.

2. Nothing in this Article shall prevent any contracting party from imposing at any time on the importation of any product:

(*a*) a charge equivalent to an internal tax imposed consistently with the provisions of paragraph 2 of Article III* in respect of the like domestic product or in respect of an article from which the imported product has been manufactured or produced in whole or in part;

(*b*) any anti-dumping or countervailing duty applied consistently with the provisions of Article VI;*

(*c*) fees or other charges commensurate with the cost of services rendered.

3. No contracting party shall alter its method of determining dutiable value or of converting currencies so as to impair the value of any of the concessions provided for in the appropriate Schedule annexed to this Agreement.

4.   If any contracting party establishes, maintains or authorizes, formally or in effect, a monopoly of the importation of any product described in the appropriate Schedule annexed to this Agreement, such monopoly shall not, except as provided for in that Schedule or as otherwise agreed between the parties which initially negotiated the concession, operate so as to afford protection on the average in excess of the amount of protection provided for in that Schedule. The provisions of this paragraph shall not limit the use by contracting parties of any form of assistance to domestic producers permitted by other provisions of this Agreement.

5.   If any contracting party considers that a product is not receiving from another contracting party the treatment which the first contracting party believes to have been contemplated by a concession provided for in the appropriate Schedule annexed to this Agreement, it shall bring the matter directly to the attention of the other contracting party. If the latter agrees that the treatment contemplated was that claimed by the first contracting party, but declares that such treatment cannot be accorded because a court or other proper authority has ruled to the effect that the product involved cannot be classified under the tariff laws of such contracting party so as to permit the treatment contemplated in this Agreement, the two contracting parties, together with any other contracting parties substantially interested, shall enter promptly into further negotiations with a view to a compensatory adjustment of the matter.

6.   (*a*)   The specific duties and charges included in the Schedules relating to contracting parties members of the International Monetary Fund, and margins of preference in specific duties and charges maintained by such contracting parties, are expressed in the appropriate currency at the par value accepted or provisionally recognized by the Fund at the date of this Agreement. Accordingly, in case this par value is reduced consistently with the Articles of Agreement of the International Monetary Fund by more than twenty per centum, such specific duties and charges and margins of preference may be adjusted to take account of such reduction; *provided* that the CONTRACTING PARTIES (*i.e.*, the contracting parties acting jointly as provided for in Article XXV) concur that such adjustments will not impair the value of the concessions provided for in the appropriate Schedule or elsewhere in this Agreement, due account being taken of all factors which may influence the need for, or urgency of, such adjustments.

(*b*)   Similar provisions shall apply to any contracting party not a member of the Fund, as from the date on which such contracting party becomes a member of the Fund or enters into a special exchange agreement in pursuance of Article XV.

7.   The Schedules annexed to this Agreement are hereby made an integral part of Part I of this Agreement.

Ad Article II

Paragraph 2 (a)

The cross-reference, in paragraph 2 (*a*) of Article II, to paragraph 2 of Article III shall only apply after Article III has been modified by the entry into force of the amendment provided for in the Protocol Modifying Part II and Article XXVI of the General Agreement on Tariffs and Trade, dated September 14, 1948.[1]

Paragraph 2 (b)

See the note relating to paragraph 1 of Article I.

Paragraph 4

Except where otherwise specifically agreed between the contracting parties which initially negotiated the concession, the provisions of this paragraph will be applied in the light of the provisions of Article 31 of the Havana Charter.

Article XVIII

The CONTRACTING PARTIES and the contracting parties concerned shall preserve the utmost secrecy in respect of matters arising under this Article.

Paragraphs 2, 3, 7, 13 and 22

The reference to the establishment of particular industries shall apply not only to the establishment of a new industry, but also to the establishment of a new branch of production in an existing industry and to the substantial transformation of an existing industry, and to the substantial expansion of an existing industry supplying a relatively small proportion of the domestic demand. It shall also cover the reconstruction of an industry destroyed or substantially damaged as a result of hostilities or natural disasters.

Paragraph 7 (b)

A modification or withdrawal, pursuant to paragraph 7 (b), by a contracting party, other than the applicant contracting party, referred to in paragraph 7 (a), shall be made within six months of the day on which the action is taken by the applicant contracting party, and shall become effective on the thirtieth day following the day on which such modification or withdrawal has been notified to the CONTRACTING PARTIES.

---

[1]   This Protocol entered into force on 14 December 1948.

Article XXIV

Territorial Application - Frontier Traffic - Customs Unions and Free-trade Areas

1.   The provisions of this Agreement shall apply to the metropolitan customs territories of the contracting parties and to any other customs territories in respect of which this Agreement has been accepted under Article XXVI or is being applied under Article XXXIII or pursuant to the Protocol of Provisional Application. Each such customs territory shall, exclusively for the purposes of the territorial application of this Agreement, be treated as though it were a contracting party; *Provided* that the provisions of this paragraph shall not be construed to create any rights or obligations as between two or more customs territories in respect of which this Agreement has been accepted under Article XXVI or is being applied under Article XXXIII or pursuant to the Protocol of Provisional Application by a single contracting party.

2.   For the purposes of this Agreement a customs territory shall be understood to mean any territory with respect to which separate tariffs or other regulations of commerce are maintained for a substantial part of the trade of such territory with other territories.

3.   The provisions of this Agreement shall not be construed to prevent:

   (*a*)   Advantages accorded by any contracting party to adjacent countries in order to facilitate frontier traffic;

   (*b*)   Advantages accorded to the trade with the Free Territory of Trieste by countries contiguous to that territory, provided that such advantages are not in conflict with the Treaties of Peace arising out of the Second World War.

4.   The contracting parties recognize the desirability of increasing freedom of trade by the development, through voluntary agreements, of closer integration between the economies of the countries parties to such agreements. They also recognize that the purpose of a customs union or of a free-trade area should be to facilitate trade between the constituent territories and not to raise barriers to the trade of other contracting parties with such territories.

5.   Accordingly, the provisions of this Agreement shall not prevent, as between the territories of contracting parties, the formation of a customs union or of a free-trade area or the adoption of an interim agreement necessary for the formation of a customs union or of a free-trade area; *Provided* that:

   (*a*)   with respect to a customs union, or an interim agreement leading to a formation of a customs union, the duties and other regulations of commerce imposed at the institution of any such union or interim agreement in respect of trade with contracting parties not parties to such union or agreement shall not on the whole be higher or more restrictive than the general incidence of the duties and regulations of commerce applicable in the constituent territories prior to the formation of such union or the adoption of such interim agreement, as the case may be;

(b)   with respect to a free-trade area, or an interim agreement leading to the formation of a free-trade area, the duties and other regulations of commerce maintained in each if the constituent territories and applicable at the formation of such free-trade area or the adoption of such interim agreement to the trade of contracting parties not included in such area or not parties to such agreement shall not be higher or more restrictive than the corresponding duties and other regulations of commerce existing in the same constituent territories prior to the formation of the free-trade area, or interim agreement as the case may be; and

(c)   any interim agreement referred to in subparagraphs (a) and (b) shall include a plan and schedule for the formation of such a customs union or of such a free-trade area within a reasonable length of time.

6.   If, in fulfilling the requirements of subparagraph 5 (a), a contracting party proposes to increase any rate of duty inconsistently with the provisions of Article II, the procedure set forth in Article XXVIII shall apply. In providing for compensatory adjustment, due account shall be taken of the compensation already afforded by the reduction brought about in the corresponding duty of the other constituents of the union.

7.   (a)   Any contracting party deciding to enter into a customs union or free-trade area, or an interim agreement leading to the formation of such a union or area, shall promptly notify the CONTRACTING PARTIES and shall make available to them such information regarding the proposed union or area as will enable them to make such reports and recommendations to contracting parties as they may deem appropriate.

(b)   If, after having studied the plan and schedule included in an interim agreement referred to in paragraph 5 in consultation with the parties to that agreement and taking due account of the information made available in accordance with the provisions of subparagraph (a), the CONTRACTING PARTIES find that such agreement is not likely to result in the formation of a customs union or of a free-trade area within the period contemplated by the parties to the agreement or that such period is not a reasonable one, the CONTRACTING PARTIES shall make recommendations to the parties to the agreement. The parties shall not maintain or put into force, as the case may be, such agreement if they are not prepared to modify it in accordance with these recommendations.

(c)   Any substantial change in the plan or schedule referred to in paragraph 5 (c) shall be communicated to the CONTRACTING PARTIES, which may request the contracting parties concerned to consult with them if the change seems likely to jeopardize or delay unduly the formation of the customs union or of the free-trade area.

8.   For the purposes of this Agreement:

(a)   A customs union shall be understood to mean the substitution of a single customs territory for two or more customs territories, so that

(i)   duties and other restrictive regulations of commerce (except, where necessary, those permitted under Articles XI, XII, XIII, XIV, XV and XX) are eliminated with respect to substantially all the trade between the constituent territories of the union or at least with respect to substantially all the trade in products originating in such territories, and,

(ii) subject to the provisions of paragraph 9, substantially the same duties and other regulations of commerce are applied by each of the members of the union to the trade of territories not included in the union;

(b)   A free-trade area shall be understood to mean a group of two or more customs territories in which the duties and other restrictive regulations of commerce (except, where necessary, those permitted under Articles XI, XII, XIII, XIV, XV and XX) are eliminated on substantially all the trade between the constituent territories in products originating in such territories.

9.   The preferences referred to in paragraph 2 of Article I shall not be affected by the formation of a customs union or of a free-trade area but may be eliminated or adjusted by means of negotiations with contracting parties affected.* This procedure of negotiations with affected contracting parties shall, in particular, apply to the elimination of preferences required to conform with the provisions of paragraph 8 (a)(i) and paragraph 8 (b).

10.   The CONTRACTING PARTIES may by a two-thirds majority approve proposals which do not fully comply with the requirements of paragraphs 5 to 9 inclusive, provided that such proposals lead to the formation of a customs union or a free-trade area in the sense of this Article.

11.   Taking into account the exceptional circumstances arising out of the establishment of India and Pakistan as independent States and recognizing the fact that they have long constituted an economic unit, the contracting parties agree that the provisions of this Agreement shall not prevent the two countries from entering into special arrangements with respect to the trade between them, pending the establishment of their mutual trade relations on a definitive basis.*

12.   Each contracting party shall take such reasonable measures as may be available to it to ensure observance of the provisions of this Agreement by the regional and local governments and authorities within its territories.

Ad Article XXIV

Paragraph 9

It is understood that the provisions of Article I would require that, when a product which has been imported into the territory of a member of a customs union or free-trade area at a preferential rate of duty is re-exported to the territory of another member of such union or area, the latter member should collect a duty equal to the difference between the duty already paid and any higher duty that would be payable if the product were being imported directly into its territory.

Paragraph 11

Measures adopted by India and Pakistan in order to carry out definitive trade arrangements between them, once they have been agreed upon, might depart from particular provisions of this Agreement, but these measures would in general be consistent with the objectives of the Agreement.

Article XXVII

Withholding or Withdrawal of Concessions

Any contracting party shall at any time be free to withhold or to withdraw in whole or in part any concession, provided for in the appropriate Schedule annexed to this Agreement, in respect of which such contracting party determines that it was initially negotiated with a government which has not become, or has ceased to be, a contracting party. A contracting party taking such action shall notify the CONTRACTING PARTIES and, upon request, consult with contracting parties which have a substantial interest in the product concerned.

Article XXVIII

Modification of Schedules

1. On the first day of each three-year period, the first period beginning on 1 January 1958 (or on the first day of any other period* that may be specified by the CONTRACTING PARTIES by two-thirds of the votes cast) a contracting party (hereafter in this Article referred to as the "applicant contracting party") may, by negotiation and agreement with any contracting party with which such concession was initially negotiated and with any other contracting party determined by the CONTRACTING PARTIES to have a principal supplying interest* (which two preceding categories of contracting parties, together with the applicant contracting party, are in this Article hereinafter referred to as the "contracting parties primarily concerned"), and subject to consultation with any other contracting party determined by the CONTRACTING PARTIES to have a substantial interest* in such concession, modify or withdraw a concession* included in the appropriate schedule annexed to this Agreement.

2. In such negotiations and agreement, which may include provision for compensatory adjustment with respect to other products, the contracting parties concerned shall endeavour to maintain a general level of reciprocal and mutually advantageous concessions not less favourable to trade than that provided for in this Agreement prior to such negotiations.

3. (*a*) If agreement between the contracting parties primarily concerned cannot be reached before 1 January 1958 or before the expiration of a period envisaged in paragraph 1 of this Article, the contracting party which proposes to modify or withdraw the concession shall, nevertheless, be free to do so and if such action is taken any contracting party with which such concession was initially negotiated, any contracting party determined under paragraph 1 to have a principal supplying interest and any contracting party determined under paragraph 1 to have a substantial interest shall then be free not later than six months after such action is taken, to withdraw, upon the expiration of thirty days from the day on which written notice of such withdrawal is received by the CONTRACTING PARTIES, substantially equivalent concessions initially negotiated with the applicant contracting party.

(*b*) If agreement between the contracting parties primarily concerned is reached but any other contracting party determined under paragraph 1 of this Article to have a substantial interest is not satisfied, such other contracting party shall be free, not later than six months after action under such agreement is taken, to withdraw, upon the expiration of thirty days from the day on which written notice of such withdrawal is received by the CONTRACTING PARTIES, substantially equivalent concessions initially negotiated with the applicant contracting party.

4. The CONTRACTING PARTIES may, at any time, in special circumstances, authorize* a contracting party to enter into negotiations for modification or withdrawal of a concession included in the appropriate Schedule annexed to this Agreement subject to the following procedures and conditions:

(*a*) Such negotiations* and any related consultations shall be conducted in accordance with the provisions of paragraph 1 and 2 of this Article.

(*b*) If agreement between the contracting parties primarily concerned is reached in the negotiations, the provisions of paragraph 3 (*b*) of this Article shall apply.

(*c*) If agreement between the contracting parties primarily concerned is not reached within a period of sixty days* after negotiations have been authorized, or within such longer period as the CONTRACTING PARTIES may have prescribed, the applicant contracting party may refer the matter to the CONTRACTING PARTIES.

(*d*) Upon such reference, the CONTRACTING PARTIES shall promptly examine the matter and submit their views to the contracting parties primarily concerned with the aim of achieving a settlement. If a settlement is reached, the provisions of paragraph 3 (*b*) shall apply as if agreement between the contracting parties primarily concerned had been reached. If no settlement is reached between the contracting parties primarily concerned, the applicant contracting party shall be free to modify or withdraw the concession, unless the CONTRACTING PARTIES determine that the applicant contracting party has unreasonably failed to offer adequate compensation.* If such action is taken, any contracting party with which the concession was initially negotiated, any contracting party determined under paragraph 4 (*a*) to have a principal supplying interest and any contracting party determined under paragraph 4 (*a*) to have a substantial interest, shall be free, not later than six months after such action is taken, to modify or withdraw, upon the expiration of thirty days from the day on which written notice of such withdrawal is received by the CONTRACTING PARTIES, substantially equivalent concessions initially negotiated with applicant contracting party.

5.   Before 1 January 1958 and before the end of any period envisaged in paragraph 1 a contracting party may elect by notifying the CONTRACTING PARTIES to reserve the right, for the duration of the next period, to modify the appropriate Schedule in accordance with the procedures of paragraph 1 to 3. If a contracting party so elects, other contracting parties shall have the right, during the same period, to modify or withdraw, in accordance with the same procedures, concessions initially negotiated with that contracting party.

Ad Article XXVIII

The CONTRACTING PARTIES and each contracting party concerned should arrange to conduct the negotiations and consultations with the greatest possible secrecy in order to avoid premature disclosure of details of prospective tariff changes. The CONTRACTING PARTIES shall be informed immediately of all changes in national tariffs resulting from recourse to this Article.

Paragraph 1

1.   If the CONTRACTING PARTIES specify a period other than a three-year period, a contracting party may act pursuant to paragraph 1 or paragraph 3 of Article XXVIII on the first day following the expiration of such other period and, unless the CONTRACTING PARTIES have again specified another period, subsequent periods will be three-year periods following the expiration of such specified period.

2.   The provision that on 1 January 1958, and on other days determined pursuant to paragraph 1, a contracting party "may ... modify or withdraw a concession" means that on such day, and on the first day after the end of each period, the legal obligation of such contracting party under Article II is altered; it does not mean that the changes in its customs tariff should necessarily be made effective on that day. If a tariff change resulting from negotiations

undertaken pursuant to this Article is delayed, the entry into force of any compensatory concessions may be similarly delayed.

3.　　Not earlier than six months, nor later than three months, prior to 1 January 1958, or to the termination date of any subsequent period, a contracting party wishing to modify or withdraw any concession embodied in the appropriate Schedule, should notify the CONTRACTING PARTIES to this effect. The CONTRACTING PARTIES shall then determine the contracting party or contracting parties with which the negotiations or consultations referred to in paragraph 1 shall take place. Any contracting party so determined shall participate in such negotiations or consultations with the applicant contracting party with the aim of reaching agreement before the end of the period. Any extension of the assured life of the Schedules shall relate to the Schedules as modified after such negotiations, in accordance with paragraphs 1, 2, and 3 of Article XXVIII. If the CONTRACTING PARTIES are arranging for multilateral tariff negotiations to take place within the period of six months before 1 January 1958, or before any other day determined pursuant to paragraph 1, they shall include in the arrangements for such negotiations suitable procedures for carrying out the negotiations referred to in this paragraph.

4.　　The object of providing for the participation in the negotiation of any contracting party with a principle supplying interest, in addition to any contracting party with which the concession was originally negotiated, is to ensure that a contracting party with a larger share in the trade affected by the concession than a contracting party with which the concession was originally negotiated shall have an effective opportunity to protect the contractual right which it enjoys under this Agreement. On the other hand, it is not intended that the scope of the negotiations should be such as to make negotiations and agreement under Article XXVIII unduly difficult nor to create complications in the application of this Article in the future to concessions which result from negotiations thereunder. Accordingly, the CONTRACTING PARTIES should only determine that a contracting party has a principal supplying interest if that contracting party has had, over a reasonable period of time prior to the negotiations, a larger share in the market of the applicant contracting party than a contracting party with which the concession was initially negotiated or would, in the judgement of the CONTRACTING PARTIES, have had such a share in the absence of discriminatory quantitative restrictions maintained by the applicant contracting party. It would therefore not be appropriate for the CONTRACTING PARTIES to determine that more than one contracting party, or in those exceptional cases where there is near equality more than two contracting parties, had a principal supplying interest.

5.　　Notwithstanding the definition of a principal supplying interest in note 4 to paragraph 1, the CONTRACTING PARTIES may exceptionally determine that a contracting party has a principal supplying interest if the concession in question affects trade which constitutes a major part of the total exports of such contracting party.

6.   It is not intended that provision for participation in the negotiations of any contracting party with a principal supplying interest, and for consultation with any contracting party having a substantial interest in the concession which the applicant contracting party is seeking to modify or withdraw, should have the effect that it should have to pay compensation or suffer retaliation greater than the withdrawal or modification sought, judged in the light of the conditions of trade at the time of the proposed withdrawal or modification, making allowance for any discriminatory quantitative restrictions maintained by the applicant contracting party.

7.   The expression "substantial interest" is not capable of a precise definition and accordingly may present difficulties for the CONTRACTING PARTIES. It is, however, intended to be construed to cover only those contracting parties which have, or in the absence of discriminatory quantitative restrictions affecting their exports could reasonably be expected to have, a significant share in the market of the contracting party seeking to modify or withdraw the concession.

Paragraph 4

1.   Any request for authorization to enter into negotiations shall be accompanied by all relevant statistical and other data. A decision on such request shall be made within thirty days of its submission.

2.   It is recognized that to permit certain contracting parties, depending in large measure on a relatively small number of primary commodities and relying on the tariff as an important aid for furthering diversification of their economies or as an important source of revenue, normally to negotiate for the modification or withdrawal of concessions only under paragraph 1 of Article XXVIII, might cause them at such time to make modifications or withdrawals which in the long run would prove unnecessary. To avoid such a situation the CONTRACTING PARTIES shall authorize any such contracting party, under paragraph 4, to enter into negotiations unless they consider this would result in, or contribute substantially towards, such an increase in tariff levels as to threaten the stability of the Schedules to this Agreement or lead to undue disturbance of international trade.

3.   It is expected that negotiations authorized under paragraph 4 for modification or withdrawal of a single item, or a very small group of items, could normally be brought to a conclusion in sixty days. It is recognized, however, that such a period will be inadequate for cases involving negotiations for the modification or withdrawal of a larger number of items and in such cases, therefore, it would be appropriate for the CONTRACTING PARTIES to prescribe a longer period.

4.   The determination referred to in paragraph 4 (*d*) shall be made by the CONTRACTING PARTIES within thirty days of the submission of the matter to them unless the applicant contracting party agrees to a longer period.

5.   In determining under paragraph 4 (*d*) whether an applicant contracting party has unreasonably failed to offer adequate compensation, it is understood that the CONTRACTING PARTIES will take due account of the special position of a contracting party which has bound a high proportion of its tariffs at very low rates of duty and to this extent has less scope than other contracting parties to make compensatory adjustment.

Article XXVIII *bis*

Tariff Negotiations

1.   The contracting parties recognize that customs duties often constitute serious obstacles to trade; thus negotiations on a reciprocal and mutually advantageous basis, directed to the substantial reduction of the general level of tariffs and other charges on imports and exports and in particular to the reduction of such high tariffs as discourage the importation even of minimum quantities, and conducted with due regard to the objectives of this Agreement and the varying needs of individual contracting parties, are of great importance to the expansion of international trade. The CONTRACTING PARTIES may therefore sponsor such negotiations from time to time.

2.   (*a*)   Negotiations under this Article may be carried out on a selective product-by-product basis or by the application of such multilateral procedures as may be accepted by the contracting parties concerned. Such negotiations may be directed towards the reduction of duties, the binding of duties at then existing levels or undertakings that individual duties or the average duties on specified categories of products shall not exceed specified levels. The binding against increase of low duties or of duty-free treatment shall, in principle, be recognized as a concession equivalent in value to the reduction of high duties.

(*b*)   The contracting parties recognize that in general the success of multilateral negotiations would depend on the participation of all contracting parties which conduct a substantial proportion of their external trade with one another.

3.   Negotiations shall be conducted on a basis which affords adequate opportunity to take into account:

(*a*)   the needs of individual contracting parties and individual industries;

(*b*)   the needs of less-developed countries for a more flexible use of tariff protection to assist their economic development and the special needs of these countries to maintain tariffs for revenue purposes; and

(*c*)   all other relevant circumstances, including the fiscal,* developmental, strategic and other needs of the contracting parties concerned.

Ad Article XXVIII *bis*

Paragraph 3

It is understood that the reference to fiscal needs would include the revenues aspect of duties and particularly duties imposed primarily for revenue purpose, or duties imposed on products which can be substituted for products subject to revenue duties to prevent the avoidance of such duties.

Article XXXV

Non-application of the Agreement between Particular Contracting Parties

1.   This Agreement, or alternatively Article II of this Agreement, shall not apply as between any contracting party and any other contracting party if:

(*a*)   the two contracting parties have not entered into tariff negotiations with each other, and

(*b*)   either of the contracting parties, at the time either becomes a contracting party, does not consent to such application.

2.   The CONTRACTING PARTIES may review the operation of this Article in particular cases at the request of any contracting party and make appropriate recommendations.

Article XXXVI

Principles and Objectives

1.   The contracting parties,

(*a*)   recalling that the basic objectives of this Agreement include the raising of standards of living and the progressive development of the economies of all contracting parties, and considering that the attainment of these objectives is particularly urgent for less-developed contracting parties;

(*b*)   considering that export earnings of the less-developed contracting parties can play a vital part in their economic development and that the extent of this contribution depends on the prices paid by the less-developed contracting parties for essential imports, the volume of their exports, and the prices received for these exports;

(*c*)   noting, that there is a wide gap between standards of living in less-developed countries and in other countries;

(*d*)   recognizing that individual and joint action is essential to further the development of the economies of less-developed contracting parties and to bring about a rapid advance in the standards of living in these countries;

(*e*)   recognizing that international trade as a means of achieving economic and social advancement should be governed by such rules and procedures - and measures in conformity with such rules and procedures - as are consistent with the objectives set forth in this Article;

(*f*) noting that the CONTRACTING PARTIES may enable less-developed contracting parties to use special measures to promote their trade and development;

agree as follows.

2. There is need for a rapid and sustained expansion of the export earnings of the less-developed contracting parties.

3. There is need for positive efforts designed to ensure that less-developed contracting parties secure a share in the growth in international trade commensurate with the needs of their economic development.

4. Given the continued dependence of many less-developed contracting parties on the exportation of a limited range of primary products,* there is need to provide in the largest possible measure more favourable and acceptable conditions of access to world markets for these products, and wherever appropriate to devise measures designed to stabilize and improve conditions of world markets in these products, including in particular measures designed to attain stable, equitable and remunerative prices, thus permitting an expansion of world trade and demand and a dynamic and steady growth of the real export earnings of these countries so as to provide them with expanding resources for their economic development.

5. The rapid expansion of the economies of the less-developed contracting parties will be facilitated by a diversification of the structure of their economies and the avoidance of an excessive dependence on the export of primary products. There is, therefore, need for increased access in the largest possible measure to markets under favourable conditions for processed and manufactured products currently or potentially of particular export interest to less-developed contracting parties.

6. Because of the chronic deficiency in the export proceeds and other foreign exchange earnings of less-developed contracting parties, there are important inter-relationships between trade and financial assistance to development. There is, therefore, need for close and continuing collaboration between the CONTRACTING PARTIES and the international lending agencies so that they can contribute most effectively to alleviating the burdens these less-developed contracting parties assume in the interest of their economic development.

7. There is need for appropriate collaboration between the CONTRACTING PARTIES, other intergovernmental bodies and the organs and agencies of the United Nations system, whose activities relate to the trade and economic development of less-developed countries.

8. The developed contracting parties do not expect reciprocity for commitments made by them in trade negotiations to reduce or remove tariffs and other barriers to the trade of less-developed contracting parties.

9.   The adoption of measures to give effect to these principles and objectives shall be a matter of conscious and purposeful effort on the part of the contracting parties both individually and jointly.

Ad Article XXXVI

Paragraph 1

This Article is based upon the objectives set forth in Article I as it will be amended by Section A of paragraph 1 of the Protocol Amending Part I and Articles XXIX and XXX when that Protocol enters into force.[2]

Paragraph 4

The term "primary products" includes agricultural products, *vide* paragraph 2 of the note *ad* Article XVI, Section B.

Paragraph 5

A diversification programme would generally include the intensification of activities for the processing of primary products and the development of manufacturing industries, taking into account the situation of the particular contracting party and the world outlook for production and consumption of different commodities.

Paragraph 8

It is understood that the phrase "do not expect reciprocity" means, in accordance with the objectives set forth in this Article, that the less-developed contracting parties should not be expected, in the course of trade negotiations, to make contributions which are inconsistent with their individual development, financial and trade needs, taking into consideration past trade developments.

This paragraph would apply in the event of action under Section A of Article XVIII, Article XXVIII, Article XXVIII *bis* (Article XXIX after the amendment set forth in Section A of paragraph 1 of the Protocol Amending Part I and Articles XXIX and XXX shall have become effective[3]), Article XXXIII, or any other procedure under this Agreement.

---

[2]   This Protocol was abandoned on 1 January 1968.

[3]   This Protocol was abandoned on 1 January 1968.

DIFFERENTIAL AND MORE FAVOURABLE TREATMENT RECIPROCITY AND FULLER PARTICIPATION OF DEVELOPING COUNTRIES

Decision of 28 November 1979
(L/4903)

Following negotiations within the framework of the Multilateral Trade Negotiations, the CONTRACTING PARTIES *decide* as follows:

1. Notwithstanding the provisions of Article I of the General Agreement, contracting parties may accord differential and more favourable treatment to developing countries[1], without according such treatment to other contracting parties.

2. The provisions of paragraph 1 apply to the following:[2]

   (*a*) Preferential tariff treatment accorded by developed contracting parties to products originating in developing countries in accordance with the Generalized System of Preferences,[3]

   (*b*) Differential and more favourable treatment with respect to the provisions of the General Agreement concerning non-tariff measures governed by the provisions of instruments multilaterally negotiated under the auspices of the GATT;

   (*c*) Regional or global arrangements entered into amongst less-developed contracting parties for the mutual reduction or elimination of tariffs and, in accordance with criteria or conditions which may be prescribed by the CONTRACTING PARTIES, for the mutual reduction or elimination of non-tariff measures, on products imported from one another

   (*d*) Special treatment of the least developed among the developing countries in the context of any general or specific measures in favour of developing countries.

3. Any differential and more favourable treatment provided under this clause:

---

[1] The words Adeveloping countries≅ as used in this text are to be understood to refer also to developing territories.

[2] It would remain open for the CONTRACTING PARTIES to consider on an *ad hoc* basis under the GATT provisions for joint action any proposals for differential and more favourable treatment not falling within the scope of this paragraph.

[3] As described in the Decision of the CONTRACTING PARTIES of 25 June 1971, relating to the establishment of Ageneralized, non-reciprocal and non discriminatory preferences beneficial to the developing countries≅ (BISD 18S/24).

(*a*)   shall be designed to facilitate and promote the trade of developing countries and not to raise barriers to or create undue difficulties for the trade of any other contracting parties;

(*b*)   shall not constitute an impediment to the reduction or elimination of tariffs and other restrictions to trade on a most-favoured-nation basis;

(*c*)   shall in the case of such treatment accorded by developed contracting parties to developing countries be designed and, if necessary, modified, to respond positively to the development, financial and trade needs of developing countries.

4.   Any contracting party taking action to introduce an arrangement pursuant to paragraphs 1, 2 and 3 above or subsequently taking action to introduce modification or withdrawal of the differential and more favourable treatment so provided shall:[4]

(*a*)   notify the CONTRACTING PARTIES and furnish them with all the information they may deem appropriate relating to such action;

(*b*)   afford adequate opportunity for prompt consultations at the request of any interested contracting party with respect to any difficulty or matter that may arise. The CONTRACTING PARTIES shall, if requested to do so by such contracting party, consult with all contracting parties concerned with respect to the matter with a view to reaching solutions satisfactory to all such contracting parties.

5.   The developed countries do not expect reciprocity for commitments made by them in trade negotiations to reduce or remove tariffs and other barriers to the trade of developing countries, i.e., the developed countries do not expect the developing countries, in the course of trade negotiations, to make contributions which are inconsistent with their individual development, financial and trade needs. Developed contracting parties shall therefore not seek, neither shall less-developed contracting parties be required to make, concessions that are inconsistent with the latters' development, financial and trade needs.

6.   Having regard to the special economic difficulties and the particular development, financial and trade needs of the least-developed countries, the developed countries shall exercise the utmost restraint in seeking any concessions or contributions for commitments made by them to reduce or remove tariffs and other barriers to the trade of such countries, and the least-developed countries shall not be expected to make concessions or contributions that are inconsistent with the recognition of their particular situation and problems.

---

[4]   Nothing in these provisions shall affect the rights of contracting parties under the General Agreement.

7.   The concessions and contributions made and the obligations assumed by developed and less-developed contracting parties under the provisions of the General Agreement should promote the basic objectives of the Agreement, including those embodied in the Preamble and in Article XXXVI. Less-developed contracting parties expect that their capacity to make contributions or negotiated concessions or take other mutually agreed action under the provisions and procedures of the General Agreement would improve with the progressive development of their economies and improvement in their trade situation and they would accordingly expect to participate more fully in the framework of rights and obligations under the General Agreement.

8.   Particular account shall be taken of the serious difficulty of the least-developed countries in making concessions and contributions in view of their special economic situation and their development, financial and trade needs.

9.   The contracting parties will collaborate in arrangements for review of the operation of these provisions, bearing in mind the need for individual and joint efforts by contracting parties to meet the development needs of developing countries and the objectives of the General Agreement.

UNDERSTANDING ON THE INTERPRETATION OF ARTICLE II:1(b) OF THE GENERAL AGREEMENT ON TARIFFS AND TRADE 1994

Members hereby *agree* as follows:

1.   In order to ensure transparency of the legal rights and obligations deriving from paragraph 1(b) of Article II, the nature and level of any "other duties or charges" levied on bound tariff items, as referred to in that provision, shall be recorded in the Schedules of concessions annexed to GATT 1994 against the tariff item to which they apply. It is understood that such recording does not change the legal character of "other duties or charges".

2.   The date as of which "other duties or charges" are bound, for the purposes of Article II, shall be 15 April 1994. "Other duties or charges" shall therefore be recorded in the Schedules at the levels applying on this date. At each subsequent renegotiation of a concession or negotiation of a new concession the applicable date for the tariff item in question shall become the date of the incorporation of the new concession in the appropriate Schedule. However, the date of the instrument by which a concession on any particular tariff item was first incorporated into GATT 1947 or GATT 1994 shall also continue to be recorded in column 6 of the Loose-Leaf Schedules.

3.   "Other duties or charges" shall be recorded in respect of all tariff bindings.

4.   Where a tariff item has previously been the subject of a concession, the level of "other duties or charges" recorded in the appropriate Schedule shall not be higher than the level obtaining at the time of the first incorporation of the concession in that Schedule. It will be open to any Member to challenge the existence of an "other duty or charge", on the ground that no such "other duty or charge" existed at the time of the original binding of the item in question, as well as the consistency of the recorded level of any "other duty or charge" with the previously bound level, for a period of three years after the date of entry into force of the WTO Agreement or three years after the date of deposit with the Director-General of the WTO of the instrument incorporating the Schedule in question into GATT 1994, if that is a later date.

5.   The recording of "other duties or charges" in the Schedules is without prejudice to their consistency with rights and obligations under GATT 1994 other than those affected by paragraph 4. All Members retain the right to challenge, at any time, the consistency of any "other duty or charge" with such obligations.

6.   For the purposes of this Understanding, the provisions of Articles XXII and XXIII of GATT 1994 as elaborated and applied by the Dispute Settlement Understanding shall apply.

7.   "Other duties or charges" omitted from a Schedule at the time of deposit of the instrument incorporating the Schedule in question into GATT 1994 with, until the date of entry into force of the WTO Agreement, the Director-General to the CONTRACTING PARTIES to GATT 1947 or,

thereafter, with the Director-General of the WTO, shall not subsequently be added to it and any "other duty or charge" recorded at a level lower than that prevailing on the applicable date shall not be restored to that level unless such additions or changes are made within six months of the date of deposit of the instrument.

8.   The decision in paragraph 2 regarding the date applicable to each concession for the purposes of paragraph 1(b) of Article II of GATT 1994 supersedes the decision regarding the applicable date taken on 26 March 1980 (BISD 27S/24).

UNDERSTANDING ON THE INTERPRETATION OF ARTICLE XXVIII OF THE GENERAL AGREEMENT ON TARIFFS AND TRADE 1994

Members hereby *agree* as follows:

1.   For the purposes of modification or withdrawal of a concession, the Member which has the highest ratio of exports affected by the concession (i.e. exports of the product to the market of the Member modifying or withdrawing the concession) to its total exports shall be deemed to have a principal supplying interest if it does not already have an initial negotiating right or a principal supplying interest as provided for in paragraph 1 of Article XXVIII. It is however agreed that this paragraph will be reviewed by the Council for Trade in Goods five years from the date of entry into force of the WTO Agreement with a view to deciding whether this criterion has worked satisfactorily in securing a redistribution of negotiating rights in favour of small and medium-sized exporting Members. If this is not the case, consideration will be given to possible improvements, including, in the light of the availability of adequate data, the adoption of a criterion based on the ratio of exports affected by the concession to exports to all markets of the product in question.

2.   Where a Member considers that it has a principal supplying interest in terms of paragraph 1, it should communicate its claim in writing, with supporting evidence, to the Member proposing to modify or withdraw a concession, and at the same time inform the Secretariat. Paragraph 4 of the "Procedures for Negotiations under Article XXVIII" adopted on 10 November 1980 (BISD 27S/26-28) shall apply in these cases.

3.   In the determination of which Members have a principal supplying interest (whether as provided for in paragraph 1 above or in paragraph 1 of Article XXVIII) or substantial interest, only trade in the affected product which has taken place on an MFN basis shall be taken into consideration. However, trade in the affected product which has taken place under non-contractual preferences shall also be taken into account if the trade in question has ceased to benefit from such preferential treatment, thus becoming MFN trade, at the time of the negotiation for the modification or withdrawal of the concession, or will do so by the conclusion of that negotiation.

4.   When a tariff concession is modified or withdrawn on a new product (i.e. a product for which three years' trade statistics are not available) the Member possessing initial negotiating rights on the tariff line where the product is or was formerly classified shall be deemed to have an initial negotiating right in the concession in question. The determination of principal supplying and substantial interests and the calculation of compensation shall take into account, *inter alia*, production capacity and investment in the affected product in the exporting Member and estimates of export growth, as well as forecasts of demand for the product in the importing Member. For the purposes of this paragraph, "new product" is understood to include a tariff item created by means of a breakout from an existing tariff line.

5.　　Where a Member considers that it has a principal supplying or a substantial interest in terms of paragraph 4, it should communicate its claim in writing, with supporting evidence, to the Member proposing to modify or withdraw a concession, and at the same time inform the Secretariat. Paragraph 4 of the above-mentioned "Procedures for Negotiations under Article XXVIII" shall apply in these cases.

6.　　When an unlimited tariff concession is replaced by a tariff rate quota, the amount of compensation provided should exceed the amount of the trade actually affected by the modification of the concession. The basis for the calculation of compensation should be the amount by which future trade prospects exceed the level of the quota. It is understood that the calculation of future trade prospects should be based on the greater of:

(a)　　the average annual trade in the most recent representative three-year period, increased by the average annual growth rate of imports in that same period, or by 10 per cent, whichever is the greater; or

(b)　　trade in the most recent year increased by 10 per cent.

In no case shall a Member's liability for compensation exceed that which would be entailed by complete withdrawal of the concession.

7.　　Any Member having a principal supplying interest, whether as provided for in paragraph 1 above or in paragraph 1 of Article XXVIII, in a concession which is modified or withdrawn shall be accorded an initial negotiating right in the compensatory concessions, unless another form of compensation is agreed by the Members concerned.

APPENDIX B

DECLARATIONS AND DECISIONS COMMENCING ROUNDS OF MULTILATERAL TRADE NEGOTIATIONS

Procedures for Giving Effect to Certain Provisions of the Charter of the International Trade Organization by Means of a General Agreement on Tariffs and Trade Among the Members of the Preparatory Committee

Annecy Tariff Conference, 1949

Memorandum on Tariff Negotiations

Procedures Adopted for Torquay Tariff Conference

Plans for Tariff Reduction and Rules and Procedures for the 1956 Tariff Conference

Rules and Procedures for the Tariff Conference Commencing in Geneva on 1 September 1960

Conclusions and Resolutions adopted on 21 May 1963

Declaration of Ministers Approved at Tokyo on 14 September 1973

Ministerial Declaration of 20 September 1986

GENEVA TARIFF NEGOTIATIONS, 1947

ANNEXURE 10[1]

MULTILATERAL TRADE-AGREEMENT NEGOTIATIONS

Procedures for Giving Effect to Certain Provisions of the Charter of the International Trade Organization by Means of a General Agreement on Tariffs and Trade Among the Members of the Preparatory Committee

Section A. - Introduction

The Preparatory Committee has resolved to recommend to the governments concerned that the Committee sponsor traffic and preference negotiations among its members to be held in Geneva commencing 8 April, 1947.[2] Upon the completion of these negotiations the Preparatory Committee would be in a position to complete its formulation of the Charter and approve and recommend it for the consideration of the International Conference on Trade and Employment which would be in a position to consider the Charter in the light of the assurance afforded as to the implementation of the tariff provisions.

Section B. - Proposed Negotiations among Members of Preparatory Committee

General

The results of the negotiations among the members of the Preparatory Committee will need to be fitted into the framework of the International Trade Organization after the Charter has been adopted. The negotiations must, therefore, proceed in accordance with the relevant provisions of the Charter as already provisionally formulated by the Preparatory Committee. In the light of these provisions, the comments and explanations which follow may be useful as a guide to the negotiations.

General Objectives

An ultimate objective of the Charter, elaborated in Article 24, is to bring about the substantial reduction of tariffs and the elimination of tariff preferences. The negotiations among the members of the Preparatory Committee should, therefore, be directed to this end and every effort should be made to achieve as much progress toward this goal as may be practicable in the circumstances, having regard to the provisions of the Charter as a whole.

---

[1] From the Report of the First Session of the Preparatory Committee of the United Nations Conference on Trade and Employment, London, October 1946.

[2] See Annexure 7.

Section C. - General Nature of Negotiations

1.   Article 24 of the Charter provides that tariff negotiations shall be on a "reciprocal" and "mutually advantageous" basis. This means that no country would be expected to grant concessions unilaterally, without action by others, or to grant concessions to others which are not adequately counterbalanced by concessions in return.

2.   The proposed negotiations arc also to be conducted on a selective, product-by-product basis which will afford an adequate opportunity for taking into account the circumstances surrounding each   product on which a concession may be considered. Under this selective procedure a particular product may or may not be made the subject of a tariff concession by a particular country. If it is decided to grant a concession on the product, the concession may either take the form of a binding of the tariff against increase or a reduction of the tariff. If the tariff on the product is reduced, the reduction may be made in greater or lesser amount. Thus, in seeking to obtain the substantial reduction of tariffs as a general objective, there is ample flexibility under the selective procedure for taking into account the needs of individual countries and individual industries.

3.   The same considerations and procedures would apply in the case of import tariff preferences, it being understood that, in accordance with the principles set forth in Article 14 of the Charter (Most-Favoured-Nation Treatment) any preferences remaining after the negotiations may not be increased.

4.   The various observations in this report regarding the negotiation of tariffs and tariff preferences should be read as applying (*mutatis mutandis*) to the negotiation of state-trading margins under Article 31 of the Charter.

Section D. - General Rules to be observed in Negotiations

Paragraph (I) of Article 24 of the Charter sets forth the following self-explanatory rules to be observed during the negotiations:-

"(*a*)   Prior International commitments shall not be permitted to stand in the way of negotiations with respect to tariff preferences, it being understood that action resulting from such negotiations shall not require the modification of existing international obligations except by agreement between the contracting parties or, failing that, by termination of such obligations in accordance with their terms.

(*b*)   All negotiated reductions in most-favoured-nation import tariffs shall operate automatically to reduce or eliminate margins of preference.

(*c*)   The binding or consolidation of low tariffs or of tariff-free treatment shall in principle be recognized as a concession equivalent in value to the substantial reduction of high tariffs or the elimination of tariff preferences."

Section E. - Miscellaneous Rules for Guidance

There are a number of additional questions which should be borne in mind in preparing for the proposed tariff negotiations among the members of the Preparatory Committee.

Base Date for Negotiations

1.   Paragraph (I) of Article 14 of the Charter would except from the most-favoured-nation provisions preferences "which do not exceed the preferences remaining after . . . negotiations." This means that all margins of preference remaining after negotiations would be bound against increase. Also, as explained above, Article 14 requires that reductions of most-favoured-nation rates of duties shall operate automatically to reduce or eliminate margins of preference.

2.   In order to determine what residual preferences shall be bound against increase under Article 14, and in order to determine what preferences shall be reduced or eliminated automatically under Article 24, it is necessary to establish a date which will fix the height of the preferences in effect prior to the negotiations.

3.   It would be desirable for such purposes to fix a single date, common to all the countries participating in the negotiations. However, the discussions during the First Session of the Preparatory Committee indicate that the establishment of a common date presents certain difficulties and may not be practicable. It is, therefore, suggested that immediately following the close of the First Session each member of the Committee concerned should inform the Secretariat of the United Nations as to the date which it proposes to use as the base date for negotiations with respect to preferences. The Secretariat will promptly inform the other members. The base date for negotiations established by any country granting preferences should hold good for its negotiations on all products with all other members of the Preparatory Committee, and should not vary from member to member or from product to product.

Avoidance of New Tariff or other Restrictive Measures

It is important that members do not effect new tariff measures prior to the negotiations which would tend to prejudice the success of the negotiations in achieving progress toward the objectives set forth in Article 24, and they should not seek to improve their bargaining position by tariff or other restrictive measures in preparation for the negotiations. Changes in the form of tariffs, or changes in tariffs owing to the depreciation or devaluation of the currency of the country maintaining the tariffs, which do not result in an increase of the protective incidence of the tariff, should not be considered as new tariff increases under this paragraph.

Principal Supplier Rule

1.   It is generally agreed that the negotiations should proceed on the basis of the "principal supplier" rule, as defined in this paragraph. This means that each country would be expected to consider the granting of tariff or preference concessions only on products of which the other members of the Preparatory Committee, are, or are likely to be, principal suppliers.

2.   In determining whether, on the basis of the "principal supplier" rule, a product is to be included in the negotiations, reference should be had not merely to whether a particular member of the Preparatory Committee is, or may become, a principal supplier, but to whether the members of the Committee, taken as a whole, supply, or are likely to supply, a principal part of the product in question.

3.   In other words, if a principal part of total imports of a particular product into the territory of a particular member is supplied by the other members of the Preparatory Committee taken together, then the importing member should, as a general rule, be willing to include that product in the negotiations, even though no single other member of the Committee, taken by itself, supplies a principal part of the total imports of the product.

4.   In estimating the future prospects of a member, or the members taken together, to become a principal supplier of a product, consideration should be given to the probable disappearance of ex-enemy countries as suppliers of certain products and of the changes in the currents of trade created by the war.

Form of Tariff Schedules

1.   It is contemplated that the tariff negotiations among the members of the Preparatory Committee will be multilateral, both in scope and in legal application. Thus, there would result from the negotiations a total of sixteen[3] schedules of tariff concessions, each schedule setting forth a description of the products and of the maximum (concession) rates of duty thereon which would be applicable in respect of the imports into a particular country. In this way each member of the Committee would he contractually entitled, in its own right and independently of the most-favoured-nation clause, to each of the concessions in rash of the schedules of the other members.

---

[3]   If the principles indicated in Article 33 of the Draft Charter should prove acceptable to the Soviet Union, these may in addition, be a schedule relating to an undertaking by the Soviet Union to purchase annually products valued at not less than an aggregate amount to be agreed upon.

2.   The multilateral form of the tariff schedules is designed to provide more stability than has existed in the past under bilateral tariff agreements, to assure certainty of broad action for the reduction of tariffs and to give to countries a right to tariff concessions on particular products which such countries might wish to obtain, but could not obtain under bilateral agreements, because of their relatively less important position as a supplier of the product concerned. The multilateral form also gives expression to the fact that each country stands to gain when another country grants tariff reductions on any product, even though primarily supplied by a third country. This point can be finally settled when the negotiations have proceeded sufficiently to enable all the varying factors to be taken into account.

Status of Preferential Rates of Duty

1.   The formulation by each member of the Preparatory Committee of a schedule of tariff concessions, which would apply to all other members, raises a question as to the method of relating to such schedules preferential rates of duty, which have been negotiated, as well as preferential rates on products for which most-favoured-nation rates have been negotiated. There appear to be two methods which might be followed:

(a)   Such preferential rates might be incorporated in the multilateral schedules, qualified by the requirement that they apply only to the products of the countries receiving preferred treatment.

(b)   Such preferential rates might be incorporated in separate schedules which would apply only to the preferred countries.

2.   It should be left to the country concerned to determine which of the two methods indicated above it desires to follow. However a single schedule containing both most-favoured-nation and preferential rates would seem to facilitate the work of both traders and governments.

Section F. - Procedures for Conducting Negotiations among the Members of the Preparatory Committee

1.   It is believed that the tariff negotiations among the members of the Preparatory Committee can best be conducted in four stages:

First Stage.

(a)   Each member should transmit to each other member, from which it desires to obtain tariff concessions, as soon as possible and preferably not later than 31 December 1946, a preliminary list of concessions which it proposes to request of such other member. This list should set forth for each product concerned

(i)   an indication of the existing rate of duty (where known) and

(ii)   an indication of the requested rate of duty. Thirty copies of this list should be sent simultaneously to the Secretariat of the United Nations, which will transmit one copy to each of the other members of the Preparatory Committee.

(b)   In order to facilitate the negotiations, each member of the Preparatory Committee should transmit to the Secretariat of the United Nations, as soon as possible and preferably not later than 31 December 1946, thirty copies of its customs tariff showing the rates of duty currently applicable. The Secretariat will promptly transmit one copy to each of the other members of the Committee.

Second Stage.

At the opening of the Second Session of the Preparatory Committee each member should submit a schedule of the proposed concessions which it would be prepared to grant to all other members in the light of the concessions it would have requested from each of them.

Third Stage.

(a)   Notwithstanding the multilateral character of the negotiations, it will usually be found that only two or three countries will be directly and primarily concerned in the concession on a particular product, and that the interest of other countries, although material, will be secondary.

(b)   It is, therefore, proposed that the third stage of the negotiations will ordinarily consist of discussions on particular products between two, or possibly three or four countries. Accordingly for the purpose of engaging in such negotiations, each country should to the extent practicable have separate groups of persons competent to negotiate with each of the other countries with which important negotiations are likely to be conducted.

(c)   The number of negotiating groups required by each country will, of course, tend to vary with the scope of its trade relations. In the case of large trading countries having important trade relations with most or all of the other members of the Committee, a large number of negotiating groups will be required. In the case of countries having less extensive trade relations, a smaller number of negotiating groups will be sufficient.

(d)   In any event the timing of negotiations between particular groups will need to be scheduled, and in order that the United Nations Secretariat may have adequate notice to prepare for such scheduling, it would be desirable for each member of the Committee to notify the Secretariat, as far in advance as may be practicable, of the number of negotiating groups, which the member proposes to send to the negotiating meeting, and of the country or countries to which each negotiating group relates.

Fourth stage

(a)   The progress of the negotiations should be subject to general review by the Committee as a whole periodically during the negotiations and also in the final stage. General review by the Committee as a whole will enable each member to assess the benefits which it is likely to receive from the series of negotiations in the light of its total contributions, and will offset the tendency toward limiting concessions which results from a comparison of benefits exchanged between two countries alone.

(b)   It is clear that the general review by the Committee as a whole cannot take the form of a detailed examination of each concession. Rather the Committee would review the general level of tariff reduction achieved as indicated in summary reports. At the same time each member should be entitled to receive, on request, detailed information as to the status of negotiations on particular products between other members in order that it may be in a position to assert an interest in such negotiations.

2.   In order that the negotiations may proceed in an orderly fashion, it is desirable that a Steering Committee be established as soon as the various delegations have assembled at the Second Session.

Section G. - Result of the Negotiations

If the tariff negotiations proceed successfully along the lines set forth above, there should emerge from the negotiations a tariff schedule for each member, each schedule containing concessions granted to all of the other members in their own right. These schedules might be identified as follows:

Names of Country[4]	*Schedule*
Australia	Schedule I
Belgo - Luxembourg - Netherlands Customs Union, Belgian Congo and Netherlands Overseas Territories	Schedule II
Brazil	Schedule III
Canada	Schedule IV
Chile	Schedule V
China	Schedule VI
Cuba	Schedule VII

---

[4]   Separate, or possibly sub-divided, schedules may be necessary in the case of certain countries in order to provide adequately for certain overseas territories.

Czechoslovakia	Schedule VIII
France and French Union	Schedule IX
India	Schedule X
New Zealand	Schedule XI
Norway	Schedule XII
Syro-Lebanese Customs Union	Schedule VIII
Union of South Africa	Schedule XIV
Union of Soviet Socialist Republics[5]	Schedule XV
United Kingdom and the overseas territories for which it has international responsibility	Schedule XVI
United States	Schedule XVII

Section H. - General Agreement on Tariffs and Trade

1.   Once agreed upon the tariff schedules resulting from the negotiations among the members of the Preparatory Committee cannot easily be held in abeyance pending action by the International Conference on Trade and Employment and the adoption of the Charter by national legislatures.

2.   It is therefore, proposed that the tariff schedules be incorporated in an agreement among the members of the Preparatory Committee which would also contain, either by reference or by reproduction, those general provisions of Chapter V of the Charter considered essential to safeguard the value of the tariff concessions and such other provisions as may be appropriate. The Agreement should contain a provision under which the signatory governments could make any adjustments in the Agreement which may be desirable or necessary in the light of the action taken by the International Conference on Trade and Employment on the Charter. A draft outline of a General Agreement on Tariffs and Trade appears in Section I. The Drafting Committee should consider this outline and prepare a more complete draft for the consideration of the Preparatory Committee at its Second Session.

3.   The General Agreement on Tariffs and Trade should be signed and made public at the close of the tariff negotiations. The Agreement should be legally independent of the Charter and should be brought into force as soon as possible after its signature and publication. Countries should be free to withdraw from the agreement at the end of three years or thereafter on giving six months'

---

[5]   If the principles indicated in Article 33 of the Charter should prove acceptable to the Soviet Union, this schedule would relate, not to tariff concessions, but to an undertaking to purchase annually products valued at not less than an aggregate amount to be agreed upon.

prior notice. This will provide an opportunity for a review of the Agreement and any adjustment of the tariff schedules which may be considered desirable.

4.   The Agreement should conform in every way to the principles laid down in the Charter and should not contain any provision which would prevent the operation of any provision of the Charter.

5.   The tariff concessions granted under the Agreement should be provisionally generalized to the trade of other countries pending the consideration by the International Conference on Trade and Employment of the question whether benefits granted under the Charter should be extended to countries which do not join the International Trade Organization and which, therefore, do not accept the obligations of Article 24.

Section I. - Creation of a Provisional Agency fending the Establishment of the International Trade Organization

Certain of the provisions of the General Agreement on Tariffs and Trade, for example, those incorporating Article 34 of the Charter (Emergency Action on Imports of Particular Products) and Article 35 of the Charter (Nullification or Impairment), will require for their successful operation the existence of an international body. It is proposed, therefore, that the members of the Preparatory Committee, which make effective the General Agreement on Tariffs and Trade, should' create a provisional international agency for this purpose. This provisional agency would go out of existence upon the establishment of the International Trade Organization.

Section J.-Relation of the General Agreement on Tariffs and Trade to the International Trade Organization after its Establishment

Interim Tariff Committee

1.   The Charter as now formulated provides in Article 67 that the countries which make effective the General Agreement on Tariffs and Trade shall constitute the original members of the Interim Tariff Committee to be set up within the International Trade Organization after the International Conference on Trade and Employment has met and the Organization has been established.

2.   The Interim Tariff Committee will have the function of determining whether (with respect to any negotiations subsequent to those culminating in the General Agreement on Tariffs and Trade) any member of the Organization has failed to live up to its obligations regarding tariff negotiations and, under paragraph (3) of Article 24 of the Charter, of authorizing complaining members to withhold tariff benefits from offending members. The following points should be noted with regard to this function:

    (a)   A member of the Organization may be admitted to membership in the Committee when the member has completed tariff negotiations "comparable in scope or effect" to the negotiations already completed by the original members of the Committee.

Thus, what is achieved by way of tariff action in the General Agreement on Tariffs and Trade will become the standard to which members of the Organization will be expected to conform in order to obtain membership of the Interim Tariff Committee. In applying this standard the Committee should have regard to the provisions of the Charter as a whole.

(b) Since it is agreed that the original members of the Interim Tariff Committee will have taken adequate steps toward fulfilment of the tariff obligations of the Charter in respect of negotiations among themselves (see Article III of the draft General Agreement on Tariffs and Trade), the Committee may not authorize one original member of the Committee to withhold tariff concessions from another original member of the Committee.[6] This would be without prejudice, of course, to any decisions reached, under the auspices of the Organization, regarding a second series of tariff negotiations among the members of the Committee.

(c) Members of the Interim Tariff Committee must, in negotiations with members of the Organization which are not members of the Committee, be prepared to consider concessions on products of interest to the latter which were not dealt with in the original negotiations. Refusal to negotiate on such products might warrant a legitimate complaint. Accordingly the Committee could in such cases authorize a member of the Organization, which is not a member of the Committee, to withhold tariff benefits from a member of the Committee. However, the extent to which a member of the Organization, which is not a member of the Committee, might withhold tariff benefits from a member of the Committee would be limited only to tariff concessions which the former had already made pursuant to Article 24 and general tariff penalties could not be applied.

(d) The authority of the Committee would in all cases be limited to granting permission to a member of the Organization to withhold tariff benefits from another member. In no event could the Committee compel a member to withhold benefits.

Procedure for Broadening Membership in the Interim Tariff Committee through Additional Tariff Negotiations.

1.   Procedures must be developed for assuring, by negotiation, action for the reduction of tariffs and the elimination of preferences by members of the Organization, which are not parties to the General Agreement on Tariffs and

---

[6]   It should be noted that the Organization, as distinct from the Committee, could authorize an original member of the Committee to withhold benefits from another original member of the Committee under certain other provisions of the Charter.

Trade and hence would not be original members of the Interim Tariff Committee. The following alternative procedures are suggested for consideration:

(a)   The original members of the Interim Tariff Committee would negotiate separate bilateral agreements with members of the Organization, which are not members of the Committee, and the latter would negotiate such agreements between themselves. The Committee would judge as to when a particular country had completed enough such agreements to entitle it to membership in the Committee.

(b)   A member of the Organization, which is not an original member of the Committee, might offer to negotiate with the Committee a multilateral schedule of concessions similar in scope and legal application -to the schedules appended to the General Agreement on Tariffs and Trade concluded among the original members of the Interim Tariff Committee and the original members of the Committee would agree to amend the multilateral schedules appended to the General Agreement on Tariffs and Trade to the extent necessary to assure appropriate concessions on products of which the country, not a member of the Committee, was a principal supplier.

2.   Whatever procedure is adopted, due weight should be given in the negotiating process to concessions already made as a result of prior negotiations.

Section K-Tentative and Partial Draft Outline of General Agreement on Tariffs and Trade

The governments in respect of which this Agreement is signed:

Having been named by the Economic and Social Council of the United Nations to prepare, for the consideration of the International Conference on Trade and Employment, a Charter for an International Trade Organization of the United Nations;

Having, as the Preparatory Committee for the Conference, recommended to the Conference the provisions of such a Charter, the text of which is set forth in the Report of the Preparatory Committee; and

Being desirious of furthering the objectives of the Conference by providing an example of concrete achievement capable of generalization to all countries on equitable terms:

Have, through their respective Plenipotentiaries, agreed as follows:

Article I

1.   During the life of the Agreement each signatory government shall make effective in respect of each other signatory government the provisions described below of the Charter for an International Trade Organization of the United Nations recommended in the report of the Preparatory Committee.

[There would follow a list of the articles to be included in the Agreement.]

2. Functions entrusted to the proposed International Trade Organization under any of the provisions of the Charter incorporated in this Agreement by virtue of paragraph I of this Article shall, pending the establishment of the Organization, be carried out by a provisional international agency consisting of delegates appointed by the signatory governments.

Article II

With regard to Articles 24, 32 and 33 of the Charter, which relate to negotiations for

1. The reduction of tariffs and the elimination of tariff preferences, and

2. Parallel action by state-trading enterprises,

the signatory governments declare that they have, by virtue of Article III of this Agreement, taken this step towards fulfilment of the obligations of these Articles in respect of themselves and that they stand ready, in conformity with the spirit of these Articles, to undertake similar negotiations with such other governments as may desire to become members of the International Trade Organization.

Article III

Each signatory government shall accord to the commerce of the customs territories of the other signatory governments the treatment provided for in the appropriate Schedule annexed to this Agreement and made an integral part thereof.

Article IV

(This Article would set forth the general exceptions provided for in Article 37 of the Charter.)

Article V

(This Article would reproduce the provisions of Article 38 of the Charter relating to territorial application.)

Article VI

(This article would permit revision of the Agreement, by agreement among the signatories, if necessary or desirable in order to take account of changes in the Charter effected by the International Conference on Trade and Employment.)

Article VII

(This Article would provide for the entry into force of this Agreement, its duration, and its termination. The Agreement would remain initially in force for three years. If not terminated at the end of the three-year period (which would require six months' prior notice), it would remain in force thereafter, subject to termination on six months' notice.

There would be a number of purely technical and of purely legal provisions.)

RESTRICTED
LIMITED B

GATT/CP.2/26
1 September 1948

ORIGINAL: ENGLISH

GENERAL AGREEMENT ON TARIFFS AND TRADE
Contracting Parties
Second Session

Memorandum on Tariff Negotiations

TO BE HELD IN GENEVA COMMENCING 11 APRIL, 1949

I.   Purpose of the Negotiations

The contracting parties to the General Agreement on Tariffs and Trade, at their Second Session in Geneva in August 1948, resolved to invite the governments which showed their interest in the proposed International Trade Organization, by accepting the invitation to the United Nations Conference on Trade and Employment at Havana, to enter into negotiations with a view to their accession to the Agreement.

In 1947 the contracting parties, in their capacity as members of the Preparatory Committee for the Trade and Employment Conference, gave effect to one of the fundamental principles of the draft Charter by carrying out negotiations directed to the substantial reduction of the general level of tariffs and to the elimination of preferences on a reciprocal and mutually advantageous basis. In order that further progress may be made towards expanding the volume of world trade, the contracting parties invite the governments referred to above to enter upon similar negotiations with them. In most cases these countries are enjoying the benefit of the tariff reductions negotiated by the contracting parties and incorporated in the Schedules to the General Agreement. But even so they will welcome the opportunity to obtain these benefits in their own right and to negotiate for further concessions on the products of most interest to them.

The main part and the final phase of the negotiations will take place in Geneva commencing on 11 April, 1949, but it will be necessary to begin preparations immediately. In order that no time will be lost in the preparatory work, the Secretariat of the contracting parties will notify by telegraph, not later than 18 September, 1948, a list of governments which will participate in the next series of negotiations, i.e. the contracting parties and the governments which wish to participate with a view to acceding to the Agreement. An acceding government should be prepared to negotiate with any contracting party and with any other acceding government. There will, generally, be no negotiations between the contracting parties themselves, but it may be that, by mutual and by general agreement, some of them will take the opportunity to complete certain negotiations which were left unfinished at the Geneva meeting in 1947 and to make certain adjustments found to be necessary in the existing Schedules to the Agreement.

II.   Scope of the Negotiations

It is intended that the countries participating in the negotiations in 1949 will propose for negotiation those of their products of which they individually, or collectively, are, or are likely to be, the principal suppliers to the countries from whom the concessions are asked. In other words, an acceding government will be expected to consider the grant of concessions, as a general rule, on products of which any participating country or any group of participating countries is, or is likely to be, the principle supplier. And a contracting party will, as a general rule, be expected to consider the grant of concessions on products of which any acceding country by itself or together with other participating countries, constitutes, or is likely to constitute, the principal source of supply, This latter rule will not apply to products which already appear in the Schedules to the Agreement, except that it is not meant to prevent an acceding government from asking for concessions on products appearing in the Schedules in which it has a special interest; in such cases, however, the government submitting the request will be expected to take fully into account the concessions already granted on the products concerned.

The Havana Charter provides that, in addition to customs tariffs and other charges on imports and exports, certain regulations, quotas, protection afforded through the operations of import and export monopolies, etc., shall be subject to negotiation in the manner provided in Article 17. The relevant provisions are contained in Articles 16 (including the Annexes thereto), 18, 19 and 31. Accordingly, requests may be submitted for concessions in respect of matters covered by these provisions in the same way as requests for tariff concessions.

III.   Methods of Negotiation

1.   The negotiations will be conducted in accordance with the rules set forth in paragraph 2 of Article 17 of the Havana Charter

(a)   The negotiations will be conducted on a selective product-by-product basis which will afford adequate opportunity to take into account the needs of individual countries and individual industries. Participating governments will be free not to grant concessions on particular products and, in the granting of a concession, they may reduce the duty, bind it at its then existing level, or undertake not to raise it above a specified higher level.

(b)   No participating government will be required to grant unilateral concessions, or to grant concessions to other governments without receiving adequate concessions in return. Account shall be taken of the value to any government of obtaining in its own right and by direct obligation the concessions already embodied in the Schedules to the General Agreement.

(c)   In negotiations relating to any specific product with respect to which a preference applies,

   (i)   when a reduction is negotiated only in the most-favoured-nation rate, such reduction shall operate automatically to reduce or eliminate the margin of preference applicable to that product;

   (ii)   when a reduction is negotiated only in the preferential rate, the most-favoured-nation rate shall automatically be reduced to the extent of such reduction;

   (iii)   when it is agreed that reductions will be negotiated in both the most-favoured-nation rate and the preferential rate, the reduction in each shall be that agreed by the parties to the negotiations;

   (iv)   no margin of preference shall be increased.

(d)   The binding against increase of low duties or of duty-free treatment will in principle be recognized as a concession equivalent in value to the substantial reduction of high duties or the elimination of tariff preferences.

(e)   Prior international obligations shall not be invoked to frustrate negotiations with respect to preferences, it being understood that agreements which result from such negotiations and which conflict with such obligations shall not require the modification or termination of such obligations except (i) with the consent of the parties to such obligations, or, in the termination of such obligations in accordance with their terms.

2.   In order to ensure the success of the negotiations, it is recommended that the participating governments should refrain from increases in tariffs and other protective measures inconsistent with the principles of the Havana Charter and designed to improve the bargaining position of those governments in preparation for the negotiations. In the event of a change in the form of tariff or a revision of rates of duties to take account of either a rise in prices or the devaluation of the currency of the country maintaining the tariff, the effects of such change or such revision would be a matter for consideration during the negotiations in order to determine, first, the change, if any, in the incidence of the duties of the country concerned, and secondly, whether the change is such as to afford a reasonable basis for negotiations.

3.   In a few exceptional cases, a general revision of tariffs prior to the negotiations may be found unavoidable. In making any such revision, the countries concerned should have regard to the principles stated in the preceding

paragraph. It is suggested that such countries should notify the Secretariat, by telegram, not later than 18 September 1948, of their decision in regard to participation in the forthcoming negotiations and the latest date by which copies of their existing and revised Customs Tariff will be supplied to other participating governments as provided in the time-table below. They should comply with all the requirements of the time-table except those relating to copies of the Customs Tariff. Negotiations will take place with such countries if the supply of copies of the revised tariff is not delayed so long as to render such negotiations impracticable and if the principles stated in the preceding paragraph have been observed.

IV.   Timetable for the Negotiation

(i)   At the earliest possible date and in no case later than 25 September 1948, each contracting party will send to each acceding government, and each of the latter will send to each other participating government, three copies of its customs tariff and one copy (if possible, three) of its latest annual import trade statistics. In addition, it is requested that every effort should be made to supply average import statistics for 1936 to 1938, or, if this is not possible, statistics for 1936, 1937 and 1938, or if neither of these is possible, statistics for the most representative pre-war year. Each participating government will advise the participating government concerned and the Secretariat, by telegram, the particulars of the documents dispatched and the date and method of dispatch.

(ii)   The United States Government are required by their statutory procedure to give public notice of all items in their tariff which are to be the subject of negotiations. Not later than 31 October 1948, therefore, each acceding government will transmit to the United States Government, by the most expeditious means available, a list of the products on which it intends to request concessions from that government. The United States Government will take reciprocal action not later than 31 October 1948. It will not be possible for the United States Government to enter into negotiations on any products which are not included in these first lists. Any other participating government which wishes to exchange preliminary and provisional lists with participating governments other than the United States in advance of the definitive lists provided for in paragraph (iv) will notify the secretariat to that effect not later than the 18 September 1948, and the last date for the transmission of such lists will be the 30 November 1948. It is hoped that exchange of such preliminary lists will not be requested except where it is considered absolutely essential, since many of the acceding governments may find it difficult to prepare a large number of such lists within the time prescribed. Forty copies of the preliminary lists, including the lists exchanged between the United States Government and acceding governments, will be sent to the Secretariat simultaneously with their transmission to the governments to which they are addressed for distribution to other participating governments.

(iii)   It is essential for the successful conduct of the forthcoming negotiations that the above time-table should be strictly adhered to. It is understood, however, that certain acceding governments may be unable, for reasons beyond their control, to notify their decisions in regard to participation by 18 September 1948, and that similarly certain participating governments may be unable to supply the necessary documents by 25 September 1948. The governments will nevertheless be expected to take the necessary action within a very short time after the dates prescribed and to conform to the remainder of the time-table so as to make the negotiations practicable.

(iv)   Not later than 15 January 1949, each government will transmit to each other participating government a final list of the tariff and other concessions which it requests from that government. Forty copies of these lists will be sent simultaneously to the Secretariat for distribution to the participating governments. When compiling lists of requests, whether preliminary or definitive, participating governments would not include products which appear in the Schedules to the Agreement unless they propose to request a concession going beyond those provided in the Schedules.

(v)   On 11 April, 1949, - that is, on the first day of the meeting in Geneva - each government will make known to all participating governments the concessions which it is prepared to offer to each government from which a request for concessions was received. These offers should include indications of the existing and the proposed rate of duty on each item.

(vi)   It will be understood that any two participating governments may arrange between themselves to conduct bilateral talks in advance of the multilateral negotiations in Geneva. In that event the exchange of preliminary requests and offers may be arranged to take place at earlier dates than those envisaged above, but the concessions offered need not be disclosed to other participating governments until the opening of the Geneva meeting. In the event that bilateral talks should be successfully concluded prior to 11 April, the results will be reported to the other participating governments at the opening of the Geneva meeting and will be subject to review and adjustment in accordance with the procedures set forth in the following paragraphs.

V.   Procedures at Geneva

When the concessions offered by all participating governments have been exchanged and distributed, negotiations between pairs of delegations will begin. Any alterations in the initial list of offers will be immediately notified to the Secretariat for the information of all participating governments. At this stage, as in the distribution of lists of requests, arrangements will be made to prevent the disclosure of any confidential material.

To follow the successful procedure adopted in 1947, the participating governments may decide to establish a "Tariff Negotiations Working Party", which will be responsible for ascertaining the progress of the negotiations and which will make recommendations on questions of procedure and other matters connected with the conduct of the negotiations and prepare the legal instruments to be signed at the conclusion of the proceedings.

As each negotiation is concluded, lists of the concessions to be exchanged will be conveyed to the Secretariat and to all other delegations. These results will be subject to review and adjustment in the light of the results of other negotiations. Each participating government will arrange through the Secretariat for the distribution to each other participating government of a consolidated list of all concessions granted.

When all the negotiations are completed the concessions will be incorporated in the Agreement, and the accession of governments, not previously contracting parties, will be effected by appropriate instruments. Each participating government will prepare for distribution through the Secretariat a supplementary list of the concessions granted showing the country with which each concession was initially negotiated.

PROCEDURES ADOPTED FOR TORQUAY TARIFF CONFERENCE

I.   Scope of the Negotiations

1.   It is intended that the countries participating in the negotiations in 1950 will propose for negotiation those of their products of which they individually, or collectively, are, or are likely to be, the principal suppliers to the countries from which the concessions are asked. This will apply to negotiations between contracting parties and, in the case of a new acceding government, the latter will be expected to consider the grant of concessions, as a general rule, on products of which any participating country or any group of participating countries, is, or is likely to be, the principal supplier. And a contracting party will, as a general rule, be expected to consider the grant of concessions on products of which any acceding country by itself or together with other participating countries, constitutes, or is likely to constitute, the principal source of supply.

2.   The Havana Charter provides that, in addition to customs tariffs and other charges on imports and exports, certain regulations, quotas, protection afforded through the operation of import and export monopolies, etc., shall be subject to negotiation in the manner provided in Article 17. The relevant provisions are contained in Articles 16 (including the Annexes thereto), 18,19 and 31. Accordingly, requests may be submitted for concessions in respect of matters covered by these provisions in the same way as requests for tariff concessions.

II.   Methods of Negotiation

3.   The negotiations will be conducted in accordance with the rules set forth in paragraph 2 of Article 17 of the Havana Charter, *i.e.*:

(a)   The negotiations shall be conducted on a selective product-by-product basis which will afford adequate opportunity to take into account the needs of individual countries and individual industries. Participating governments will be free not to grant concessions on particular products and, in the granting of a concession, they may reduce the duty, bind it at its then existing level, or undertake not to raise it above a specified higher level.

(b)   No participating government shall be required to grant unilateral concessions, or to grant concession to other governments without receiving adequate concessions in return. Account shall be taken of the value to any government of obtaining in its own right and by direct obligation the indirect concessions already embodied in the Schedules to the General Agreement.

(c)   In negotiations relating to any specific product with respect to which a preference applies,

        (i)   when a reduction is negotiated only in the most-favoured-nation rate, such reduction shall operate automatically to reduce or eliminate the margin of preference applicable to that product;

        (ii)   when a reduction is negotiated only in the preferential rate, the most-favoured-nation rate shall automatically be reduced to the extent of such reduction;

        (iii)   when it is agreed that reductions will be negotiated in both the most-favoured-nation rate and the preferential rate, the reduction in each shall be that agreed by the parties to the negotiations; and

        (iv)   no margin of preference shall be increased.

(d)   The binding against the increase of low duties or of duty-free treatment shall be in principle be recognized as a concession equivalent in value to the substantial reduction of high duties or the elimination of tariff preferences.

(e)   Prior international obligations shall not be invoked to frustrate negotiations with respect to preferences, it being understood that agreements which result from such negotiations and which conflict with such obligations shall not require the modification or termination of such obligation except with the consent of the parties to such obligations or in the absence of such consent by modification or termination of such obligations in accordance with their terms.

    4.   An important consideration to be taken into account by the acceding governments in their negotiations with contracting parties is the indirect benefit they are enjoying as a result of the concessions exchanged by the latter at Geneva and Annecy. It will be expected, therefore, that, in granting tariff concessions, acceding governments will take into consideration these indirect benefits and those which will result from new negotiations among contracting parties. Similarly, all the participating governments will be expected to take into consideration the indirect benefits which they will receive from the negotiations between the acceding governments themselves and between them and the contracting parties.

    5.   In order to ensure the success of the negotiations, the participating governments shall refrain from increases in tariffs and other protective measures inconsistent with the principles of the Havana Charter and designed to improve the bargaining position of these governments in preparation for the negotiations. As a general rule, the basis for negotiations shall be the rates of duty in effect on November 15, 1949.

    6.   In exceptional cases, a country may find that a general revision of its tariff prior to the negotiations is unavoidable. In making any such revision, the country concerned should have regard to the principles stated in the preceding paragraph. In the event of a change in the form of tariff or a general

revision of rates of duties to take account of either a rise in prices or the devaluation of the currency of the country which has introduced the new tariff, the effects of such change or such revision would be a matter for consultation between the acceding country and the other participating countries, acting jointly, in order to determine first, the change, if any, in the incidence of the duties of the country concerned, and secondly, whether the change affords a reasonable basis for a reciprocal and mutually advantageous conclusion of the negotiations. Moreover, except in special circumstances, any general revision in tariff nomenclature or rates of duty shall not be considered a satisfactory basis for negotiations unless it has been promulgated prior to September 28, 1950.

III.   Time-Table for the Negotiations

7.   At the earliest possible date and in no case later than November 22, 1949, each participating government will send to each other participating government and to the Secretariat three copies of its current customs tariff, details of other import charges or taxes and one copy (if possible, three) of its annual import trade statistics for post-war years. In addition, it is requested that every effort should be made to supply average import statistics for 1936 to 1938 or, if this is not possible, statistics for 1936, 1937 and 1938, or if neither of these is possible, statistics for the most representative pre-war year. Governments which participated in the Geneva and/or Annecy negotiations will not be expected to supply copies to governments to which they were supplied on those previous occasions, but they will be expected to supply details of subsequent tariff changes and copies of any more recent trade statistics that may be available. In cases where transmission by surface post would occupy more than one week, the documents should be dispatched by air mail. Each participating government will advise the other participating governments and the Secretariat, by telegram, the particulars of the documents dispatched and the date and method of dispatch.

8.   It must be recognized that the foreign trade statistics of many countries are not compiled on the basis of their customs tariffs and therefore it cannot be reliably ascertained from the statistics of trade to which customs duties the various statistical items are subject. Consequently, participating governments will, in some cases, experience difficulty in determining the articles on which to request concessions and in calculating the value of concessions offered. Moreover, the customs tariffs of some countries contain the general , but not the conventional, rates of duty, and the texts of many statistical and customs publications are not available in any of the well-known languages. In order to avoid these difficulties, and to assist in the preparations for the negotiations and also in the actual conduct of the negotiations, participating governments are asked to do their best to meet all requests which may be directed to them for additional information relating to their tariffs and statistics.

9.   Not later than January 15, 1950 each participating government will transmit, by the most expeditious means available, to each other participating

government with which it wishes to negotiate, a list of the products on which it intends to request concessions. Sixty copies of each list will be sent simultaneously to the Secretariat for distribution to the other participating governments. In order to facilitate preparations for the negotiations, it is important that the date of January 15 be adhered to. The United States Government is required by its statutory procedure to give public notice of all items in its tariff which are to be the subject of negotiations, and therefore it will not be possible for that government to enter into negotiations on any products which are not included in these lists. A similar situation may exist for certain other governments and therefore items not included in these lists may be excluded from the negotiations.

10.   Not later than June 15 1950, each government will transmit to each other participating government a final list of the tariff and other concessions which it requests from that government. Sixty copies of each list will be sent simultaneously to the Secretariat for distribution to the other participating governments. It is strongly recommended that all countries send their lists as early as possible in advance of June 15, 1950.

11.   On September 28, 1950 - that is, on the first day of the meeting in Torquay - each government should be ready to make known the concessions it is prepared to offer to each government from which a request for concessions is received. These offers should include an indication of the existing and of the proposed rate of duty on each item. When the offers have been exchanged, negotiations between pairs of delegations will begin.

12.   It will be understood that any two participating governments may arrange between themselves to conduct bilateral talks in advance of the multilateral negotiations in Torquay. In that event, the exchange of requests and offers may be arranged to take place at earlier dates than those stipulated above. In the event that bilateral talks should be successfully concluded prior to September 28, 1950, the results will be reported at the opening of the Torquay meeting.

IV.   Arrangements for the Conduct of Negotiations

13.   In accordance with the successful procedure adopted at Geneva in 1947 and at Annecy in 1949, a "Tariff Negotiations Working Party" will be established at the opening of the conference. This Working Party will be responsible for ascertaining the progress of the negotiations and will make recommendations on questions of procedure and other matters connected with the conduct and the conclusion of the negotiations. In addition, arrangements will be made to prevent the disclosure of confidential material.

14.   Each participating government will prepare for distribution through the Secretariat a consolidated list of the concessions it has granted and a supplementary list showing the country or countries with which each concession was initially negotiated.

15.   When all the negotiations are completed, the accession of governments, not previously contracting parties, will be effected by appropriate instruments. The concessions granted will thereby be incorporated in the Agreement.

V.   Negotiations Under Article XXVIII[1]

16.   If a contracting party finds it necessary to modify a concession provided for in its Schedule, it should send a notification, accompanied by details of the proposed modification, to the contracting party with which the concession was initially negotiated and, as far as possible, to the other contracting parties believed to be substantially interested, by August 1, 1950. It is recognized that particular contracting parties may not be in a position to give the notification by that date. In such exceptional cases, the notification of a modification may be given after this date; but contracting parties, in formulating their offers for the Torquay negotiations, will be entitled to assume that this deadline has been met, and to exchange their offers on the basis of this assumption or delay such exchange with other contracting parties until assurances have been received that the latter have no intention of giving any subsequent notification affecting products of substantial interest to them. Any notification as to proposed action under Article XXVIII shall, whenever practicable, be accompanied by a statement as to compensatory adjustments with respect to other products which the notifying country is prepared to offer. Forty-five copies of such notification should be sent simultaneously to the Secretariat for distribution to the other participating governments.

17.   At the opening of the tariff negotiations or within six weeks of the receipt of the notification, whichever is later, the contracting party with which the concession was initially negotiated will indicate to the contracting party which has given the notification any compensation which it wishes to obtain from that contracting party. At the same time, the contracting party which has given the notification will indicate to the contracting party with which the concession was initially negotiated any compensatory adjustments with respect to other products which is prepared to offer, and annex to its communication a detailed description of the compensation proposed, to the extent that such information had not previously been communicated by it. The communications provided for in this sub-paragraph will be circulated through the Secretariat to all participating governments in the same manner as the lists of offers.

18.   The negotiations on requests for adjustments under Article XXVIII will be conducted within the framework of the Torquay negotiations, and should

---

[1]   This section contains rules for the guidance of the contracting parties involved in such negotiations in order to ensure that the discussions relating to the adjustments under Article XXVIII, while being duly coordinated with the third round of tariff negotiations, do not unduly interfere with them and that all the necessary modifications are agreed upon before the close of the Torquay conference.

be concluded before the end of those negotiations; results of such negotiations will be communicated simultaneously with the final exchange of lists of concessions, but in a separate list.

19.   Other contracting parties having a substantial interest in the proposed adjustments will be given an opportunity, at as early a stage as possible in the course of the Torquay Conference, to be consulted in accordance with the provisions of Article XXVIII.

20.   The adjustments on which agreement has been reached with the contracting parties concerned will not become final until the multilateral stage of the negotiations is completed.

21.   The adjustments made in accordance with the provisions of Article XXVIII will be listed in an Annex to the Declaration to be signed at the close of the Torquay conference.

PLANS FOR TARIFF REDUCTION AND RULES AND PROCEDURES FOR THE 1956 TARIFF CONFERENCE

Report adopted on 18 November 1955

1.   The Working Party was appointed on 4 March 1955 with the following terms of reference:

   (*a*)   to study generally the possibilities of future action directed to the reduction of the general level of tariffs, with special consideration being given to the reduction of unreasonably high tariffs;

   (*b*)   to examine various particular plans or procedures which may be proposed for carrying out the objectives set forth in paragraph (*a*);

   (*c*)   to recommend to the CONTRACTING PARTIES the convening of a tariff conference as soon as it is felt by the Working Party that progress in this field is possible, and to make preparations for such a conference, and

   (*d*)   to report to the CONTRACTING PARTIES at their Tenth Session.

PROPOSED TARIFF CONFERENCE COMMENCING 18 JANUARY 1956

2.   At the meeting of the Intersessional Committee in June, the United States representative stated that his Government wished that the CONTRACTING PARTIES would give consideration to further tariff negotiations in the light of the new powers granted to the President of the United States and that, in order to meet the time-limit prescribed by United States legislation and practices, any tariff negotiations that might be arranged should start early in 1956. Accordingly a meeting of the Working Party was convened without delay. The Working Party considered unanimously that every effort should be made to carry out another round of multilateral negotiations on as broad a basis as possible and that these should be conducted in time to permit full participation by the United States Government under its new powers.

3.   The Working Party decided to *recommend* that the CONTRACTING PARTIES convene a tariff conference to begin in January 1956, instructed the Executive Secretary to enquire of contracting parties whether they wished to participate and laid down a provisional time-table for the preparations for the conference. At a second meeting of the Working Party in September the Executive Secretary reported (L/395) that the following governments had indicated that they wished to take part in such a conference:

Australia	Dominican Republic	Japan
Austria	Finland	Nicaragua
Belgium	France	Norway
Luxemburg	Federal Republic	Sweden
Kingdom of the	of Germany	Turkey
Netherlands	Greece	United Kingdom
Canada	Haiti	Union of South Africa
Ceylon	India	United States
Cuba	Italy	of America
Denmark		

4. The Working Party noted the statement by the Government of France that it intended to negotiate with the United States but was not in a position to participate in negotiations with other contracting parties. The French representative informed the Working Party that his Government intended to bring about very soon a customs union of all the territories of the French Union, which would involve unilateral reduction in the tariff of Metropolitan France; for this reason, and also because the abandonment of the GATT plan appeared to it to limit considerably the scope of the forthcoming negotiations, the French Government had taken the decision notified to the Executive Secretary. The other members of the Working Party expressed their disappointment that the participation of France should be thus limited, and strongly expressed the hope that the French Government would reconsider its decision in the light of paragraph 2 (*b*) of Article XXIX. Some members stated that their governments were preparing lists of concessions which they wished to obtain from France in the negotiations and enquired of the representative of France whether such lists would be received and considered by the French Government. The French representative replied that his Government could not refuse to accept such lists, but this acceptance would not involve any commitment by his Government. He agreed to communicate to his Government the wishes of the other members that France should reconsider its decision on participation in the conference.

5. The Executive Secretary was also asked to ascertain from governments which had displayed an interest in the work of the CONTRACTING PARTIES whether, at the same time, they would be willing to initiate negotiations with a view to acceding to the General Agreement. The Executive Secretary has been in contact with a number of governments but thus far none of them has indicated a desire to negotiate with a view to accession at the present time.

6. The Working Party *recommends* that the conference begin on 18 January 1956 and the United States representative has indicated that the timetable prescribed by United States legislation and practices will require that a target date of 1 May be set for completion of the negotiations.

7. The Executive Secretary informed the Working Party that, on the information available at the present time, it appeared that accommodation for the conference would be available in Geneva. The Working Party accordingly *recommends* that the conference be held in Geneva and that the Executive

Secretary be authorized to make the necessary arrangements. However, if as a result of a change in circumstances it should prove impracticable to meet in Geneva, the Executive Secretary should consult with governments before recommending an alternative site.

RULES AND PROCEDURES

8.   At its meeting in June, the Working Party discussed the method of negotiation to be followed in the January conference. A majority expressed a preference for the application of multilateral procedures along the lines of the GATT plan[1], which they considered to be the only satisfactory solution for the tariff problem, but as the United States and United Kingdom Governments were not in a position to proceed on that basis in these negotiations, the Working Party came to the conclusion that it was not practicable to consider the introduction of such procedures at the conference in 1956.

9.   On the other hand, the majority felt that to proceed in accordance with the rules followed in previous tariff negotiations would not result in a substantial contribution to the objectives set out in Article XXIX of the revised Agreement, particularly as regards reduction of excessive rates of duty and the recognition of the equivalence of the binding of low rates to reductions in high rates of duty. They recalled, moreover, that the discussions which had led to the formulation of the GATT plan had been based upon a widespread feeling that the former rules were unlikely to lead to satisfactory results. The Working Party agreed that it would be desirable to consider to what extent and in what manner the negotiating rules should be amended in order to ensure the attainment of the objectives of Article XXIX. At the meeting in June, a set of revised procedures was prepared and in addition the United Kingdom representative submitted a draft of procedures which would be acceptable to his Government. These two plans were referred to governments for consideration.[2]

10.   At the September meeting it was found that neither of these plans was wholly acceptable and the Working Party therefore decided to recommend procedures based upon three features which were common to both of them, namely:

(i)   that the negotiations should be based on the principles of Article XXIX;

(ii)   that each participating government should present a consolidated list of offers, and

(iii)   that the Tariff Negotiations Committee should have broader functions than in previous tariff negotiations in order to strengthen the multilateral aspect of the conference.

---

[1]   BISD, second Supplement, page 75.

[2]   The discussions at the June meeting are reported more fully in the Working Party's interim report (L/373). The two plans are annexed to that report.

The United States representative made suggestions for the functions and terms of reference of the proposed Tariff Negotiations Committee.

11.   The rules and procedures developed by the Working Party on the basis of these three principles and the United States suggestions for the terms of reference of the Committee, as recommended for adoption by the CONTRACTING PARTIES, are set out in the annex to this report. Comments on certain points are given in the following paragraphs.

12.   The proposed rules for the negotiations have been drafted on the basis of the provisions of Article XXIX which stipulate that negotiations sponsored by the CONTRACTING PARTIES shall be conducted on a basis which affords adequate opportunity to take certain considerations into account. The fact that paragraph 3 (*a*) of that Article is stipulated in the proposed rules, whereas paragraphs 3 (*b*) and (*c*) are not cited, does not mean that the latter are any less relevant. In fact, it is stated in the rules and procedures that the negotiations are to be based on the principles of Article XXIX.

13.   It is stated in rule 5 that overall concessions granted by a participating government should be commensurate with the overall concessions received. This phrase is intended to be interpreted broadly and not in the sense of requiring any form of mathematical equivalence.[3]

14.   While it was recognized that various factors might in practice restrict the negotiating possibilities of participating governments, it was agreed that it was desirable to enlarge the scope of the negotiations as much as possible so as to achieve the maximum progress towards the objectives of Article XXIX. In particular, it was agreed that the fact that the negotiating powers of the United States were in general limited to 15 per cent over a period of three years should not preclude other governments from negotiating for greater reductions among themselves.

15.   With reference to rule 6, the Working Party wishes to stress that governments should observe as closely as possible the date of 1 October 1955 for the submission of their lists of requests in order that other governments should be able to prepare their lists of offers by 18 January. Some members proposed an earlier date for the submission of the lists of consolidated offers in order to avoid any delay in the initial review of the lists by the Committee and thereby, from the very outset, strengthen the multilateral aspects of the negotiations. Members, however, were unable to agree on an earlier date. The United States representative indicated his willingness to submit with the list of concessions being offered by the United States a statistical analysis showing the value of imports of the products included in the list from the various participating countries. The Working Party considered that this information would be helpful to participating countries, and also to the secretariat in preparing for the

---

[3]   Some members stressed that the inclusion of this phrase does not prejudice in any way what countries may consider, in terms of the principles of Article XXIX, to be an acceptable overall balance of concessions and advantages.

Committee's review of the offer lists, and therefore recommends that participating countries should, if possible, furnish such statistical analyses concerning their import trade in the items on which concessions are being offered.

16.   Regarding rule 11 (*c*), the countries described in the second sentence continue to believe that the only satisfactory method of meeting their problems would be by the adoption of an automatic formula for tariff reduction. The statement that the rule in question "takes account of" these problems is only a recognition of the special problems of these countries in negotiations of the kind contemplated. The rule in itself affords no solution of these problems and the position of the countries concerned will only be improved to the extent to which the rule is effectively applied.

ANNEX

RULES AND PROCEDURES FOR THE TARIFF CONFERENCE COMMENCING IN GENEVA ON 18 JANUARY 1956

I.   Objectives of the Negotiations

1.   The CONTRACTING PARTIES, recognizing that customs duties often constitute serious obstacles to trade, have decided to sponsor a tariff negotiations conference based on the principles of Article XXIX of the revised General Agreement and conducted with due regard to the objectives of the General Agreement.

2.   The negotiations shall be directed towards the reduction of the general level of tariffs and other charges on imports and, in particular, to the reduction of such high tariffs as discourage the importation of even minimum quantities and shall aim at the exchange of reciprocal and mutually advantageous concessions. Governments participating in the negotiations shall endeavour through common effort to ensure that the results of the negotiations are as great as practicable.

II.   Scope of the Negotiations

3.   Participating countries may request concessions on products of which they individually, or collectively are, or are likely to be, the principal suppliers to the countries from which the concessions are asked. This rule shall not apply to prevent a country not a principal supplier from making a request, but the country concerned may invoke the principal supplier rule if the principal supplier of the product is not participating in the negotiations or is not a contracting party to the General Agreement.

4.   In addition to customs tariffs and other charges on imports, certain regulations, protection afforded through the operation of import monopolies, etc.,

as provided in Articles II (including the Annexes thereto), III and IV of the revised General Agreement, shall be subject to negotiation in accordance with these rules. Accordingly, requests may be submitted for concessions in respect of these matters in the same way as requests for tariff concessions.

5.   Participating governments agree to make a maximum effort towards achieving the objectives of the negotiations in accordance with Article XXIX and to this end shall cooperate to further their multilateral character by making overall concessions commensurate with the overall concessions received.

III.   The Opening of the Conference

6.   On the first day of the Conference each participating government should submit a consolidated list of the concessions it is prepared to offer, with an indication for each item of the country or countries to which the concession is offered. Forty copies of each consolidated list of offers shall be sent to the Executive Secretary who will furnish one copy to each other government which has submitted its consolidated list.

IV.   The Tariff Negotiations Committee

7.   With a view to facilitating the negotiations and ensuring the fullest possible multilateral effort to achieve their objectives, a Tariff Negotiations Committee, composed of all the governments which have submitted consolidated lists of offers in accordance with paragraph 6, shall be established. The functions and terms of reference of the Committee shall be the following:

(a)   The Committee shall exercise its good offices for the purpose of achieving the maximum practicable progress towards the objectives of the Conference.

(b)   The Committee shall review the consolidated offers as soon as practicable after the opening of the negotiations, at any time deemed appropriate and useful during the Conference and again in the final phase of the negotiations; *provided* that the opening of negotiations bilaterally shall in no way be conditioned upon the carrying out of the initial review referred to above.

(c)   The Committee shall be at the disposal of any country or group of countries to arrange for negotiations on a triangular or multilateral basis to improve the scope of concessions.

(d)   Upon the request of any participating country, the Committee shall consider any problems that such country may believe are impeding or unduly delaying the successful conclusion of negotiations.

(e)   The Committee may give advice and make recommendations on any of the foregoing matters and in so doing shall be guided by the principles of Article XXIX.

8.   Participating governments shall give full consideration to the advice and recommendations of the Tariff Negotiations Committee. Each country retains the right to determine for itself whether to accept such advice or recommendations and to decide on the basis of its own assessment whether to accept the results of the negotiations.

9.   The Committee shall appoint a Tariff Negotiations Working Party to assist in the conduct of the negotiations and may appoint such other subsidiary bodies as may assist the Committee in carrying out its functions.

10.   The Committee shall make arrangements to prevent the disclosure of confidential material.

V.   Methods of Negotiation

11.   The negotiations shall be conducted in accordance with the following rules:

(a)   The negotiations shall be conducted on a selective product-by-product basis which will afford adequate opportunity to take into account the needs of individual countries and individual industries. Participating governments will be free not to grant concessions on particular products and, in the granting of a concession, they may reduce the duty, bind it at its then existing, level, or undertake not to raise it above a specified higher level.

(b)   No participating government shall be required to grant unilateral concessions, or to grant concessions to other governments without receiving adequate concessions in return.

(c)   The binding against increase of low duties or of duty-free treatment shall, in principle, be recognized as a concession equivalent in value to the reduction of high duties. This rule takes account *inter alia*, of the position of countries which, whilst maintaining low or moderate duties on all or most of the products imported from their principal suppliers, find their exports or potential exports generally impeded by high rates of duty.

(d)   In so far as negotiations relate to preferences, the applicable provisions of the General Agreement shall be applied in accordance with the rules, as relevant, followed hitherto in negotiations sponsored by the CONTRACTING PARTIES.

(e)   Participating governments will be expected to take into consideration the indirect benefits which they will receive from the negotiations between other governments.

12.   The participating governments shall refrain from increases in tariffs and other protective measures inconsistent with the principles of the General Agreement and designed to improve their bargaining position in preparation for the negotiations.

VI.   Preparations for the Conference

13.   Not later than 1 October 1955 each government intending to participate in the Conference shall transmit:

(*a*)   A list of requests to each government with which it desires to negotiate. (Forty copies shall be sent simultaneously to the Executive Secretary for distribution to the other governments intending to participate.)

(*b*)   To the Executive Secretary, two copies of the latest edition of its customs tariff and of its foreign trade statistics for 1953 and 1954. (The same information shall be sent to any other government intending to participate which requests it, together with such additional information as may be requested and is readily available.)

VII.   Incorporation of the Results in the General Agreement

14.   Before the close of the Conference each participating government shall prepare for distribution through the secretariat a consolidated list of the concessions granted and a supplementary list showing the country or countries with which each concession was initially negotiated .

15.   The results of the Conference shall be incorporated in the General Agreement by means of a protocol to which will be annexed the schedules of concessions of the participating governments.

RULES AND PROCEDURES FOR THE TARIFF CONFERENCE COMMENCING IN GENEVA ON I SEPTEMBER 1960

I. Scope and Time-Table of the Conference

The CONTRACTING PARTIES, wishing to hold at the same conference:

(a) a general round of negotiations between contracting parties for new concessions;

(b) negotiations for accession to the General Agreement of Cambodia Israel, Tunisia and any other government invited for this purpose by the CONTRACTING PARTIES;

(c) re-negotiations by the Members of the European Economic Community under Article XXIV:6;

(d) re-negotiations under Article XXVIII,

decided, at the fourteenth session:

(i) to convene the conference on 1 September 1960 and that the first part of the conference will be devoted to the carrying out of re-negotiations under Article XXIV:6 with the European Economic Community with a view to concluding such re-negotiations by Christmas 1960, and thereby initiating the negotiations for new concessions in good time;

(ii) to urge all the participating governments to make the necessary arrangements and to give the necessary instructions to enable their delegations to conclude the re-negotiations under Article XXIV:6 by Christmas 1960;

(iii) taking into account what is said in paragraph (i) and (ii) above, to set 2 January 1961 as a target date for the opening of negotiations for new concessions;

(iv) to agree that, for reasons of convenience, any re-negotiations which governments intend to undertake before the end of the three-year period of firm validity, should take place during the first part of the tariff conference, i.e. from 1 September to 24 December 1960; and that, to that effect, these governments be invited to submit any notifications under Article XXVIII as early as possible and not later than 15 July 1960;

(v) to give to Cambodia, Israel, Tunisia and to any other government invited to negotiate with a view to accession at this time, an opportunity to carry out such negotiations during the second part of the conference, i.e. during the early part of 1961.

II.   General Round of Negotiations

(a)   *Aim of the negotiations*

The CONTRACTING PARTIES, recognizing that customs duties and other measures often constitute serious obstacles to the balanced expansion of trade, have decided to hold negotiations based on the principles of Article XXVIII *bis* of the General Agreement and conducted with due regard to the objectives of the General Agreement.

The negotiations shall be directed towards the reduction of the general level of tariffs and other charges on imports and, in particular, to the reduction of such high tariffs as discourage the importation of even minimum quantities and shall aim at the exchange of reciprocal and mutually advantageous concessions. To the extent that contracting parties are able to negotiate mutually satisfactory concessions, negotiations may also be held on non-tariff barriers as provided in (b) (ii) below. Governments participating in the negotiations shall endeavour through common effort to ensure that the results of the negotiations are as great as practicable.

(b)   *Scope of the negotiations*

(i)   Participating countries may request concessions on products of which they individually, or collectively are, or are likely to be, the principal suppliers to the countries from which the concessions are asked. This rule shall not apply to prevent a country not a principal supplier from making a request, but the country concerned may invoke the principal supplier rule if the principal supplier of the product is not participating in the negotiations or is not a contracting party to the General Agreement.

(ii)   Participating countries may also enter into negotiations in accordance with these rules in respect of the following matters:

-   the protection afforded through the operation of import monopolies, as provided in Articles II and XVII (including the interpretative notes thereto);

-   internal quantitative regulations as provided in paragraph 6 of Article III (mixing regulations);

-   the level of screen quotas as provided in Article IV;

-   import restrictions as provided in paragraph 2 (c) of Article XI;

-   the level of a subsidy which operates directly or indirectly to reduce imports;

-   internal taxes.

(c)   Multilateral character of the negotiations

Participating governments agree to make a maximum effort towards achieving the objectives of the negotiations in accordance with Article XXVIII *bis* of the General Agreement and other relevant provisions; and to this end shall cooperate to further their multilateral character by making overall concessions commensurate with the overall concessions received.

III.   Accession to the General Agreement

As mentioned above, Cambodia, Israel, Tunisia and any other government which may be invited by the CONTRACTING PARTIES will be given an opportunity to carry out negotiations with a view to acceding to the General Agreement, The procedural steps are the same as those for contracting parties. In granting tariff concessions, acceding governments will take into consideration the indirect benefits which they will receive from the concessions exchanged between contracting parties at earlier conferences and those which will result from new negotiations among contracting parties. Similarly, all the participating governments will be expected to take into consideration the indirect benefits which they will receive from the negotiations between the acceding governments themselves and between them and the contracting parties.

IV.   Negotiations under Article XXIV:6

The time-table for these negotiations is contained in Sections I and VIII.

V.   Renegotiations under Article XXVIII

The time-table for these negotiations is contained in Section I.

VI.   The Tariff Negotiations Committee

With a view to facilitating the negotiations and ensuring the fullest possible multilateral effort to achieve their objectives, a Tariff Negotiations Committee, composed of all the governments which have submitted consolidated lists of offers, shall be established. When dealing with the re-negotiations mentioned under (d) below, the Committee shall be composed of all interested parties within the terms of Article XXVIII:1. The functions and terms of reference of the Committee shall be the following:

(a)   The Committee shall exercise its good offices for the purpose of achieving the maximum practicable progress towards the objectives of the conference.

(b)   The Committee shall review the consolidated offers as soon as practicable after the opening of the negotiations, at any time deemed appropriate and useful during the conference and again in the final phase of the negotiations; *provided* that the opening of negotiations bilaterally shall in no way be conditioned upon the carrying out of the initial review referred to above.

(c)   The Committee should consider the possibilities of furthering the multilateral character of the negotiations, for example through examining the lists of requests before the opening of the second stage of the conference. Furthermore, the Committee shall be at the disposal of any country or group of countries to arrange for negotiations on a triangular or multilateral basis to improve the scope of concessions.

(d)   The Committee shall follow closely the course of the re-negotiations under Article XXIV:6 and those under Article XXVIII, review their progress from time to time, and assist participating countries in eliminating difficulties which might be holding up their re-negotiations.

(e)   Upon the request of any participating country, the Committee shall consider any problems that such country may believe are impeding or unduly delaying the successful conclusion of negotiations.

(f)   The Committee may give advice and make recommendations on any of the foregoing matters and in so doing shall be guided by the principles of Article XXVIII *bis* and any other relevant provisions.

(g)   The Committee will draft the instrument or instruments, which will embody the results of the negotiations. The draft or drafts will be submitted, if necessary by postal ballot, to the CONTRACTING PARTIES for their approval.

Participating governments shall give full consideration to the advice and recommendations of the Tariff Negotiations Committee. Each country retains the right to determine for itself whether to accept such advice or recommendations and to decide on the basis of its own assessment whether to accept the results of the negotiations.

The Committee shall appoint a Tariff Negotiations Working Party to assist in the conduct of the negotiations and may appoint such other subsidiary bodies as may assist the Committee in carrying out its functions.

The Committee shall make arrangements to prevent the disclosure of confidential material.

VII.   Methods of Negotiation

The negotiations shall be conducted in accordance with the following rules:

a)   The negotiations shall be conducted on a selective product-by-product basis which will afford adequate opportunity to take into account the needs of individual countries and individual industries. Participating governments will be free not to grant concessions on particular products and, in the granting of a concession they may reduce the duty or other form of protection, bind it at its then existing level, or undertake not to raise it above a specified higher level.

(b)   No participating government shall be required to grant unilateral concessions, or to grant concessions to other governments without receiving adequate concessions in return.

(c)   The binding against increase of low duties or of duty-free treatment shall, in principle, be recognized as a concession equivalent in value to the reduction of high duties. This rule takes account, *inter alia*, of the position of countries which, whilst maintaining low or moderate duties on all or most of the products imported from their principal suppliers, find their exports or potential exports generally impeded by high rates of duty.

(d)   Insofar as negotiations relate to preferences, the applicable provisions of the General Agreement shall be applied in accordance with the rules, as relevant, followed hitherto in negotiations sponsored by the CONTRACTING PARTIES.

(e)   Participating governments will be expected to take into consideration the indirect benefits which they will receive from the negotiations between other governments.

The participating governments shall refrain from increasing tariffs and other protective measures inconsistently with the principles of the General Agreement and with the object of improving their bargaining position in preparation for the negotiations.

VIII. Preparations for the Conference

In preparation for the negotiations the following time-table shall be observed:

A.   General round of negotiations

1.   In order to facilitate the task of the United States authorities preliminary lists of products were to be sent to the United States Government in August or September 1959. If a country should need more time the United States would still take into consideration lists received before 31 October 1959. Forty copies should be sent to the secretariat at least by 31 October 1959 for distribution to contracting parties.

2.   Lists of requests with the indication of the rates requested would be submitted not later than 1 August 1960. Fifty copies should be sent simultaneously to the secretariat for distribution to contracting parties.

3.   As early as possible, but at the latest simultaneously with the lists of requests, each participating government shall send to the Executive Secretary two copies of the latest edition of its customs tariff and of its foreign trade statistics for 1958 and 1959. The same information should be sent to any other

contracting party which requests it, together with such additional information as may be requested and is readily available.

4.　　　Consolidated lists of offers should be prepared in time for distribution on the day the general round of negotiations opens.

5.　　　Models for the lists mentioned in paragraphs 1, 2 and 4 of Section A above are shown below.

B.　　Negotiations for accession

Procedurally, acceding governments are required to submit the same kinds of lists and to follow the same time-table as contracting parties. Models for the lists mentioned in paragraphs 1, 2 and 4 of Section A above are shown below.

C.　　Negotiations on the common tariff the European Economic Community under Article XXIV:6

1.　　　The Commission of the EEC agreed to submit towards the end of 1959 its common tariff, including rates for the large part if not all of the products contained in List G annexed to the Rome Treaty.

2.　　　The Community will submit by 1 May 1960 a list of the items bound by the Six under the GATT indicating opposite each item: the contracting party with which each item was initially negotiated; and (a) whether it considers the "internal compensation" to be adequate; (b) whether it considers the "internal compensation", if any, to be inadequate; or (c) whether it considers the "internal compensation" to exceed the compensation actually required.

3.　　　At the same time as the list of bound items the Community will furnish statistical information on imports into the territories of the Six as a whole for 1958; statistical information relating to 1959 might have to be sent at a later date. The Community would, of course, supply supplementary data on request in the course of the negotiations.

4.　　　Contracting parties which so wish may submit to the Community as soon as possible after receipt of the May 1960 list, a notification of the items of which they are initial negotiators or in which they consider themselves to have a principal supplying or substantial interest. At the same time, contracting parties may submit to the Community for its guidance lists of items on which they would wish to request compensation.

5.　　　At the opening of the conference on 1 September 1960 the Community will make offers of compensation for all those modifications for which compensation was promised under 2 (b) above in the list submitted on 1 May.

Models of lists mentioned above, Section VIII B

GATT TARIFF NEGOTIATIONS 1960/61

List of the products on which ... (country) ...
intends to request concessions from the United States

Tariff item number	Description of products

GATT TARIFF NEGOTIATIONS 1960/61

Tariff concessions which ... (country) ...
requests from ... (country) ...

Tariff item number	Description of products	Present rate of duty	Requested rate of duty

GATT TARIFF NEGOTIATIONS 1960/61

Consolidated list of offers by ... (country) ...

Tariff item number	Description of products	Present rate of duty	Requested rate of duty	Offers	
				Concession offered	Countries to which offer is made

CONCLUSIONS AND RESOLUTIONS ADOPTED ON 21 MAY 1963

At the close of the ministerial meeting held at Geneva from 16 to 21 May, the Ministers adopted the following conclusions and resolutions relating to the three items of their agenda:

....

....

II. ARRANGEMENTS FOR THE REDUCTION OR ELIMINATION OF TARIFFS AND OTHER BARRIERS TO TRADE, AND RELATED MATTERS

and

III. MEASURES FOR ACCESS TO MARKETS FOR AGRICULTURAL AND OTHER PRIMARY PRODUCTS

Resolution adopted

The Ministers agreed:

A. *Principles*

1.   That a significant liberalization of world trade is desirable, and that, for this purpose, comprehensive trade negotiations, to be conducted on a most-favoured-nation basis and on the principle of reciprocity, shall begin at Geneva on 4 May 1964, with the widest possible participation.

2.   That the trade negotiations shall cover all classes of products, industrial and non-industrial, including agricultural and primary products.

3.   That the trade negotiations shall deal not only with tariffs but also with non-tariff barriers.

4.   That, in view of the limited results obtained in recent years from item-by-item negotiations, the tariff negotiations, subject to the provisions of paragraph B 3, shall be based upon a plan of substantial linear tariff reductions with a bare minimum of exceptions which shall be subject to confrontation and justification. The linear reductions shall be equal. In those cases where there are significant disparities in tariff levels, the tariff reductions will be based upon special rules of general and automatic application.

5.   That in the trade negotiations it shall be open to each country to request additional trade concessions or to modify its own offers where this is necessary to obtain a balance of advantages between it and the other participating countries. It shall be a matter of joint endeavour by all participating countries to negotiate for a sufficient basis of reciprocity to maintain the fullest measure of trade concessions.

6.   That during the trade negotiations a problem of reciprocity could arise in the case of countries the general incidence of whose tariffs is unquestionably lower than that of other participating countries.

7.   That, in view of the importance of agriculture in world trade, the trade negotiations shall provide for acceptable conditions of access to world markets for agricultural products.

8.   That in the trade negotiations every effort shall be made to reduce barriers to exports of the less-developed countries, but that the developed countries cannot expect to receive reciprocity from the less-developed countries.

B.   *Procedures*

1.   That a Trade Negotiations Committee, composed of representatives of all participating countries, shall be set up, and that it shall be the function of the Trade Negotiations Committee, directly or through committees (including the Special Groups referred to in paragraph 3(d) below):

(a)   to elaborate a trade negotiating plan in the light of the principles in paragraphs A 1-8 above, with a view to reaching agreement on the details of the plan of tariff reductions referred to in paragraph A 4 above by 1 August 1963, and to completing the remainder of the task by the date of the beginning of the twenty-first session of the Contracting Parties.

(b)   to supervise the conduct of the trade negotiations.

2.   That the trade negotiating plan will have to take into account the issues raised by the Ministers, and that the acceptability of the trade negotiating plan, from the point of view of individual countries, will depend upon the degree to which it succeeds in dealing with such issues.

3.   That the Trade Negotiations Committee in elaborating the trade negotiating plan, shall deal *inter alia* with the following issues and special situations:

(a)   the depth of the tariff reductions, and the rules for exceptions.

(b)   the criteria for determining significant disparities in tariff levels and the special rules applicable for tariff reductions in these cases.

(c)   the problem for certain countries with a very low average level of tariffs or with a special economic or trade structure such that equal linear tariff reductions may not provide an adequate balance of advantages.

(d)   the rules to govern, and the methods to be employed in, the creation of acceptable conditions of access to world markets for agricultural products in furtherance of a significant development and expansion of world trade in such products. Since cereals and meats are amongst the commodities for which general arrangements may be required, the Special Groups on Cereals and Meats shall convene at early dates to negotiate appropriate arrangements. For similar reasons a special group on dairy products shall also be established.

(e)   the rules to govern and the methods to be employed in the treatment of non-tariff barriers, including *inter alia* discriminatory treatment applied to products of certain countries and the means of assuring that the value of tariff reductions will not be impaired or nullified by non-tariff barriers. Consideration shall be given to the possible need to review the application of certain provisions of the General Agreement, in particular Articles XIX and XXVIII, or the procedures thereunder, with a view to maintaining, to the largest extent possible, trade liberalization and the stability of tariff concessions.

DECLARATION OF MINISTERS
APPROVED AT TOKYO ON 14 SEPTEMBER 1973

(MIN(73)1)

1.　　The Ministers, having considered the report of the Preparatory Committee for the Trade Negotiations and having noted that a number of governments have decided to enter into comprehensive multilateral trade negotiations in the framework of GATT and that other governments have indicated their intention to make a decision as soon as possible, declare the negotiations officially open. Those governments which have decided to negotiate have notified the Director-General of GATT to this effect, and the Ministers agree that it will be open to any other government, through a notification to the Director-General, to participate in the negotiations. The Ministers hope that the negotiations will involve the active participation of as many countries as possible. They expect the negotiations to be engaged effectively as rapidly as possible, and that, to that end, the governments concerned will have such authority as may be required.

2.　　The negotiations shall aim to:

-　　achieve the expansion and ever-greater liberalization of world trade and improvement in the standard of living and welfare of the people of the world, objectives which can be achieved, *inter alia*, through the progressive dismantling of obstacles to trade and the improvement of the international framework for the conduct of world trade.

-　　secure additional benefits for the international trade of developing countries so as to achieve a substantial increase in their foreign exchange earnings, the diversification of their exports, the acceleration of the rate of growth of their trade, taking into account their development needs, an improvement in the possibilities for these countries to participate in the expansion of world trade and a better balance as between developed and developing countries in the sharing of the advantages resulting from this expansion, through, in the largest possible measure, a substantial improvement in the conditions of access for the products of interest to the developing countries and, wherever appropriate, measures designed to attain stable, equitable and remunerative prices for primary products.

To this end, co-ordinated efforts shall be made to solve in an equitable way the trade problems of all participating countries, taking into account the specific trade problems of the developing countries.

3.　　To this end the negotiations should aim, inter alia, to:

(a)　　conduct negotiations on tariffs by employment of appropriate formulae of as general application as possible;

(b)　　reduce or eliminate non-tariff measures or, where this is not appropriate, to reduce or eliminate their trade restricting or distorting effects, and to bring such measures under more effective international discipline;

(c)   include an examination of the possibilities for the co-ordinated reduction or elimination of all barriers to trade in selected sectors as a complementary technique;

(d)   include an examination of the adequacy of the multilateral safeguard system, considering particularly the modalities of application of Article XIX, with a view to furthering trade liberalization and preserving its results;

(e)   include, as regards agriculture, an approach to negotiations which, while in line with the general objectives of the negotiations, should take account of the special characteristics and problems in this sector;

(f)   treat tropical products as a special and priority sector.

4.   The negotiations shall cover tariffs, non-tariff barriers and other measures which impede or distort international trade in both industrial and agricultural products, including tropical products and raw materials, whether in primary form or at any stage of processing including in particular products of export interest to developing countries and measures affecting their exports.

5.   The negotiations shall be conducted on the basis of the principles of mutual advantage, mutual commitment and overall reciprocity, while observing the most-favoured-nation clause, and consistently with the provisions of the General Agreement relating to such negotiations. Participants shall jointly endeavour in the negotiations to achieve, by appropriate methods, an overall balance of advantage at the highest possible level. The developed countries do not expect reciprocity for commitments made by them in the negotiations to reduce or remove tariff and other barriers to the trade of developing countries, i.e., the developed countries do not expect the developing countries, in the course of the trade negotiations, to make contributions which are inconsistent with their individual development, financial and trade needs. The Ministers recognize the need for special measures to be taken in the negotiations to assist the developing countries in their efforts to increase their export earnings and promote their economic development and, where appropriate, for priority attention to be given to products or areas of interest to developing countries. They also recognize the importance of maintaining and improving the Generalized System of Preferences. They further recognize the importance of the application of differential measures to developing countries in ways which will provide special and more favourable treatment for them in areas of the negotiation where this is feasible and appropriate.

6.   The Ministers recognize that the particular situation and problems of the least developed among the developing countries shall be given special attention, and stress the need to ensure that these countries receive special treatment in the context of any general or specific measures taken in favour of the developing countries during the negotiations.

7.   The policy of liberalizing world trade cannot be carried out successfully in the absence of parallel efforts to set up a monetary system which shields the world economy from the shocks and imbalances which have previously occurred. The Ministers will not lose sight of the fact that the efforts which are to be made in the trade field imply continuing efforts to maintain orderly conditions and to establish a durable and equitable monetary system.

The Ministers recognize equally that the new phase in the liberalization of trade which it is their intention to undertake should facilitate the orderly functioning of the monetary system.

The Ministers recognize that they should bear these considerations in mind both at the opening of and throughout the negotiations. Efforts in these two fields will thus be able to contribute effectively to an improvement of international economic relations, taking into account the special characteristics of the economies of the developing countries and their problems.

8.   The negotiations shall be considered as one undertaking, the various elements of which shall move forward together.

9.   Support is reaffirmed for the principles, rules and disciplines provided for under the General Agreement.[1] Consideration shall be given to improvements in the international framework for the conduct of world trade which might be desirable in the light of progress in the negotiations and, in this endeavour, care shall be taken to ensure that any measures introduced as a result are consistent with the overall objectives and principles of the trade negotiations and particularly of trade liberalization.

10.   A Trade Negotiations Committee is established, with authority, taking into account the present Declaration, *inter alia*:

(*a*)   to elaborate and put into effect detailed trade negotiating plans and to establish appropriate negotiating procedures, including special procedures for the negotiations between developed and developing countries;

(*b*)   to supervise the progress of the negotiations.

The Trade Negotiations Committee shall be open to participating governments.[2] The Trade Negotiations Committee shall hold its opening meeting not later than 1 November 1973.

11.   The Ministers intend that the trade negotiations be concluded in 1975.

---

[1]   This does not necessarily represent the views of representatives of countries not now parties to the General Agreement.

[2]   Including the European Communities.

MINISTERIAL DECLARATION OF 20 SEPTEMBER 1986

(Min.Dec)

Ministers, meeting on the occasion of the Special Session of the CONTRACTING PARTIES at Punta del Este, have decided to launch Multilateral Trade Negotiations (The Uruguay Round). To this end, they have adopted the following Declaration. The Multilateral Trade Negotiations will be open to the participation of countries as indicated in Parts I and II of this Declaration. A Trade Negotiations Committee is established to carry out the negotiations. The Trade Negotiations Committee shall hold its first meeting not later than 31 October 1986. It shall meet as appropriate at Ministerial level. The Multilateral Trade Negotiations will be concluded within four years.

PART I

NEGOTIATIONS ON TRADE IN GOODS

The CONTRACTING PARTIES meeting at Ministerial level

Determined to halt and reverse protectionism and to remove distortions to trade

Determined also to preserve the basic principles and to further the objectives of the GATT

Determined also to develop a more open, viable and durable multilateral trading system

Convinced that such action would promote growth and development

Mindful of the negative effects of prolonged financial and monetary instability in the world economy, the indebtedness of a large number of less developed contracting parties, and considering the linkage between trade, money, finance and development

Decide to enter into Multilateral Trade Negotiations on trade in goods within the framework and under the aegis of the General Agreement on Tariffs and Trade.

A. *Objectives*

Negotiations shall aim to:

(i) bring about further liberalization and expansion of world trade to the benefit of all countries, especially less-developed contracting parties, including the improvement of access to markets by the reduction and elimination of tariffs, quantitative restrictions and other non-tariff measures and obstacles;

(ii) strengthen the rôle of GATT, improve the multilateral trading system based on the principles and rules of the GATT and bring about a wider coverage of world trade under agreed, effective and enforceable multilateral disciplines;

(iii) increase the responsiveness of the GATT system to the evolving international economic environment, through facilitating necessary structural adjustment, enhancing the relationship of the GATT with the relevant international organizations and taking account of changes in trade patterns and prospects, including the growing importance of trade in high technology products, serious difficulties in commodity markets and the importance of an improved trading environment providing, *inter alia*, for the ability of indebted countries to meet their financial obligations;

(iv) foster concurrent cooperative action at the national and international levels to strengthen the inter-relationship between trade policies and other economic policies affecting growth and development, and to contribute towards continued, effective and determined efforts to improve the functioning of the international monetary system and the flow of financial and real investment resources to developing countries.

B. *General Principles Governing Negotiations*

(i) Negotiations shall be conducted in a transparent manner, and consistent with the objectives and commitments agreed in this Declaration and with the principles of the General Agreement in order to ensure mutual advantage and increased benefits to all participants.

(ii) The launching, the conduct and the implementation of the outcome of the negotiations shall be treated as parts of a single undertaking. However, agreements reached at an early stage may be implemented on a provisional or a definitive basis by agreement prior to the formal conclusion of the negotiations. Early agreements shall be taken into account in assessing the overall balance of the negotiations.

(iii) Balanced concessions should be sought within broad trading areas and subjects to be negotiated in order to avoid unwarranted cross-sectoral demands.

(iv) The CONTRACTING PARTIES agree that the principle of differential and more favourable treatment embodied in Part IV and other relevant provisions of the General Agreement and in the Decision of the CONTRACTING PARTIES of 28 November 1979 on Differential and More Favourable Treatment, Reciprocity and Fuller Participation of Developing Countries applies to the negotiations. In the implementation of standstill and rollback, particular care should be given to avoiding disruptive effects on the trade of less-developed contracting parties.

(v) The developed countries do not expect reciprocity for commitments made by them in trade negotiations to reduce or remove tariffs and other barriers to the trade of developing countries, i.e. the developed countries do not expect the developing countries, in the course of trade negotiations, to make contributions which are inconsistent with their individual development, financial and trade needs. Developed contracting parties shall therefore not seek, neither shall less-developed contracting parties be required to make, concessions that are inconsistent with the latter's development, financial and trade needs.

(vi)   Less-developed contracting parties expect that their capacity to make contributions or negotiated concessions or take other mutually agreed action under the provisions and procedures of the General Agreement would improve with the progressive development of their economies and improvement in their trade situation and they would accordingly expect to participate more fully in the framework of rights and obligations under the General Agreement.

(vii)   Special attention shall be given to the particular situation and problems of the least-developed countries and to the need to encourage positive measures to facilitate expansion of their trading opportunities. Expeditious implementation of the relevant provisions of the 1982 Ministerial Declaration concerning the least-developed countries shall also be given appropriate attention.

C.   Standstill and Rollback

Commencing immediately and continuing until the formal completion of the negotiations, each participant agrees to apply the following commitments:

Standstill

(i)   not to take any trade restrictive or distorting measure inconsistent with the provisions of the General Agreement or the Instruments negotiated within the framework of GATT or under its auspices;

(ii)   not to take any trade restrictive or distorting measure in the legitimate exercise of its GATT rights, that would go beyond that which is necessary to remedy specific situations, as provided for in the General Agreement and the Instruments referred to in (i) above;

(iii)   not to take any trade measures in such a manner as to improve its negotiating positions.

Rollback

(i)   that all trade restrictive or distorting measures inconsistent with the provisions of the General Agreement or Instruments negotiated within the framework of GATT or under its auspices, shall be phased out or brought into conformity within an agreed timeframe not later than by the date of the formal completion of the negotiations, taking into account multilateral agreements, undertakings and understandings, including strengthened rules and disciplines, reached in pursuance of the Objectives of the Negotiations;

(ii)   there shall be progressive implementation of this commitment on an equitable basis in consultations among participants concerned, including all affected participants. This commitment shall take account of the concerns expressed by any participant about measures directly affecting its trade interests;

(iii)   there shall be no GATT concessions requested for the elimination of these measures.

Surveillance of standstill and rollback

Each participant agrees that the implementation of these commitments on standstill and rollback shall be subject to multilateral surveillance so as to ensure that these commitments are being met. The Trade Negotiations Committee will decide on the appropriate mechanisms to carry out the surveillance, including periodic reviews and evaluations. Any participant may bring to the attention of the appropriate surveillance mechanism any actions or omissions it believes to be relevant to the fulfilment of these commitments. These notifications should be addressed to the GATT secretariat which may also provide further relevant information.

D.   Subjects for Negotiation

Tariffs

Negotiations shall aim, by appropriate methods, to reduce or, as appropriate, eliminate tariffs including the reduction or elimination of high tariffs and tariff escalation. Emphasis shall be given to the expansion of the scope of tariff concessions among all participants.

Non-tariff measures

Negotiations shall aim to reduce or eliminate non-tariff measures, including quantitative restrictions, without prejudice to any action to be taken in fulfilment of the rollback commitments.

Tropical products

Negotiations shall aim at the fullest liberalization of trade in tropical products, including in their processed and semi-processed forms and shall cover both tariff and all non-tariff measures affecting trade in these products.

The CONTRACTING PARTIES recognize the importance of trade in tropical products to a large number of less developed contracting parties and agree that negotiations in this area shall receive special attention, including the timing of the negotiations and the implementation of the results as provided for in B(ii).

Natural resource-based products

Negotiations shall aim to achieve the fullest liberalization of trade in natural resource-based products, including in their processed and semi-processed forms. The negotiations shall aim to reduce or eliminate tariff and non-tariff measures, including tariff escalation.

Textiles and clothing

Negotiations in the area of textiles and clothing shall aim to formulate modalities that would permit the eventual integration of this sector into GATT on the basis of strengthened GATT rules and disciplines, thereby also contributing to the objective of further liberalization of trade.

Agriculture

The CONTRACTING PARTIES agree that there is an urgent need to bring more discipline and predictability to world agricultural trade by correcting and preventing restrictions and distortions including those related to structural surpluses so as to reduce the uncertainty, imbalances and instability in world agricultural markets.

Negotiations shall aim to achieve greater liberalization of trade in agriculture and bring all measures affecting import access and export competition under strengthened and more operationally effective GATT rules and disciplines, taking into account the general principles governing the negotiations, by:

(i)   improving market access through, *inter alia*, the reduction of import barriers;

(ii)   improving the competitive environment by increasing discipline on the use of all direct and indirect subsidies and other measures affecting directly or indirectly agricultural trade, including the phased reduction of their negative effects and dealing with their causes;

(iii)   minimizing the adverse effects that sanitary and phytosanitary regulations and barriers can have on trade in agriculture, taking into account the relevant international agreements.

In order to achieve the above objectives, the negotiating group having primary responsibility for all aspects of agriculture will use the Recommendations adopted by the CONTRACTING PARTIES at their Fortieth Session, which were developed in accordance with the GATT 1982 Ministerial Work Programme, and take account of the approaches suggested in the work of the Committee on Trade in Agriculture without prejudice to other alternatives that might achieve the objectives of the negotiations.

GATT Articles

Participants shall review existing GATT Articles, provisions and disciplines as requested by interested contracting parties, and, as appropriate, undertake negotiations.

Safeguards

(i)   A comprehensive agreement on safeguards is of particular importance to the strengthening of the GATT system and to progress in the Multilateral Trade Negotiations.

(ii)   The agreement on safeguards:

-    shall be based on the basic principles of the General Agreement;

-    shall contain, *inter alia*, the following elements: transparency, coverage, objective criteria for action including the concept of serious injury or threat thereof, temporary nature, degressivity and structural adjustment, compensation and retaliation, notification, consultation, multilateral surveillance and dispute settlement; and

-    shall clarify and reinforce the disciplines of the General Agreement and should apply to all contracting parties.

MTN Agreements and Arrangements

Negotiations shall aim to improve, clarify, or expand, as appropriate, Agreements and Arrangements negotiated in the Tokyo Round of Multilateral Negotiations.

Subsidies and countervailing measures

Negotiations on subsidies and countervailing measures shall be based on a review of Articles VI and XVI and the MTN Agreement on subsidies and countervailing measures with the objective of improving GATT disciplines relating to all subsidies and countervailing measures that affect international trade. A negotiating group will be established to deal with these issues.

Dispute settlement

In order to ensure prompt and effective resolution of disputes to the benefit of all contracting parties, negotiations shall aim to improve and strengthen the rules and the procedures of the dispute settlement process, while recognizing the contribution that would be made by more effective and enforceable GATT rules and disciplines. Negotiations shall include the development of adequate arrangements for overseeing and monitoring of the procedures that would facilitate compliance with adopted recommendations.

Trade-related aspects of intellectual property rights, including trade in counterfeit goods

In order to reduce the distortions and impediments to international trade, and taking into account the need to promote effective and adequate protection of intellectual property rights, and to ensure that measures and procedures to enforce intellectual property rights do not themselves become barriers to legitimate trade, the negotiations shall aim to clarify GATT provisions and elaborate as appropriate new rules and disciplines.

Negotiations shall aim to develop a multilateral framework of principles, rules and disciplines dealing with international trade in counterfeit goods, taking into account work already undertaken in the GATT.

These negotiations shall be without prejudice to other complementary initiatives that may be taken in the World Intellectual Property Organization and elsewhere to deal with these matters.

Trade-related investment measures

Following an examination of the operation of GATT Articles related to the trade restrictive and distorting effects of investment measures, negotiations should elaborate, as appropriate, further provisions that may be necessary to avoid such adverse effects on trade.

E.   *Functioning of the GATT System*

Negotiations shall aim to develop understandings and arrangements:

(i)   to enhance the surveillance in the GATT to enable regular monitoring of trade policies and practices of contracting parties and their impact on the functioning of the multilateral trading system;

(ii)   to improve the overall effectiveness and decision-making of the GATT as an institution, including, inter alia, through involvement of Ministers;

(iii)   to increase the contribution of the GATT to achieving greater coherence in global economic policy-making through strengthening its relationship with other international organizations responsible for monetary and financial matters.

F.   *Participation*

(a)   Negotiations will be open to:

(i)   all contracting parties,

(ii)   countries having acceded provisionally,

(iii)   countries applying the GATT on a *de facto* basis having announced, not later than 30 April 1987, their intention to accede to the GATT and to participate in the negotiations,

(iv)   countries that have already informed the CONTRACTING PARTIES, at a regular meeting of the Council of Representatives, of their intention to negotiate the terms of their membership as a contracting party, and

(v)   developing countries that have, by 30 April 1987, initiated procedures for accession to the GATT, with the intention of negotiating the terms of their accession during the course of the negotiations.

(b)   Participation in negotiations relating to the amendment or application of GATT provisions or the negotiation of new provisions will, however, be open only to contracting parties.

G.   *Organization of the Negotiations*

A Group of Negotiations on Goods (GNG) is established to carry out the programme of negotiations contained in this Part of the Declaration. The GNG shall, *inter alia*:

(i)   elaborate and put into effect detailed trade negotiating plans prior to 19 December 1986;

(ii)   designate the appropriate mechanism for surveillance of commitments to standstill and rollback;

(iii)   establish negotiating groups as required. Because of the interrelationship of some issues and taking fully into account the general principles governing the negotiations as stated in B(iii) above it is recognized that aspects of one issue may be discussed in more than one negotiating group. Therefore each negotiating group should as required take into account relevant aspects emerging in other groups;

(iv)   also decide upon inclusion of additional subject matters in the negotiation;

(v)   co-ordinate the work of the negotiating groups and supervise the progress of the negotiations. As a guideline not more than two negotiating groups should meet at the same time;

(vi)   the GNG shall report to the Trade Negotiations Committee.

In order to ensure effective application of differential and more favourable treatment the GNG shall, before the formal completion of the negotiations, conduct an evaluation of the results attained therein in terms of the Objectives and the General Principles Governing Negotiations as set out in the Declaration, taking into account all issues of interest to less-developed contracting parties.

PART II
NEGOTIATIONS ON TRADE IN SERVICES

Ministers also decide, as part of the Multilateral Trade Negotiations, to launch negotiations on trade in services.

Negotiations in this area shall aim to establish a multilateral framework of principles and rules for trade in services, including elaboration of possible disciplines for individual sectors, with a view to expansion of such trade under conditions of transparency and progressive liberalization and as a means of promoting economic growth of all trading partners and the development of developing countries. Such framework shall respect the policy objectives of national laws and regulations applying to services and shall take into account the work of relevant international organizations.

GATT procedures and practices shall apply to these negotiations. A Group of Negotiations on Services is established to deal with these matters. Participation in the negotiations under this Part of the Declaration will be open to the same countries as under Part I. GATT secretariat support will be provided, with technical support from other organizations as decided by the Group of Negotiations on Services.

The Group of Negotiations on Services shall report to the Trade Negotiations Committee.

IMPLEMENTATION OF RESULTS UNDER PARTS I AND II

When the results of the Multilateral Trade Negotiations in all areas have been established, Ministers meeting also on the occasion of a Special Session of CONTRACTING PARTIES shall decide regarding the international implementation of the respective results.

APPENDIX C

PROTOCOLS EMBODYING THE RESULTS OF MULTILATERAL TRADE NEGOTIATIONS [1]

The Annecy Protocol

The Torquay Protocol

The Sixth Protocol of Supplementary Concessions

Protocol Embodying the Results of the 1960-61 Tariff Conference

Geneva (1967) Protocol

Geneva (1979) Protocol

Geneva (1979) Supplementary Protocol

Marrakesh Protocol

---

[1]   The Tariff Schedules embodying the results of Geneva 1947 negotiations were annexed to GATT

THE ANNECY PROTOCOL OF TERMS OF ACCESSION TO THE GENERAL AGREEMENT ON TARIFFS AND TRADE

The governments of the Commonwealth of Australia, the Kingdom of Belgium, the United States of Brazil, Burma, Canada, Ceylon, the Republic of Chile, the Republic of China, the Republic of Cuba, the Czechoslovak Republic, the French Republic, India, Lebanon, the Grand-Duchy of Luxemburg, the Kingdom of the Netherlands, New Zealand, the Kingdom of Norway, Pakistan,

Southern Rhodesia, Syria, the Union of South Africa, the United Kingdom of Great Britain and Northern Ireland, and the United States of America, which are the present contracting parties to the General Agreement on Tariffs and Trade (hereinafter called "the present contracting parties" and "the General Agreement" respectively), and the Governments of the Kingdom of Denmark, the Dominican Republic, the Republic of Finland, the Kingdom of Greece, the Republic of Haiti, the republic of Italy, the Republic of Liberia, the Republic of Nicaragua, the Kingdom of Sweden, and the oriental republic of Uruguay (hereinafter called "the acceding governments"),

HAVING REGARD to the results of the negotiations directed towards the accession of the acceding governments to the General Agreement,

In accordance with the provisions of Article XXXIII of the General Agreement:

HEREBY AGREE upon the terms on which the acceding governments may so accede, which terms are embodied in this Protocol,

AND the present contracting parties DECIDE by decisions of two-thirds majorities, taken in the manner provided in paragraph II of this Protocol, upon the accession to the General Agreement of the acceding governments

    1.   (a)   Subject to the provisions of this Protocol, each of the acceding governments shall, upon the entry into force of this Protocol with respect to it, apply provisionally:

        (i)   Parts I and III of the General Agreement, and

        (ii)   Part II of the General Agreement to the fullest extent not inconsistent with its legislation existing on the date of this Protocol.

    (b)   The obligations incorporated in paragraph I of Article I of the General Agreement by reference to Article III thereof and those incorporated in paragraph 2 (b) of Article II by reference to Article VI shall be considered as falling within Part II of the General Agreement for the purpose of this paragraph.

    (c)   For the purposes of the General Agreement, the Schedules contained in Annex B to this Protocol shall be regarded as Schedules to the General Agreement relating to acceding governments.

    (d)   Notwithstanding the provisions of paragraph I of Article I of the General Agreement, signature of this Protocol by an acceding government shall not require the elimination of any preferences in respect of import duties or charges which do not exceed the levels provided for in paragraph 4 of Article I of the General Agreement as modified and which are in force exclusively between Uruguay and Paraguay.

2.　　Upon the entry into force of this Protocol with respect to each acceding government, that government shall become a contracting party as defined in Article XXXII of the General Agreement.

3.　　Notwithstanding the provisions of paragraph 12, the concessions provided for in the Schedule relating to each present contracting party and contained in Annex A to this Protocol shall not enter into force for that contracting party unless notification of the intention to apply these concessions has first been received by the Secretary-General of the United Nations from that contracting party. Such concessions shall thereafter enter into force for that contracting party either on the date or which this Protocol first enters into force pursuant to paragraph 12 or on the thirtieth day following the day upon which such notification is received by the Secretary-General, whichever is the later. Such notification shall only be effective if received by the Secretary-General not later than April 30, 1950. Upon the entry into force of such concessions the appropriate Schedule shall be regarded as a Schedule to the General Agreement relating to that contracting party.

4.　　Any present contracting party which has given the notification referred to in paragraph 3 or any acceding government which has signed this Protocol shall be free at any time to withhold or to withdraw in whole or in part any concession, provided for in the appropriate Schedule contained in Annex A or B to this Protocol, in respect of which such contracting party or government determines that it was initially negotiated with an acceding government which has not signed this Protocol or a present contracting party which has not given such notification; *Provided* that the present contracting party or acceding government withholding or withdrawing in whole or in part any such concession shall give notice to all other present contracting parties and acceding governments within thirty days after the date of such withholding or withdrawal and, upon request, shall consult with the contracting parties which have a substantial interest in the product concerned; and *Provided further* that, without prejudice to the provisions of Article XXXV of the General Agreement, any concession so withheld or withdrawn shall be applied from the thirtieth day following the day upon which the acceding government or present contracting party with which it was initially negotiated signs this Protocol or gives the notification referred to in paragraph 3.

5　　(a)　　In each case in which Article II of the General Agreement refers to the date of that Agreement, the applicable date in respect of the Schedules annexed to this Protocol shall be the date of this Protocol.

(b)　　In each case in which paragraph 6 of Article V, subparagraph 4 (d) of Article VII and sub-paragraph 3 (c) of Article X of the General Agreement refers to the date of that Agreement, the applicable date in respect of each acceding government shall be March 24, 1948.

(c)　　In the case of the references in paragraph II of Article XVIII of the General Agreement to September 1, 1947, and October 10, 1947, the applicable dates in respect of each acceding government shall be May 14, 1949 and July 30, 1949, respectively.

6.   The provisions of the General Agreement to be applied by an acceding government shall be those contained in the text annexed to the Final Act of the Second Session of the Preparatory Committee of the United Nations Conference on Trade and Employment as rectified, amended, or otherwise modified on the day on which this Protocol is signed by such acceding government. Signature of this Protocol by an acceding government, to be effective, shall be accompanied by appropriate action accepting any rectification, amendment, or other modification which has been drawn up by the CONTRACTING PARTIES for submission to governments for acceptance but which has not become effective by the date of signature of this Protocol by that acceding government.

7.   Any acceding government which has signed this Protocol shall be free to withdraw its provisional application of the General Agreement and such withdrawal shall take effect on the sixtieth day following the day on which written notice of such withdrawal is received by the Secretary-General of the United Nations.

8.   (a)   Any acceding government which has signed this Protocol and has not given notice of withdrawal under paragraph 7, may, on or after the date on which the General Agreement enters into force pursuant to Article XXVI thereof, accede to that Agreement upon the terms of this Protocol by deposit of an instrument of accession with the Secretary-General of the united nations. Such accession shall take effect on the day on which the General Agreement enters into force pursuant to Article XXVI, or on the thirtieth day following the day of the deposit of the instrument of accession, whichever shall be the later.

(b)   Accession to the General Agreement pursuant to paragraph 8 (a) of this Protocol shall, for the purpose of paragraph 2 of Article XXXII of that Agreement, be regarded as acceptance of the Agreement pursuant to paragraph 3 of Article XXVI thereof.

9.   (a)   Each acceding government signing this Protocol, or depositing an instrument of accession under paragraph 8 (a), and each present contracting party giving the notification referred to in paragraph 3, does so in respect of its metropolitan territory and of the other territories for which it has international responsibility, except such separate customs territories as it shall notify to the Secretary-General of the United Nations at the time of such signature, deposit, or notification under paragraph 3.

(b)   Any acceding government or present contracting party which has notified the Secretary-General, under the exception in subparagraph (a) of this paragraph, may at any time give notice to the Secretary-General that such signature, accession, or notification under paragraph 3 shall be effective in respect of any separate customs territory or territories so excepted and such notice shall take effect on the thirtieth day following the day on which it is received by the Secretary-General.

(c)   If any of the customs territories, in respect of which an acceding government has made the General Agreement effective, possesses or acquires full autonomy in the conduct of its external commercial relations and of the other matters provided for in the General Agreement, such territory shall, upon sponsorship through a declaration by the responsible acceding government establishing the above-mentioned fact, be deemed to be a contracting party.

10.   (a)   The original text of this Protocol shall be deposited with the Secretary-General of the United Nations and shall be open for signature at the Headquarters of the United Nations by present contracting parties from October 10, 1949, until November 30, 1949 and by acceding governments from October 10, 1949, until April 30, 1950.

(b)   The Secretary-General of the United Nations shall promptly furnish a certified copy of this Protocol, and a notification of each signature thereto, of each deposit of an instrument of accession under paragraph 8 (a), and of each notification or notice under paragraph 3, 7, 9 (a) or 9 (b), to each Member of the United Nations and to each other government which participated in the United Nations conference on Trade and Employment.

(c)   The Secretary-General is authorized to register this Protocol in accordance with Article 102 of the Charter of the United Nations.

11.   Upon signature of this Protocol in respect of an acceding government by two-thirds of the present contracting parties, it shall constitute a decision taken under Article XXXIII of the General Agreement agreeing to the accession of that government.

12.   Subject to the provisions of paragraph 3, this Protocol shall, for each acceding government in respect of which it has been signed by November 30, 1949, by two-thirds of the present contracting parties, enter into force:

(a)   if it has been signed by that acceding government by November 30, 1949, on January 1, 1950, or,

(b)   if it has not been signed by that acceding government by November 30, 1949, on the thirtieth day following the day upon which it shall have been signed by such acceding government.

13. The date of this Protocol shall be October 10, 1949.

Done at Annecy, in a single copy, in the English and French languages, both texts authentic except as otherwise specified with respect to Schedules annexed hereto.

THE TORQUAY PROTOCOL
TO THE GENERAL AGREEMENT ON TARIFFS AND TRADE

The Governments which are contracting parties to the General Agreement on Tariffs and Trade on the date of this Protocol (hereinafter called "the present contracting parties" and "the General Agreement" respectively), the Governments of the Republic of Austria, the Federal Republic of Germany, the Republic of Korea, Peru, the Republic of the Philippines and the Republic of Turkey (hereinafter called "the acceding governments"), and the Oriental Republic of Uruguay, which may accede to the General Agreement under the Annecy Protocol of Terms of Accession in accordance with the Decision of the CONTRACTING PARTIES of November 9, 1950 (hereinafter called "Uruguay"),

HAVING REGARD to the results of the negotiations concluded at Torquay,

HAVE through their representatives agreed as follows:

1.   (a)   Each of the acceding governments, with respect to the accession of which a decision under Article XXXIII of the General Agreement has been taken shall, upon the entry into force of this Protocol with respect to it pursuant to paragraph II, apply provisionally and subject to the provisions of this Protocol:

(i)   Parts I and III of the General Agreement, and

(ii)   Part II of the General Agreement to the fullest extent not inconsistent with its legislation existing on the date of this Protocol.

(b)   The obligations incorporated in paragraph I of Article I of the General Agreement by reference to Article III thereof and those incorporated in paragraph 2 (b) of Article II by reference to Article VI shall be considered as falling within Part II of the General Agreement for the purpose of this paragraph.

(c)   For the purposes of the General Agreement, the schedules contained in Annex B upon their entry into force pursuant to paragraph II shall be regarded as schedules to the General Agreement relating to acceding governments.

2.   Upon the entry into force of this Protocol with respect to each acceding government, pursuant to paragraph II hereof, that government shall become a contracting party as defined in Article XXXII of the General Agreement.

3.   (a)   On the thirtieth day following the day upon which this Protocol shall have been signed by a present contracting party or Uruguay, or on the forty-sixth day following the date of this Protocol, whichever is the later, the schedule relating to that contracting party or Uruguay contained in Annex A shall enter into force.

(b)   Portions of the schedules contained in Annex A which are the result of negotiations and agreement pursuant to paragraph I of Article XXVIII of the General Agreement may be made effective, by agreement of the negotiating parties, after the date of this Protocol and prior to the date determined pursuant to subparagraph (a) *Provided* that

(i)   compensatory adjustments negotiated in return for withdrawals of or reductions in concessions contained in the existing schedules to the General Agreement may not be made effective later than such withdrawals or reductions, and

(ii)   any government proposing to make a portion of its schedule effective pursuant to this subparagraph shall give the Secretary-General of the United Nations at least thirty days' notice of the date on which the proposed action will become effective.

(c)   Portions of the schedules contained in Annex A which are the result of negotiations and agreement pursuant to procedures established by the CONTRACTING PARTIES may be made effective, by agreement of the negotiating parties, prior to the date determined pursuant to subparagraph (a), *Provided* that compensatory adjustments negotiated in return for withdrawals of or reductions in concessions contained in the existing schedules to the General Agreement may not be made effective later than such withdrawals or reductions.

(d)   When a schedule has entered into force pursuant to subparagraph (a) or when any portion of a schedule has been made effective pursuant to subparagraph (b) or (c), such schedule, or portion (together with all provisions of the schedule in Annex A relevant thereto), shall become a schedule to the General Agreement relating to the government in question. In the case of any difference between the treatment provided for a product in a schedule contained in Annex A, and the treatment provided for the same product in an existing schedule to the General Agreement relating to the same government, the treatment provided in the schedule contained in Annex A shall prevail when and so long as effect is given thereto pursuant to the provisions of this Protocol.

(e)   For the purposes of this Protocol, the "existing schedules to the General Agreement" shall mean the schedules annexed to the General Agreement and to the Annecy Protocol of Terms of Accession, as modified by: (i) provisions of any protocol relating to their rectification or modification, or (ii) any other action, which was effective on September 28, 1950, taken pursuant to a specific provision of the General Agreement or to procedures established by the CONTRACTING PARTIES.

4.   Any government which has signed this Protocol shall be free at any time to withhold or to withdraw in whole or in part any concession, provided for in the appropriate schedule annexed to this Protocol, in respect of which such government determines that it was initially negotiated with a government which has not signed this Protocol, *Provided* that

(i)   the government withholding or withdrawing in whole or in part any such concession shall give notice to all contracting parties, acceding governments and Uruguay within thirty days after the date of such withholding or withdrawal and, upon request, shall consult with any contracting party having a substantial interest in a product involved;

(ii)   any such withholding or withdrawal shall cease to be effective on the thirtieth day following the day upon which the government with which it was initially negotiated signs this Protocol; and

(iii)   this paragraph shall not authorize the withdrawal or withholding of any compensatory adjustments resulting from any negotiations and agreement described in subparagraphs (b) and (c) of paragraph 3, unless all withdrawals of or reductions in concessions contained in the existing schedules to the General Agreement, in return for which such compensatory adjustments were negotiated, are withheld or withdrawn for the same period of time.

5.   (a)   In each case in which Article II of the General Agreement refers to the date of that Agreement, the applicable date in respect of the schedules annexed to this Protocol shall be the date of this Protocol.

(b)   In each case in which paragraph 6 of Article V, subparagraph 4 (d) of Article VII, and subparagraph 3 (c) of Article X of the General Agreement, refer to the date of that Agreement, the applicable date in respect of each acceding government shall be March 24, 1948.

(c)   In the case of the references in paragraph II of Article XVIII of the General Agreement to September 1, 1947, and October 10, 1947, the applicable dates in respect of each acceding government shall be November 1, 1950, and January 15, 1951, respectively.

(d)   In the case of the reference in paragraph I of Article XXVIII of the General Agreement to January 1, 1951, the applicable date in respect of the schedules annexed to this Protocol shall be January 1, 1954.

6.   (a)   The text of paragraph I of Article XXVIII of the General Agreement shall be amended by the deletion of "On or after January 1, 1951" and the substitution therefor of "On or after January 1, 1954".

(b)   Signature of this Protocol in accordance with paragraph 10 shall be deemed to constitute the deposit of an instrument of acceptance of the amendment set forth in subparagraph (a), within the meaning of Article XXX, paragraph 2, of the General Agreement.

(c)   The amendment set forth in subparagraph (a) shall become effective, in accordance with Article XXX, paragraph I, of the General Agreement, when this Protocol shall have been signed by two-thirds of the governments which are at that time contracting parties.

(d)   Notwithstanding the provisions of subparagraph (c), the amendment set forth in subparagraph (a) shall not become effective in respect of concessions initially negotiated by a contracting party which has signed this Protocol with a contracting party which has not signed either this Protocol or the Declaration on the Continued Application of the Schedules of the General Agreement annexed to the Final Act signed at Torquay on April 21, 1951.

7.   (a)   The provisions of the General Agreement to be applied by an acceding government shall be those contained in the text annexed to the Final Act of the Second Session of the Preparatory Committee of the United Nations Conference on Trade and Employment as rectified, amended, supplemented, or otherwise modified by such of the following instruments:

Protocol Modifying Certain Provisions, signed at Havana on March 24, 1948;

Special Protocol relating to Article XXIV, signed at Havana on March 24, 1948;

Special Protocol Modifying Article XIV, signed at Havana on March 24, 1948;

Protocol of Rectifications, signed at Havana on March 24, 1948;

Protocol Modifying Part I and Article XXIX, signed at Geneva on September 14, 1948;

Protocol Modifying Part II and Article XXVI, signed at Geneva on September 14, 1948;

Second Protocol of Rectifications, signed at Geneva on September 14, 1948;

Declaration of May 9, 1949, relating to Section E of Schedule XIX;

Declaration of August II, 1949, relating to Section B of Schedule XIX;

Protocol Modifying Article XXVI, signed at Annecy on August 13, 1949;

Protocol Replacing Schedule I (Australia), signed at Annecy on August 13, 1949;

Protocol Replacing Schedule VI (Ceylon), signed at Annecy on August 13, 1949;

First Protocol of Modifications, signed at Annecy on August 13, 1949;

Third Protocol of Rectifications, signed at Annecy on August 13, 1949;

Annecy Protocol of Terms of Accession, signed at Annecy on October 10, 1949;

Fourth Protocol of Rectifications, signed at Geneva on April 3, 1950;

Fifth Protocol of Rectifications, signed at Torquay on December 16, 1950;

and by such other instruments drawn up by the CONTRACTING PARTIES, as may have become effective by the day on which this Protocol enters into force for that government.

(b)   Signature of this Protocol by an acceding government shall constitute an acceptance of the rectifications, amendments, supplementations or other modifications of the General Agreement by such of the instruments named in subparagraph (a), and by such other instruments drawn up by the CONTRACTING PARTIES and open for acceptance, as may not have become effective by the date on which this Protocol enters into force for that government, such acceptance to take effect upon the same day as the signature of this Protocol by that government.

(c)   Without prejudice to any action taken by a contracting party under Article XXXV, signature of this Protocol by a contracting party or Uruguay shall constitute, except as it may specify otherwise at the time of signature, an acceptance of the rectifications, amendments, supplementations or other modifications of the General Agreement by such of the instruments named in subparagraph (a) and by such other instruments drawn up by the CONTRACTING PARTIES and open for acceptance, as had not been signed or accepted by that contracting party or Uruguay, such acceptance to take effect on the day of signature.

8.   Any acceding government which has signed this Protocol shall be free to withdraw its provisional application of the General Agreement and such withdrawal shall take effect on the sixtieth day following the day on which written notice of such withdrawal is received by the Secretary-General of the United Nations.

9.   (a)   Any acceding government which has signed this Protocol and has not given notice of withdrawal under paragraph 8 may, on or after the date on which the General Agreement enters into force pursuant to Article XXVI thereof, accede to that Agreement upon the applicable terms of this Protocol by deposit of an instrument of accession with the Secretary-General of the United Nations. Such accession shall take effect on the day on which the General Agreement enters into force pursuant to Article XXVI, or on the thirtieth day following the day of the deposit of the instrument of accession, whichever shall be the later.

(b)   Accession to the General Agreement pursuant to subparagraph (a) shall, for the purpose of paragraph 2 of Article XXXII of that Agreement, be regarded as acceptance of the Agreement pursuant to paragraph 3 of Article XXVI thereof.

10.   (a)   The original text of this Protocol shall be opened for signature at Torquay by present contracting parties and acceding governments on April 21, 1951. It shall thereafter be deposited with the Secretary-General of the United Nations and shall be open for signature at the Headquarters of the United Nations from May 7, 1951, to October 21, 1951, by present contracting parties and acceding governments, and by Uruguay, provided Uruguay shall previously have signed the Annecy Protocol of Terms of Accession in accordance with the decision of the Contracting Parties of November 9, 1950.

(b)   The Secretary-General of the United Nations shall promptly furnish a certified copy of this Protocol, and a notification of each signature to this Protocol, of each deposit of an instrument of accession under paragraph 9 (a), and of each notice under paragraph 3 (b) or 8, to each Member of the United Nations, to each government which participated in the United Nations Conference on Trade and Employment, and to any other interested government.

(c)   The Secretary-General is authorized to register this Protocol in accordance with Article 102 of the Charter of the United Nations.

11.   Provided a decision under Article XXXIII of the General Agreement has been taken agreeing to the accession of an acceding government, this Protocol, including the schedule relating to that acceding government contained in Annex B, shall enter into force for that acceding government

(a)   on July 20, 1951, if this Protocol has been signed by that acceding government by June 20, 1951, or

(b)   on the thirtieth day following the day upon which it shall have been signed by that acceding government, if it has not been signed by that acceding government by June 20, 1951.

12.   The date of this Protocol shall be April 21, 1951.

DONE at Torquay, in a single copy, in the English and French languages, both texts authentic except as otherwise specified with respect to schedules annexed hereto.

SIXTH PROTOCOL
OF SUPPLEMENTARY CONCESSIONS
TO THE GENERAL AGREEMENT ON TARIFFS AND TRADE

The governments which are contracting parties to the General Agreement on Tariffs and Trade (hereinafter referred to as "the contracting parties" and "the General Agreement" respectively), having agreed upon procedures for the conduct of tariff negotiations by two or more contracting parties under the General Agreement and for putting into effect under the General Agreement the results of such negotiations,

The Governments of the Commonwealth of Australia, the Republic of Austria, the Kingdom of Belgium, Canada, the Republic of Chile, the Republic of Cuba, the Kingdom of Denmark, the Dominican Republic, the Republic of Finland, the French Republic, the Federal Republic of Germany, the Republic of Haiti, the Republic of Italy, Japan, the Grand-Duchy of Luxemburg, the Kingdom of the Netherlands, the Kingdom of Norway, Peru, the Kingdom of Sweden, the Republic of Turkey, the United Kingdom of Great Britain and Northern Ireland, and the United States of America, which are contracting parties to the General Agreement (hereinafter referred to as "negotiating contracting parties"), having carried out tariff negotiations under these procedures, and being desirous of so giving effect to the results of these negotiations,

IT IS AGREED:

1.   The schedule of each negotiating contracting party annexed to this Protocol shall upon its entry into force in accordance with the provisions of paragraph 2 be regarded as a schedule to the General Agreement relating to that contracting party.

2.   Subsequent to the signature of this Protocol by a negotiating contracting party the annexed schedule which relates to that contracting party shall enter into force on the thirtieth day following the day upon which notification has been received by the Executive Secretary from that contracting party of its intention to apply its concessions in that schedule or on such earlier date as may be specified by the contracting party giving such notification, and the concessions included in that schedule shall, except as specified therein, then enter into force.

3.   Any negotiating contracting party which has given the notification referred to in, paragraph 2 shall be free at any time to withhold or to withdraw in whole or in part any concession provided for in the appropriate schedule annexed to this Protocol, in respect of which such contracting party determines that it was initially negotiated with a negotiating contracting party which has not given such notification; *Provided* that

(a)   the negotiating contracting party withholding in whole or in part any such concessions shall give notice to the CONTRACTING PARTIES within thirty days after the date of such withholding and, upon request, shall consult with any contracting party having a substantial interest in the product involved;

(b)   the negotiating contracting party withdrawing in whole or is part any such concessions shall, before taking such action, give not less than thirty days notice to the CONTRACTING PARTIES and, upon request, shall consult with any contracting party having a substantial interest in the product involved; and

(c)   any concession so withheld or withdrawn shall be applied on and after the thirtieth day following the day upon which the notification referred to in paragraph 2 relating to a contracting party with which the concession was initially negotiated is received by the Executive Secretary.

4.   In each case in which Article II of the General Agreement refers to the date of that Agreement, the applicable date in respect of the schedules annexed to this Protocol shall be the date of this Protocol.

5.   (a)   This Protocol shall be deposited with the Executive Secretary and shall be open for signature at the Headquarters of the CONTRACTING PARTIES in Geneva from 23 May 1956 until 31 December 1956.

(b)   The Executive Secretary shall promptly furnish a certified copy of this Protocol, and a notification of each signature of this Protocol and of each notification referred to in paragraph 2, to each contracting party to the General Agreement.

6.   The date of this Protocol shall be 23 May 1956. Its provisions will become effective in accordance with paragraphs 2 and 3 hereof.

DONE at Geneva, in a single copy in the English and French languages, both texts authentic except as otherwise specified in schedules annexed hereto.

PROTOCOL EMBODYING THE RESULTS
OF THE 1960-61 TARIFF CONFERENCE

The governments which are contracting parties to the General Agreement on Tariffs and Trade (hereinafter referred to as "contracting parties" and "the General Agreement", respectively), the European Economic Community, and the Government of the Swiss Confederation (hereinafter referred to as "Switzerland"),

Having carried out at the 1960-61 Tariff Conference negotiations pursuant to paragraph 6 of Article XXIV, Article XXVIII, Article XXVIII *bis*, and other relevant provisions of the General Agreement,

Have through their representatives agreed as follows:

1.   The schedule in Annex A[1] relating to any contracting party shall, upon the entry into force of this Protocol with respect to such contracting party, become a Schedule to the General Agreement relating to that contracting party.

2.   The schedule in Annex B relating to the European Economic Community shall, upon the entry into force of this Protocol with respect to the Community, become a Schedule to the General Agreement relating to the European Economic Community.

3.   The schedule in Annex C relating to any contracting party, the European Economic Community, or Switzerland shall, upon the date on which both the Declaration on the Provisional Accession of the Swiss Confederation to the General Agreement on Tariffs and Trade, of 22 November 1958 (hereinafter referred to as the Swiss Declaration of 22 November 1958) and this Protocol shall have entered into force with respect to such contracting party, the European Economic Community, or Switzerland, as the case may be, become a schedule to the Swiss Declaration of 22 November 1958 relating to such contracting party, the European Economic Community, or Switzerland.

4.   In each case in which a schedule in Annex A or C to this Protocol provides for any product imported into the territory of a contracting party treatment less favourable than was provided for such product in a schedule applicable to such contracting party on 1 September 1960, such provision for less favourable treatment in the schedule annexed to this Protocol shall, when such schedule becomes a Schedule to the General Agreement pursuant to paragraph 1 or 3 above, terminate the provision for such product in such prior schedule.

5.   (a)   In each case in which paragraph 1 of Article II of the General Agreement refers to the date of that Agreement:

(i)   the applicable date in respect of each product which is the subject of a concession provided for in the schedule annexed to this Protocol of a contracting party or of Switzerland, if such product

---

[1]   The Annexes to this Protocol have not been reproduced in this Supplement.

was not the subject of a concession provided for in the same part or section, of a Schedule to the General Agreement of such contracting party or Switzerland on 1 September 1960, shall be the date of this Protocol;

(ii)   the applicable date in respect of each product which is the subject of a concession provided for in the schedule of the Community shall, when imported into the Kingdom of Belgium, the French Republic, the Federal Republic of Germany, the Republic of Italy, the Grand Duchy of Luxemburg, or the Kingdom of the Netherlands, be:

    (I)   if the product was provided for in Part I of a schedule (or of a relevant section of a schedule) applicable to such contracting party on 1 September 1960: the date of the instrument by which such product was first provided for therein; *Provided* that a concession on such product has been continuously in effect since the entry into force of the concession provided for in such instrument;

    (II)   if the product was not so provided for on 1 September 1960: the date of this Protocol.

(b)   For the purpose of the reference in paragraph 6(a) of Article II of the General Agreement to the date of that Agreement, the applicable date in respect of the schedules annexed to this Protocol shall be the date of this Protocol.

6.   Any contracting party, the European Economic Community, and Switzerland, after a schedule relating to it annexed to this Protocol has become a Schedule to the General Agreement or to the Swiss Declaration of 22 November 1958 pursuant to the provisions of paragraphs 1, 2, or 3 of this Protocol, shall be free at any time to withhold or to withdraw in whole or in part any concession in such schedule which it determines to have been initially negotiated with a contracting party, the European Economic Community, or Switzerland, the schedule relating to which annexed to this Protocol has not yet become a Schedule to the General Agreement or to the Swiss Declaration of 22 November 1958, as the case may be; *Provided* that:

(a)   this paragraph shall only apply to concessions negotiated pursuant to Article XXVIII *bis* of the General Agreement;

(b)   written notice of any such withholding of a concession shall be given to the CONTRACTING PARTIES (or to the parties to the Swiss Declaration of 22 November 1958, in the case of a concession in a schedule to that Declaration) within thirty days after the date of such withholding;

(c)   written notice of intention to make any such withdrawal of a concession shall be given to the CONTRACTING PARTIES (or to the parties to the Swiss Declaration of 22 November 1958) at least thirty days before the date of such intended withdrawal;

(d)   consultations shall be held upon request, with any contracting party, the European Economic Community, or Switzerland, the relevant schedule relating to which has become a Schedule to the General Agreement or the Swiss Declaration of 22 November 1958, as the case may be, and which has a substantial interest in the product involved;

(e)   any concession so withheld or withdrawn shall be applied on and after the day on which the schedule of the contracting party, the European Economic Community, or Switzerland with which such concession was initially negotiated becomes a Schedule to the General Agreement or to the Swiss Declaration of 22 November 1958, as the case may be, or if it should be a later date, on and after the thirtieth day following the day on which this Protocol shall have been accepted by such contracting party, the European Economic Community, or Switzerland, as the case may be.

7.   (a)   This Protocol shall be deposited with the Executive Secretary of the CONTRACTING PARTIES. It shall be open to acceptance, by signature or otherwise, by contracting parties, by the European Economic Community, and by Switzerland.

(b)   Acceptance of this Protocol by a contracting party, to the extent that it shall not have already taken final action to become a party to the following instruments and except as it may otherwise notify the Executive Secretary in writing at the time of such acceptance, shall constitute final action to become a party to each of the following instruments:

(i)   Protocol Amending Part I and Articles XXIX and XXX, Geneva, 10 March 1955;

(ii)   Protocol Amending the Preamble and Parts II and III, Geneva, 10 March 1955;

(iii)   Protocol of Rectifications to the French Text, Geneva, 15 June 1955;

(iv)   Procès-Verbal of Rectifications Concerning the Protocol Amending Part I and Articles XXIX and XXX, the Protocol Amending the Preamble and Parts II and III and the Protocol of Organizational Amendments, Geneva, 3 December 1955;

(v)   Fifth Protocol of Rectifications and Modifications to the Texts of the Schedules, Geneva, 3 December 1955;

(vi)   Sixth Protocol of Rectifications and Modifications to the Texts of the Schedules, Geneva, 11 April 1957;

(vii)   Seventh Protocol of Rectifications and Modifications to the Texts of the Schedules, Geneva, 30 November 1957;

(viii) Protocol Relating to the Negotiations for the Establishment of New Schedule III - Brazil, Geneva, 31 December 1958;

(ix)   Eighth Protocol of Rectifications and Modifications to the Texts of the Schedules, Geneva, 18 February 1959; and

(x)   Ninth Protocol of Rectifications and Modifications to the Texts of the Schedules, Geneva, 17 August 1959.

8.   This Protocol shall enter into force for any contracting party, the European Economic Community or Switzerland, on the thirtieth day following the day upon which it shall have been accepted by that contracting party, the European Economic Community or Switzerland, or on such earlier date following such acceptance as may be notified to the Executive Secretary in writing at the time of such acceptance.

9.   The Executive Secretary shall promptly furnish a certified copy of this Protocol, a notification of each acceptance thereof pursuant to sub-paragraph (a) of paragraph 7, and of each notice or notification pursuant to sub-paragraph (b) or (c) of paragraph 6, sub-paragraph (b) of paragraph 7, or paragraph 8, to each contracting party, to each government which has negotiated during the 1960-61 Tariff Conference for accession to the General Agreement, to the European Economic Community, to each government which shall have acceded provisionally to the General Agreement, and to each other government with respect to which an instrument establishing special relations with the CONTRACTING PARTIES to the General Agreement shall have entered into force.

Done at Geneva this sixteenth day of July, one thousand nine hundred and sixty-two, in a single copy in the English and French languages, both texts being authentic except as otherwise specified with respect to Schedules annexed hereto.

GENEVA (1967) PROTOCOL TO THE GENERAL AGREEMENT
ON TARIFFS AND TRADE[1]

The contracting parties to the General Agreement on Tariffs and Trade and the European Economic Community which participated in the 1964-67 Trade Conference (hereinafter referred to as "participants"),

Having carried out negotiations pursuant to paragraph 6 of Article XXIV, Article XXVIII *bis*, Article XXXIII and other relevant provisions of the General Agreement on Tariffs and Trade (hereinafter referred to as "the General Agreement"),

Have, through their representatives, agreed as follows:

I - *Provisions Relating to Schedules*

1.   The schedule annexed[2] to this Protocol relating to a participant shall become a Schedule to the General Agreement relating to that participant on the day on which this Protocol enters into force for it pursuant to paragraph 6.

2.   Each participant shall ensure that, in so far as any rate specified in the column of its schedule setting out the concession rate (hereinafter referred to as the "final rate") does not become effective on 1 January 1968, each final rate shall become effective not later than 1 January 1972. Within the period of 1 January 1968 to 1 January 1972 a participant shall make rate reductions in amounts not less than and on dates not later than those laid down in one of the following sub-paragraphs, except as may be otherwise clearly provided for in its schedule:

(*a*)   A participant which begins rate reductions on 1 January 1968 shall make effective one fifth of the total reduction to the final rate on that date and four fifths of the total reduction in four equal instalments on 1 January of 1969, 1970, 1971 and 1972.

(*b*)   A participant which begins rate reductions on 1 July 1968, or on a date between 1 January and 1 July 1968, shall make effective two fifths of the total reduction to the final rate on that date and three fifths of the total reduction in three equal instalments on 1 January of 1970, 1971 and 1972.

3.   Any participant, after the schedule relating to it annexed to this Protocol has become a Schedule to the General Agreement pursuant to the provisions of paragraph 1 of this Protocol, shall be free at any time to withhold or to withdraw in whole or in part the concession in such schedule with respect to any product in which a participant or a government having negotiated for accession during the 1964-67 Trade Conference (hereinafter referred to as an

---

[1]   The Protocol entered into force on 1 January 1968.

[2]   See BISD/S37/8 for a list of the Schedules annexed.

"acceding government"), but the schedule of which annexed to this Protocol or to the protocol for the accession of the acceding government has not yet become a Schedule to the General Agreement, has a principal supplying interest; provided that:

(a)   Written notice of any such withholding of a concession shall be given to the CONTRACTING PARTIES within thirty days after the date of such withholding.

(b)   Written notice of intention to make any such withdrawal of a concession shall be given to the CONTRACTING PARTIES at least thirty days before the date of such intended withdrawal.

(c)   Consultations shall be held upon request, with any participant or any acceding government, the relevant schedule relating to which has become a Schedule to the General Agreement and which has a substantial interest in the product involved.

(d)   Any concession so withheld or withdrawn shall be applied on and after the day on which the schedule of the participant or the acceding government which has the principal supplying interest becomes a Schedule to the General Agreement.

4.   (a)   In each case in which paragraph 1 (b) and (c) of Article II of the General Agreement refers to the date of that Agreement, the applicable date in respect of each product which is the subject of a concession provided for in a schedule annexed to this Protocol shall be the date of this Protocol, but without prejudice to any obligations in effect on that date.

(b)   For the purpose of the reference in paragraph 6 (a) of Article II of the General Agreement to the date of that Agreement, the applicable date in respect of a schedule annexed to this Protocol shall be the date of this Protocol.

II - *Final Provisions*

5.   (a)   This Protocol shall be open for acceptance by participants, by signature or otherwise, until 30 June 1968.

(b)   The period during which this Protocol may be accepted by a participant may be extended, but not beyond 31 December 1968, by a decision of the Council of Representatives. Such decision shall lay down the rules and conditions for the implementation of the schedule annexed to this Protocol relating to that participant.

6.   This Protocol shall enter into force on 1 January 1968 for those participants which have accepted it before 1 December 1967, and for participants accepting after that date it shall enter into force on the dates of acceptance, provided that not later than 1 December 1967 the participants which have accepted or are then prepared to accept this Protocol shall consider whether they constitute a sufficient number of participants to justify the beginning of rate reductions according to paragraph 2, and if they consider that they do not constitute a sufficient number they shall so notify the Director-General who shall

request all participants to review the situation with a view to securing the greatest possible number of acceptances at the earliest practicable date.

7.   This Protocol shall be deposited with the Director-General to the CONTRACTING PARTIES who shall promptly furnish a certified copy thereof and a notification of each acceptance thereof, pursuant to paragraph 5 above, to each contracting party to the General Agreement and to the European Economic Community.

8.   This Protocol shall be registered in accordance with the provisions of Article 102 of the Charter of the United Nations.

Done at Geneva this thirtieth day of June one thousand nine hundred and sixty-seven, in a single copy, in the English and French languages, except as otherwise specified with respect to the schedules annexed hereto, both texts being authentic.

Schedules annexed

I.	Australia	XXVII.	Italie
II.	Benelux	XXX.	Sweden
	(Belgique, Luxembourg,	XXXII.	Austria
	Royaume des Pays-Bas)	XXXIII.	République fédérale
III.	Brazil		d'Allemagne
V.	Canada	XXV.	Peru
VII.	Chile	XXXVII.	Turkey
X.	Czechoslovakia	XXXVIII.	Japan
XI.	France	XL.	Communauté économique
XII.	India		européenne
XIII.	New Zealand	XL *bis*	Etats membres de la
XIV.	Norway		Communauté européenne
XVIII.	South Africa		du Charbon et de l'Acier
XIX.	United Kingdom	XLII.	Israel
	Section A -	XLIV.	Portugal
	Metropolitan Territory	XLV.	Espagne
	Section C -	LVII.	Yugoslavia
	Hong Kong	LVIII.	Malawi
XX.	United States of America	LIX.	Suisse
XXII.	Denmark	LX.	Republic of Korea
XXIII.	Dominican Republic	LXVI.	Jamaica
XXIV.	Finland	LXVII.	Trinidad and Tobago

GENEVA (1979) PROTOCOL
TO THE GENERAL AGREEMENT ON TARIFFS AND TRADE

(L/4875)

The contracting parties to the General Agreement on Tariffs and Trade and the European Economic Community which participated in the Multilateral Trade Negotiations 1973-79 (hereinafter referred to as "participants"),

Having carried out negotiations pursuant to Article XXVIII *bis*, Article XXXIII and other relevant provisions of the General Agreement on Tariffs and Trade (hereinafter referred to as "the General Agreement"), Have, through their representatives, agreed as follows:

1.   The schedule of tariff concessions[1] annexed to this Protocol relating to a participant shall become a Schedule to the General Agreement relating to that participant on the day on which this Protocol enters into force for it pursuant to paragraph 5.

2.   (*a*)   The reductions agreed upon by each participant shall, except as may be otherwise specified in a participant's schedule, be implemented in equal annual rate reductions beginning 1 January 1980 and the total reduction become effective not later than 1 January 1987. A participant which begins rate reductions on 1 July 1980 or on a date between 1 January and 1 July 1980 shall, unless otherwise specified in that participant's schedule, make effective two-eighths of the total reduction to the final rate on that date followed by six equal instalments beginning 1 January 1982. The reduced rate should in each stage be rounded off to the first decimal. The provisions of this paragraph shall not prevent participants from implementing reductions in fewer stages or at earlier dates than indicated above.

(*b*)   The implementation of the annexed schedules in accordance with paragraph 2(*a*) above shall, upon request, be subject to multilateral examination by the participants having accepted this Protocol. This would be without prejudice to the rights and obligations of contracting parties under the General Agreement.

3.   After the schedule of tariff concessions annexed to this Protocol relating to a participant has become a Schedule to the General Agreement pursuant to the provisions of paragraph 1, such participant shall be free at any time to withhold or to withdraw in whole or in part the concession in such schedule with respect to any product for which the principal supplier is any other participant or any government having negotiated for accession during the Multilateral Trade Negotiations, but the schedule of which, as established in the Multilateral Trade Negotiations, has not yet become a Schedule to the General Agreement. Such action can, however, only be taken after written notice of any such withholding or withdrawal of a concession has been given to the

---

[1]   See page 5 for a list of the Schedules annexed.

CONTRACTING PARTIES and after consultations have been held, upon request, with any participant or any acceding government, the relevant schedule of tariff concessions relating to which has become a Schedule to the General Agreement and which has a substantial interest in the product involved. Any concessions so withheld or withdrawn shall be applied on and after the day on which the schedule of the participant or the acceding government which has the principal supplying interest becomes a Schedule to the General Agreement.

4.   (*a*)   In each case in which paragraph 1(*b*) and (*c*) of Article II of the General Agreement refers to the date of that Agreement, the applicable date in respect of each product which is the subject of a concession provided for in a schedule of tariff concessions annexed to this Protocol shall be the date of this Protocol, but without prejudice to any obligations in effect on that date.

(*b*)   For the purpose of the reference in paragraph 6(*a*) of Article II of the General Agreement to the date of that Agreement, the applicable date in respect of a schedule of tariff concessions annexed to this Protocol shall be the date of this Protocol.

5.   (*a*)   This Protocol shall be open for acceptance by participants, by signature or otherwise, until 30 June 1980.

(*b*)   This Protocol shall enter into force on 1 January 1980 for those participants which have accepted it before that date, and for participants accepting after that date, it shall enter into force on the dates of acceptance.

6.   This Protocol shall be deposited with the Director-General to the CONTRACTING PARTIES who shall promptly furnish a certified copy thereof and a notification of each acceptance thereof, pursuant to paragraph 5, to each contracting party to the General Agreement and to the European Economic Community.

7.   This Protocol shall be registered in accordance with the provisions of Article 102 of the Charter of the United Nations.

Done at Geneva this thirtieth day of June one thousand nine hundred and seventy-nine, in a single copy, in the English and French languages, both texts being authentic. The Schedules annexed hereto are authentic in the English, French and Spanish language as specified in each Schedule.

Schedules annexed

V	- Canada	LVII	- Yugoslavia
X	- Czechoslovakia	LIX	- Switzerland
XIII	- New Zealand	LXII	- Iceland
XIV	- Norway	LXIV	- Argentina
XVIII	- South Africa	LXVI	- Jamaica
XX	- United States of America	LXIX	- Romania
XXIV	- Finland	LXXI	- Hungary
XXX	- Sweden	LXXII	- European Communities
XXXII	- Austria	and	
XXXVIII	- Japan	LXXII *bis*	
XLV	- Spain		

MARRAKESH PROTOCOL TO THE
GENERAL AGREEMENT ON TARIFFS AND TRADE 1994

Members,

Having carried out negotiations within the framework of GATT 1947, pursuant to the Ministerial Declaration on the Uruguay Round,

Hereby *agree* as follows:

1.   The schedule annexed to this Protocol relating to a Member shall become a Schedule to GATT 1994 relating to that Member on the day on which the WTO Agreement enters into force for that Member. Any schedule submitted in accordance with the Ministerial Decision on measures in favour of least-developed countries shall be deemed to be annexed to this Protocol.

2.   The tariff reductions agreed upon by each Member shall be implemented in five equal rate reductions, except as may be otherwise specified in a Member's Schedule. The first such reduction shall be made effective on the date of entry into force of the WTO Agreement, each successive reduction shall be made effective on 1 January of each of the following years, and the final rate shall become effective no later than the date four years after the date of entry into force of the WTO Agreement, except as may be otherwise specified in that Member's Schedule. Unless otherwise specified in its Schedule, a Member that accepts the WTO Agreement after its entry into force shall, on the date that Agreement enters into force for it, make effective all rate reductions that have already taken place together with the reductions which it would under the preceding sentence have been obligated to make effective on 1 January of the year following, and shall make effective all remaining rate reductions on the schedule specified in the previous sentence. The reduced rate should in each stage be rounded off to the first decimal. For agricultural products, as defined in Article 2 of the Agreement on Agriculture, the staging of reductions shall be implemented as specified in the relevant parts of the schedules.

3.   The implementation of the concessions and commitments contained in the schedules annexed to this Protocol shall, upon request, be subject to multilateral examination by the Members. This would be without prejudice to the rights and obligations of Members under Agreements in Annex 1A of the WTO Agreement.

4.   After the schedule annexed to this Protocol relating to a Member has become a Schedule to GATT 1994 pursuant to the provisions of paragraph 1, such Member shall be free at any time to withhold or to withdraw in whole or in part the concession in such Schedule with respect to any product for which the principal supplier is any other Uruguay Round participant the schedule of which has not yet become a Schedule to GATT 1994. Such action can, however, only be taken after written notice of any such withholding or withdrawal of a concession has been given to the Council for Trade in Goods and after consultations have been held, upon request, with any Member, the relevant schedule relating to which has become a Schedule to GATT 1994 and which has

a substantial interest in the product involved. Any concessions so withheld or withdrawn shall be applied on and after the day on which the schedule of the Member which has the principal supplying interest becomes a Schedule to GATT 1994.

5. (a) Without prejudice to the provisions of paragraph 2 of Article 4 of the Agreement on Agriculture, for the purpose of the reference in paragraphs 1:(b) and 1(c) of Article II of GATT 1994 to the date of that Agreement, the applicable date in respect of each product which is the subject of a concession provided for in a schedule of concessions annexed to this Protocol shall be the date of this Protocol.

(b) For the purpose of the reference in paragraph 6(a) of Article II of GATT 1994 to the date of that Agreement, the applicable date in respect of a schedule of concessions annexed to this Protocol shall be the date of this Protocol.

6. In cases of modification or withdrawal of concessions relating to non-tariff measures as contained in Part III of the schedules, the provisions of Article XXVIII of GATT 1994 and the "Procedures for Negotiations under Article XXVIII" adopted on 10 November 1980 (BISD 27S/26-28) shall apply. This would be without prejudice to the rights and obligations of Members under GATT 1994.

7. In each case in which a schedule annexed to this Protocol results for any product in treatment less favourable than was provided for such product in the Schedules of GATT 1947 prior to the entry into force of the WTO Agreement, the Member to whom the schedule relates shall be deemed to have taken appropriate action as would have been otherwise necessary under the relevant provisions of Article XXVIII of GATT 1947 or 1994. The provisions of this paragraph shall apply only to Egypt, Peru, South Africa and Uruguay.

8. The Schedules annexed hereto are authentic in the English, French or Spanish language as specified in each Schedule.

9. The date of this Protocol is 15 April 1994.

[The agreed schedules of participants will be annexed to the Marrakesh Protocol in the treaty copy of the WTO Agreement.]

APPENDIX D

DECISIONS ON PROCEDURES ON RENEGOTIATIONS, RECTIFICATIONS, MODIFICATIONS AND RELATED SUBJECTS

Procedures for Negotiations under Article XXVIII - Guidelines Proposed by the Committee on Tariff Negotiations (3 November 1980)

Procedures for Modification and Rectification of Schedules of Tariff Concessions (Decision of 26 March 1980)

Introduction of Loose-Leaf System for the Schedules of Tariff Concessions (Decision of 26 March 1980)

GATT Concessions Under the Harmonized Commodity Description and Coding System (Decision of 12 July 1983)

GATT Concessions Under the Harmonized Commodity Description and Coding System – Procedures to Implement Changes in the Harmonized System (Decision of 8 October 1991)

Establishment of Consolidated Loose-leaf Schedule on Goods (Decision of 29 November 1996)

PROCEDURES FOR NEGOTIATIONS UNDER ARTICLE XXVIII

GUIDELINES PROPOSED BY THE COMMITTEE ON TARIFF CONCESSIONS

On 31 May 1957 the Executive Secretary in compliance with instructions given to him by the CONTRACTING PARTIES (L/641, BISD 6S/158), issued a note concerning arrangements for negotiations under Article XXVIII in 1957 (document L/635). This note has served as a guideline for the procedural arrangements for all subsequent negotiations under Article XXVIII.

In the more than twenty years that have passed since document L/635 was circulated, there have, however, been introduced a number of technical amendments in the procedures as set out in that document. The Director-General therefore prepared revised procedural guidelines for renegotiations under Article XXVIII which were contained in document L/4651, dated 22 June 1978.[1] After discussion of this document in the Council (see C/M/127), a revised proposal by the Director-General was circulated in document L/4651/Rev.1, dated 13 September 1978. Some delegations had suggestions for amendments to this proposal which were circulated in L/4651/Rev.1/Add.1-3. The revised proposal and the amendments were examined by the Council on 18 October 1978 without any final decision being taken (C/M/128).

At the meeting of the Committee on Tariff Concessions on 28 February 1980, it was agreed that the proposal by the Director-General should be examined at a future meeting of the Committee (TAR/M/1, page 16). The Committee discussed this question at its meeting of 7 July (TAR/M/2, pages 5-8) and 3 November 1980 and agreed on the following text which it proposes for adoption by the Council.

---

1.   A contracting party intending to negotiate for the modification or withdrawal of concessions in accordance with the procedures of Article XXVIII, paragraph 1 - which are also applicable to negotiations under paragraph 5 of that Article - should transmit a notification to that effect to the Secretariat which will distribute the notification to all other contracting parties in a secret document.[2] In the case of negotiations under paragraph 4 of Article XXVIII the request for authority to enter into negotiations should be transmitted to the Secretariat to be circulated in a secret document and included in the agenda of the next meeting of the Council.

---

[1]   A note by the Secretariat comparing the 1957 procedures and the new proposal was circulated in document C/W/306.

[2]   The date for submission of a notification for negotiation under Article XXVIII, paragraph 1, shall comply with the provisions of interpretative note 3 to paragraph 1 of Article XXVIII.

2. The notification or request should include a list of items, with corresponding tariff line numbers, which it is intended to modify or withdraw indicating for each item the contracting parties, if any, with which the item was initially negotiated. It should be indicated whether the intention is to modify a concession or withdraw it, in whole or in part, from the schedule. If a concession is to be modified, the proposed modification should be stated in the notification or circulated as soon as possible thereafter to those contracting parties with which the concession was originally negotiated and those which are recognized, in accordance with paragraph 4 below, to have a principal or a substantial supplying interest. The notification or request should be accompanied by statistics of imports of the products involved, by country of origin, for the last three years for which statistics are available. If specific or mixed duties are affected, both values and quantities should be indicated, if possible.

3. At the same time as the notification is transmitted to the Secretariat or when the authorization to enter into negotiation has been granted by the Council - or as soon as possible thereafter - the contracting party referred to in paragraph 1 above should communicate to those contracting parties, with which concessions were initially negotiated, and those which have a principal supplying interest, the compensatory adjustments which it is prepared to offer.

4. Any contracting party which considers that it has a principal or a substantial supplying interest in a concession which is to be the subject of negotiation and consultation under Article XXVIII should communicate its claim in writing to the contracting party referred to in paragraph 1 above and at the same time inform the Secretariat. If the contracting party referred to in paragraph 1 above recognizes the claim, the recognition will constitute a determination by the CONTRACTING PARTIES of interest in the sense of Article XXVIII:1.[3] If a claim of interest is not recognized, the contracting party making the claim may refer the matter to the Council. Claims of interest should be made within ninety days following the circulation of the import statistics referred to in paragraph 2 above.

5. Upon completion of each bilateral negotiation the contracting party referred to in paragraph 1 above should send to the Secretariat a joint letter on the lines of the model in Annex A attached hereto signed by both parties. To this letter shall be attached a report on the lines of the model in Annex B attached hereto. The report should be initialled by both parties. The Secretariat will distribute the letter and the report to all contracting parties in a secret document.

6. Upon completion of all its negotiations the contracting party referred to in paragraph 1 above should send to the Secretariat, for distribution in

---

[3] If, in exceptional circumstances, the contracting party referred to in paragraph 1 above is not in a position to supply relevant import statistics, it shall give due consideration to export statistics provided by contracting parties claiming an interest in the concession or concessions concerned.

a secret document, a final report on the lines of the model in Annex C attached hereto.

7.   Contracting parties will be free to give effect to the changes agreed upon in the negotiations as from the first day of the period referred to in Article XXVIII:1, or, in the case of negotiations under paragraph 4 or 5 of Article XXVIII, as from the date on which the conclusion of all the negotiations have been notified as set out in paragraph 6 above. A notification shall be submitted to the Secretariat, for circulation to contracting parties, of the date on which these changes will come into force.

8.   Formal effect will be given to the changes in the schedules by means of Certifications in accordance with the Decision of the CONTRACTING PARTIES of 19 November 1968 (BISD 16S/16).

9.   The Secretariat will be available at all stages to assist the governments involved in the negotiations and consultations.

10.   These procedures are in relevant parts also valid for renegotiations under Article XVIII, paragraph 7, and Article XXIV, paragraph 6.

ANNEX A

MODEL

To the Director-General,   SECRET

GATT,

Geneva.   _____

                                          (Date)

NEGOTIATIONS RELATING TO SCHEDULE ....[1]

The Delegations of _____ and

_____, have concluded their negotiations under

Article XXVIII for the modification or withdrawal of concessions provided for

in Schedule _____as set out in the report[2] attached.

_____   _____

signed for the Delegation of   signed for the Delegation of

_____   _____

---

[1]   Insert number of Schedule and name of country.

[2]   See Annex B

ANNEX B

MODEL

SECRET[1]

Results of Negotiations under Article XXVIII for the Modification or Withdrawal of Concessions in the Schedule of........ Initially Negotiated with ....

CHANGES IN SCHEDULE.......[2]

A.   Concessions to be withdrawn

Tariff item number	Description of products	Rates of duty bound in existing schedule

B.   Bound rates to be increased[3]

Tariff item number	Description of products	Rates of duty bound in existing schedule	Rates of duty to be bound

C.   Reduction of rates bound in the existing schedules[3]

Tariff item number	Description of products	Rates of duty bound in existing schedule	Rates of duty to be bound

D. New concessions on items not in existing schedules

Tariff item number	Description of products	Rates of duty at present in force	Rates of duty to be bound

---

[1]   Each page should be marked SECRET.

[2]   Insert number of schedule and name of country.

[3]   If the modification implies an extension of an initial negotiating right to a further country or countries or is a change in the description of the product rather than an increase or a decrease in the bound rate of duty, or if the modification is a conversion of the type of duty that is considered to constitute neither an increase nor a decrease in the margin of protection or is of any other character not falling under the headings "B" or "C", such modifications should be reported under a separate, appropriate heading.

ANNEX C

MODEL

<u>SECRET</u>

NEGOTIATIONS UNDER ARTICLE XXVIII

Report by the delegation of _____ relating to

negotiations under Article XXVIII with respect to

Schedule _____

1.   <u>Negotiations resulted in agreement with:</u>

Country ...... (SECRET/-/Add.-)
   "   ......   (SECRET/-/Add.-)
etc.

2.   <u>Agreement was not reached with:</u>

.......……………………………..

3.   <u>Consultations have been held with:</u>

……...........………………………

PROCEDURES FOR MODIFICATION AND RECTIFICATION
OF SCHEDULES OF TARIFF CONCESSIONS

Decision of 26 March 1980

(L/4962)

Recalling that the CONTRACTING PARTIES established on 19 November 1968 a procedure for the certification of changes to Schedules annexed to the General Agreement.[1]

Considering the importance of keeping the authentic texts of Schedules annexed to the General Agreement up to date and of ensuring that they tally with the texts of corresponding items in national customs tariffs;

Considering that, in consequence, changes in the authentic texts of Schedules which record rectifications of a purely formal character or modifications resulting from action taken under Article II, Article XVIII, Article XXIV, Article XXVII and Article XXVIII shall be certified without delay;

The CONTRACTING PARTIES decide that:

1. Changes in the authentic texts of Schedules annexed to the General Agreement which reflect modifications resulting from action under Article II, Article XVIII, Article XXIV, Article XXVII or Article XXVIII shall be certified by means of Certifications. A draft of such change shall be communicated to the Director-General within three months after the action has been completed.

2. Changes in the authentic texts of Schedules shall be made when amendments or rearrangements which do not alter the scope of a concession are introduced in national customs tariffs in respect of bound items. Such changes and other rectifications of a purely formal character shall be made by means of Certifications. A draft of such changes shall be communicated to the Director-General where possible within three months but not later than six months after the amendment or rearrangement has been introduced in the national customs tariff or in the case of other rectifications, as soon as circumstances permit.

3. The draft containing the changes described in paragraphs 1 and 2 shall be communicated by the Director-General to all the contracting parties and shall become a Certification provided that no objection has been raised by a contracting party within three months on the ground that, in the case of changes described in paragraph 1, the draft does not correctly reflect the modifications or, in the case of changes described in paragraph 2, the proposed rectification is not within the terms of that paragraph.

4. Whenever practicable Certifications shall record the date of entry into force of each modification and the effective date of each rectification.

5. The procedure of Certification under this Decision may be applied for the establishment of consolidated Schedules or of new Schedules under

---

[1] BISD 16S/16.

paragraph 5(*c*) of Article **XXVI**, wherein all changes are modifications or rectifications referred to in paragraphs 1 or 2.

6.   This Decision supersedes the Decision of 19 November 1968.

INTRODUCTION OF A LOOSE-LEAF SYSTEM FOR THE
SCHEDULES OF TARIFF CONCESSIONS

Proposal by the Director-General

Adopted on 26 March 1980

(C/107/Rev.1)

1.   As can be seen from document L/4821 and Addenda 1 and 2, the existing system for the publication of the tariff concessions has become out-dated. There are at present more than forty legal instruments (Protocols, Certifications) containing valid tariff concessions. Extensive and time-consuming efforts are necessary under the present system to find out the status of a particular concession.

2.   In view of this, I suggest that henceforth the schedules of tariff concessions be published in the form of a loose-leaf system which can continuously be kept up to date when rectifications, modifications, withdrawals and new concessions are made. The CONTRACTING PARTIES have given their approval of the financial consequences for the introduction of such a system.

3.   In order to establish such a loose-leaf system a number of decisions would have to be taken. The basis for the creation of a loose-leaf system for the schedules of tariff concessions must be a general consolidation of schedules. I would consequently propose that the *Council agree that contracting parties submit consolidated schedules of tariff concessions as soon as possible and not later than 30 September 1980.*

4.   In order to draw the full advantages of the loose-leaf system and to ensure as complete a transparency as possible of the tariff concessions, some particular decisions would have to be taken to that effect. I would suggest that *the Council agree on a format for the schedules as set out in the Annex to document L/4821/Add.1.*

5.   The schedules should comprise a complete description of the products covered. Furthermore, it is, in my view, desirable that the entries in the schedules should, as far as possible, correspond with the entries in the customs tariffs, not only for the descriptions but also in respect of the numeration used. For example, if a heading is only partially bound, then sub-headings should be created and should have their own numbers.

6.   In order to maintain as far as possible the information in the schedules in conformity with the corresponding data in the national customs tariffs, there is in my view also a need for a new decision for procedures for modifications and rectifications of schedules. The present decision (BISD, 16S/16) does not contain provisions sufficiently precise to encourage contracting

parties to up-date continuously their schedules. Therefore, I suggest that *the proposed decision in the Annex[1] be adopted.*

7.   So far, initial negotiating rights (INRs) have only been indicated in working documents on schedules in connexion with renegotiations or with consolidation of schedules. In the final, published schedules the indication of the INRs has so far been deleted. In order to make the loose-leaf system as transparent as possible and to remove the need for contracting parties to consult underlying documents, I propose that *the INRs be indicated in the loose-leaf schedules* as foreseen in the fifth column of the proposed format annexed to document L/4821/Add.1. The secretariat's files and assistance will be available to help delegations in establishing records of initial negotiating rights granted by or to their countries.

8.   There is an understanding in the GATT concerning consolidated schedules that earlier schedules and negotiating records should be considered as proper sources in interpreting concessions in consolidated schedules. [2] This understanding is valid inter alia, for INR's regarding earlier bindings made at a higher level than the present bound rate on a certain item. In order to make the loose-leaf system as transparent as possible and to remove the need for contracting parties to consult underlying documents, I propose that *this understanding will cease to be valid as regards the previous INRs when the loose-leaf schedules have been established and that all these previous INRs must, in order to maintain a legal value, be indicated in the loose-leaf schedules.* If the inclusion of previous INRs would necessitate the creation of additional sub-items that would otherwise not be necessary, the reference to the existence of such INRs could be made in the form of a footnote to the relevant heading or in any other suitable way. As the incorporation of previous INRs into the Schedules will necessitate time-consuming research in old negotiating records, I suggest that such INRs be indicated in the loose-leaf schedules only one year after the date for the submission of the consolidated schedules, i.e. not later than 30 September 1981 and that earlier schedules and negotiating records will remain proper sources for interpreting concessions until 1 January 1987.

9.   A similar question arises with respect to the date applicable to each concession for the purpose of Article II:1(*b*) of the General Agreement. It has been agreed that the date, as of which "other duties or charges" on importation are bound, applicable to any concession in a consolidated schedule should be, for the purposes of Article II, the date of the instrument by which the concession on any particular item was first incorporated into the General Agreement (cf. BISD 7S/115-116). In order to draw full advantage of the loose-leaf system by making it as transparent as possible as to the status of all concessions, I propose that *the instrument by which the concession was first incorporated into a GATT Schedule be indicated in a special column* (column 6 of the proposed format in the annex

---

[1]   The Annex is not reproduced. See BISD 27S/25 for the text of the Decision.

[2]   Cf. BISD 7S/115-116.

to document L/4821/Add.1) *of the loose-leaf schedules.* I wish to point out in this connexion that such "other duties or charges" are in principle only those that discriminate against imports. As can be seen from Article II:2 of the General Agreement, such "other duties or charges" concern neither charges equivalent to internal taxes, nor anti-dumping or countervailing duties, nor fees or other charges commensurate with the cost of services rendered.

GATT CONCESSIONS UNDER THE HARMONIZED
COMMODITY DESCRIPTION AND CODING SYSTEM

Decision of 12 July 1983

(L/5470/Rev.1)

1.   Introduction

1.1   The Harmonized Commodity Description and Coding System (H.S.), which was developed in the Customs Co-operation Council, is envisaged by the CCC timetable to be applied, for those countries which decide to adopt it, as the basis for customs tariffs and international trade statistics nomenclatures with effect from 1 January 1987[1].

1.2   In addition to the benefits for trade facilitation and analysis of trade statistics, from a GATT point of view adoption of the Harmonized System would ensure greater uniformity among countries in customs classification and thus a greater ability for countries to monitor and protect the value of tariff concessions.

1.3   The introduction of the Harmonized System implies considerable changes in the GATT schedules of tariff concessions. Some of the changes will be made through the rectification procedure; others are likely to require renegotiation of existing schedules.

1.4   In order to facilitate the wide adoption of the Harmonized System, contracting parties should aim to complete any necessary negotiations under Article XXVIII sufficiently in advance (approximately one year) of the scheduled entry into force of the Harmonized System so as to allow contracting parties adequate time for their required domestic procedures. Based upon past experience, Article XXVIII negotiations should begin a minimum of eighteen months earlier if they are to be completed within this time frame. In order to cope with the amount and complexity of the work involved, considerable discipline will be required and the traditional GATT procedures will have to be simplified and accelerated as much as possible.

1.5   The purpose of this note is to outline the tasks involved and to suggest arrangements for simplifying and facilitating the exercise to the greatest extent possible.

2.   Basic principles

2.1   The main principle to be observed in connexion with the introduction of the Harmonized System in national tariffs is that existing GATT bindings should be maintained unchanged. The alteration of existing bindings should only be envisaged where their maintenance would result in undue

---

[1]   See Appendix (not reproduced).

complexity in the national tariffs and should not involve a significant or arbitrary increase of customs duties collected on a particular product.

2.2　In order to avoid complicating the introduction of the Harmonized System, contracting parties should endeavour to avoid modifying or renegotiating, in the context of the introduction of the Harmonized System, their bindings for reasons not associated with the System.

2.3　In light of paragraphs 2.1 and 2.2 contracting parties should be ready to explain and discuss the reason for their proposed changes where requested. Interested contracting parties will be free to raise specific cases, which the party which has notified the change will examine, taking into account all relevant factors with a view to finding a mutually acceptable solution. If such agreement cannot be reached, the contracting party which has notified the change shall proceed under Article XXVIII and subject to the rights under that Article of contracting parties with initial negotiating rights or principal or substantial supplying interests.

2.4　To the extent that the value of existing concessions is not impaired, the conversion of present nomenclatures to the Harmonized System can be done through the rectification procedure[2].

3.　Negotiations

3.1　It is very difficult to forecast the number of cases where renegotiations will be required. The fact that one bound tariff line is divided up into a number of new lines, without changing the content of the original line, will not create any problem for the maintenance of the concession. Since, however, the introduction of the Harmonized System will result in a considerable number of cases where tariff lines with different bound rates are combined or bound rates combined with unbound rates, renegotiations under Article XXVIII will in many cases be necessary.

3.2　The guidelines relating to procedures for negotiations under Article XXVIII, adopted by the Council on 10 November[3] will be the basis for this exercise. The objective should be to maintain in these bilateral negotiations a general level of reciprocal and mutually advantageous concessions not less favourable to trade than that provided for prior to such negotiations. However, because of the amount and complexity of the work involved, and the exceptional nature of the exercise, it will be necessary to simplify the guidelines, as indicated below, in order to facilitate the implementation of the Harmonized System.

---

[2]　See BISD 27S/25-26.

[3]　BISD 27S/26.

4. Proposed Special Procedures

4.1   Each contracting party adopting the Harmonized System shall supply to the GATT secretariat the following information[4]:

4.1.1   An up-to-date consolidated schedule of concessions in the existing nomenclature in loose-leaf form[5].

4.1.2   A proposed consolidated schedule of concessions in the nomenclature of the Harmonized System. This schedule should incorporate the Harmonized System nomenclature in the proper order, form, and layout. This document should contain the following information: new tariff schedule number; a complete product description; the proposed rate of duty for the item; and the proposed INR(s) for the item. If practicable, this document should also contain information on historical initial negotiating rights and other information required for loose-lease schedules.

4.1.3   A concordance table from the existing to the proposed consolidated schedules of concessions. For each item in the contracting party's existing schedule, this document should indicate the following information: (1) the item number and an abbreviated product description; (2) the corresponding item(s) in Annex 2; (3) the existing and the proposed rates of duty (with an asterisk aside the proposed rate(s) of duty when it (they) differ(s) from the existing rate); (4) the initial negotiating right status for the existing item; (5) the percent of total imports in the existing item which has been allocated to each of the proposed items; and (6) the value of trade allocated to each of the proposed new items for the most recent three years for which import statistics are available[6]. Items (5) and (6) above need not be supplied if there is no change in either the proposed rate of duty or the initial negotiating right status from the existing tariff line. The proposed new concession rates should be annotated with a symbol indicating how they were arrived at.

4.1.4   A concordance table from the proposed to the existing consolidated schedules of concessions. For each item in the contracting party's proposed schedule, this document should contain the following information: (1) the item number and a brief product description; (2) the corresponding item number(s) from Annex 1; (3) the existing and the proposed rates of duty (with an asterisk aside the proposed rate(s) when different from the existing rate(s); (4) the INR status for the existing item; (5) the percent of trade in the existing item allocated to the proposed item; and (6) for the most recent three years, the value of trade of the existing item(s) allocated to the new item and the percent of trade

---

[4]   The question of the presentation of the data mentioned in this paragraph is subject to further discussion in the Committee on Tariff Concessions but it has already been agreed that delegations should have a certain flexibility in this regard. Samples of the annexes can be found in document TAR/W/25/Rev.2.

[5]   See BISD 27S/22.

[6]   Apart from import figures for each separate year, there should also be an indication of the average figure for the three-year period.

in the proposed item accounted for by each component existing item[1].
Information required under (5) and (6) above need not be supplied for items
where there are no proposed changes in rates of duty or in INR status.

4.1.5   A list of items proposed for certification. For each item in the
contracting party's existing schedule proposed for certification, this document
should contain the information specified in paragraph 4.1.3 above.

4.1.6   A list of items for renegotiation. For each item in the contracting
party's existing schedule which requires renegotiation, this document should
contain the information specified in paragraph 4.1.3 above.

4.2   Where contracting parties consider it unavoidable to combine
headings or parts of headings in implementing the Harmonized System they may
have to modify certain of their existing concessions. Possible ways of arriving at
new rates include:

4.2.1   Applying the lowest rate of any previous heading to the whole of
the new heading.

4.2.2   Applying the rate previously applied to the heading or headings
with the majority of trade.

4.2.3   Applying the trade weighted average rate of duty for the new
heading.

4.2.4   Applying the arithmetic average of the previous rates of duty,
where no basis exists for establishing reasonably accurate trade allocations.

4.3   If a contracting party considers that the conversion of a
concession, which has been notified as a rectification case by another contracting
party, in effect impairs the value of the concessions and should have been
notified for renegotiation under Article XXVIII, the first contracting party,
having demonstrated at least its substantial interest in the concession, is free to
request, in accordance with normal practice in rectification exercises, that the
concession be restored (or, failing, that the item concerned be notified for
renegotiation).

4.4   Contracting parties should, as soon as possible, provide
information on their envisaged timetable and domestic procedures for the
implementation of the Harmonized System.

4.5   Consistent with Part IV of the GATT special account would be
taken of the needs of developing countries.

Conclusion

5.1   It is clear that the implementation of the Harmonized System will
involve a great deal of work for contracting parties both domestically and in the
GATT. It will speed up the examination of the documentation listed under 4
above by other contracting parties, if the submitting contracting party would
send the documentation in instalments, even if in a preliminary form, rather than
wait until the complete documentation is available. It is not, however, envisaged
that renegotiations could start until contracting parties have an overall view of

modifications to be made in another contracting party's schedule. It would, nevertheless, be a considerable gain if the examination of the "rectification part" of the new schedules could begin at as early a date as possible.

5.2   The complexity of this exercise should not be underestimated and it is, therefore, essential that contracting parties should recognize the timing constraints mentioned in Section 1 and respect the procedures set out in Section 4.

GATT CONCESSIONS UNDER THE HARMONIZED COMMODITY DESCRIPTION AND CODING SYSTEM

PROCEDURES TO IMPLEMENT CHANGES IN THE HARMONIZED SYSTEM

Decision of 8 October 1991

(Annex to L/6905)

Contracting parties to the GATT[1] which are also contracting parties to the International Convention on the Harmonized Commodity Description and Coding System (Harmonized System), in order to keep the authentic texts of their GATT schedules up to date and in conformity with their national customs tariffs, adopt the following procedures:

1.   The implementation of revisions of the nomenclature of the Harmonized System adopted by the Customs Co-operation Council (CCC) shall not involve any alteration in the scope of concessions nor any increase in bound rates of duty unless their maintenance results in undue complexity in the national tariffs. In such cases the contracting parties concerned shall inform the other contracting parties of the technical difficulties in question, e.g. why it has not been possible to create a new subheading to maintain the existing concession on a product or products transferred from within one HS 6-digit heading to another.

2.   No later than 120 days after the circulation by the secretariat of both

(1)   a communication concerning the acceptance by the CCC of a recommendation to revise the Harmonized System nomenclature made in accordance with Article 16 of the Harmonized System Convention, and

(2)   correlation tables prepared by the CCC secretariat,

contracting parties shall submit to the GATT secretariat a notification which includes the pages of their loose-leaf schedules containing proposed changes. The relevant pages of the loose-leaf schedules shall be presented as follows:

(a)   Items in relation to which the proposed changes do not, in the view of the contracting party in question, alter the scope of a concession (e.g. changes or other rectifications of a purely formal character), should be indicated by underlining or shading the item.

(b)   Items in relation to which the proposed changes will, in the view of the contracting party in question, alter the scope of a concession (e.g. through an increase in the bound rate of duty or a change in the product description of the item) should be indicated by an

---

[1]   Including the European Communities.

asterisk. For these items, the following information shall also be submitted (in separate annexes):

(i)   a concordance table between the existing and the proposed schedule;

(ii)   a concordance table between the proposed and the existing schedule;

(iii)   an indication of contracting party or parties with which the existing concession was initially negotiated;

(iv)   import statistics by country of origin, for the most recent three-year period for which statistics are available (import figures for each separate year and average figures for the three-year period). If specific or mixed duties are affected, both values and volumes should be indicated, if possible.

At the same time as the notification is submitted to the secretariat, or as soon as possible thereafter, the contracting party in question should communicate to those contracting parties with which the concessions were initially negotiated and those with a principal supplying interest the compensatory adjustments which it is prepared to offer.

3.   The documentation listed in paragraph 2 above should be submitted to the secretariat in 230 copies. The secretariat will distribute the documentation to all contracting parties in a secret document.

4.   A proposed change in the authentic text of a GATT schedule described in paragraph 2(a) above shall be certified provided no objection has been raised by a contracting party within ninety days on the ground that the proposed change or rectification is not of a purely formal character. If such objection is raised and in the absence of agreement among the contracting parties concerned, the contracting party in question shall without delay submit to the secretariat, for circulation to all contracting parties, the documentation described in paragraph 2(b) above.

5.   A proposed change in the authentic text of a GATT schedule described in paragraph 2(b) above shall be certified provided no request for negotiation or consultation under Article XXVIII has been made to the contracting party in question within ninety days following the circulation of the documentation described in paragraph 2(b) above.

6.   In cases where an objection under paragraph 4 above is raised or where a request for negotiation or consultation under paragraph 5 has been made, the Procedures for Negotiations Under Article XXVIII (BISD 27S/26) shall apply. Any such objection or request shall at the same time be sent to the secretariat. After the completion of these procedures, a comprehensive list of all changes and the corresponding amended pages of the GATT schedule shall be sent to the secretariat for certification.

ESTABLISHMENT OF CONSOLIDATED LOOSE-LEAF
SCHEDULES ON GOODS

Decision of 29 November 1996

Members,

Having regard to Articles XI, XII and XIV of the *Agreement Establishing the WTO*, Articles II and XXVIII of GATT 1994, and the *Decision on Measures in Favour of Least-Developed Countries*;

Recalling the proposal by the Director-General adopted by the CONTRACTING PARTIES of GATT 1947 on 26 March 1980[1] concerning the *Introduction of a Loose-Leaf System for the Schedules of Tariff Concessions* (BISD 27S/22);

Recalling further the modifications proposed by the Director-General adopted by the CONTRACTING PARTIES of GATT 1947 on 6 November 1986[2] (BISD 33S/135);

Considering the developments which took place in the context of the introduction of the *International Convention on the Harmonized Commodity Description and Coding System* by the World Customs Organization and its subsequent changes;[3]

Noting that the Committee on Market Access, at its meeting of 22 November 1995, has accepted the revised proposals by the Chairman with regard to the preparation of consolidated schedules in loose-leaf format as included in document G/MA/TAR/W/4/Rev.2;

Agree as follows:

Objectives

1.   The consolidated loose-leaf schedules on goods as described in the Annex to this Decision shall be binding instruments, replacing all previous schedules for all purposes relating to a Member's rights and obligations under the WTO, except with respect to historical Initial Negotiating Rights (INRs). The schedules therefore shall contain all necessary information in order to reflect the exact situation in respect of each tariff concession and commitment.

---

[1]   C/107/Rev.1 and L/4821 + Add.1-2.

[2]   C/107/Rev.1/Add.1 and C/M/204.

[3]   L/6905 and L/5470/Rev.1.

Coverage of Unbound Items

2.   It is understood that WTO schedules do not create obligations with respect to unbound items, and that Members are not required to include unbound items in their schedules.

3.   Notwithstanding paragraph 2, with a view to ensuring the complete coverage of all tariff items, Members may include all items in their loose-leaf schedule, including any unbound items.

4.   Where a Member decides to include unbound items, "U" (unbound) shall be indicated in column 3 "Rate of duty". No obligations shall thereby be created with respect to such unbound items. *Description of bound items*

5.   In the case of concessions that have been bound on the basis of "ex-out" items, a complete description of the concession shall be provided. Where necessary, in order to provide a complete description of a bound item, a Member shall include in the description any relevant unbound items. In the case where only a sub-item is bound, the description provided in column 2 shall ensure that as many elements of the description as necessary are provided as described in paragraphs 3 and 4 of Document G/MA/TAR/W/4/Rev.2.

Ad valorem, specific and mixed duties

6.   Where both ad valorem and specific duties are shown in a Member's schedule, both shall be indicated in the loose-leaf schedule. In that case, specific rates may be shown in brackets. However, it is preferable to indicate both rates in an identical manner. Where necessary, Members shall indicate how ad valorem, specific and mixed rates are to be applied. Members may do so, *inter alia*, through a headnote.

Base and final tariff rates and staging

7.   With a view to reflecting fully Members' Uruguay Round schedules, the loose-leaf schedule shall contain in column 3 both base and final Uruguay Round rates, along with any necessary information on staging. Supplementary information on staging may be provided in the schedules or in an annex to the schedules. The schedule shall also include unbound base rates for products that have been bound in a Member's Uruguay Round schedule, and that will be subject to staging. In the case of final bound rates that entered into effect on January 1, 1995, and that are not subject to staging, only the final bound rate shall be shown.

Other duties and charges (ODCs)

8.   Members shall indicate ODCs in column 8 of their loose-leaf schedule. Where a Member's schedule does not contain any ODCs, it may so indicate at the beginning of its schedule and dispense with column 8. Members whose ODCs cover a limited number of products,[4] and Members that apply a common ODC to all products, may provide such information either through a headnote or appropriate footnotes to their schedule.

Treatment of agriculture

9.   Any Member whose Uruguay Round schedule contains specific commitments in agriculture shall indicate such commitments in its loose-leaf schedule. Agricultural tariffs shall be indicated separately from those of non-agricultural products. Tariff and agricultural commitments (i.e. tariff quotas and the domestic support and export subsidy commitments) shall follow the same format as in the Uruguay Round schedules.

Initial negotiating rights (INRs)

10.   Each Member shall include in its schedule all INRs at the current bound rate. Other Members may request the inclusion of any INR that had been granted to them. Historical INRs different from the current bound rate not specifically identified shall remain valid where a Member modifies its concession at a rate different from the rate at which the INR was granted.

Date of first instrument including a concession

11.   Members shall include in column 6 of their loose-leaf schedule the date of the legal instrument by means of which the concession was first incorporated in a GATT schedule.

Verification

12.   Until a methodology for the verification of consolidated loose-leaf schedules is agreed upon by the Market Access Committee, existing procedures will continue to apply.

Modification and Rectification

13.   With respect to modifications and rectifications of loose-leaf schedules, the *Procedures for Modification and Rectification of Schedules of Tariff Concessions*[5] shall apply. A request for the correction of minor clerical

---

[4]   It is understood that a "limited number of products" shall mean 10 to 20 tariff lines under the Harmonized System.

[5]   Decision of 26 March 1980, GATT Document L/4962 (BISD 27S/25).

errors that have occurred in the transposition of existing schedules into loose-leaf schedules through these *Procedures* may be submitted at any time.

ANNEX

SCHEDULE (Number - Country)

Date of loose leaf

This schedule is authentic only in ...

Part I/II

Most-favoured-nation tariff/Preferential tariff

Tariff item number	Description of product	Rate of duty		Present concession established	Initial negotiating right (INR) on the concession	Concession first incorporated in a GATT	INRs on earlier concession	Other duties and charges (ODCs)
		Base rate	Bound rate					
1	2	3		4	5	6	7	8

Index

Locators show the page number followed by the paragraph number. Where discussion continues onto the following page but within the same paragraph, subsequent page number[s] are not usually indicated. Conversely, where discussion begins on a page subsequent to the beginning of the paragraph, it is that page number which is given together with the relevant paragraph number.

A

accession to GATT/WTO

Annecy Tariff Conference 25.2, 73.1

Austria 25.2

binding of tariffs 10.10, 74.2 (v), 78.4 (i), 78.4 (iv)

comparable products, equivalence of treatment 78.4 (iii)

Bulgaria 73.2

Colombia 99.7

Czech Republic 77.2 (xi)

delay 73.2

Denmark 25.2

dependent territories 10.11

Dominican Republic 25.2

Finland 25.2

FRG 25.2

GATT 1947 accession negotiations 73.2-3

bilateral nature 74.2 (iii), 74.2 (v), 74.2 (vi)

developing countries, concessions and 74.2 (ii)

non-tariff measures and 75.2 (viii)

notifications to Secretariat 74.2 (vi)

reciprocity of concessions, developments 73.2 (i), 111.2

Schedules of concessions 73.2 (i)

Geneva Tariff Conference (1960-61) 26.4

Greece 25.2

Haiti 25.2

INRs and 12.4, 74.2 (iv)

Italy 25.2

ITNs and 78.4 (ii)

Korea 25.2, 99.7

Nicaragua 25.2

non-application of GATT 1947/WTO Agreement 11.12, 75.2 (ix)

Printed in the United States
125407LV00005B/6/A